Y0-AHH-381

"A MAN AND WOMAN LIE FACING EACH OTHER NAKED IN BED. HESITANTLY, ONE REACHES OUT TO GENTLY TOUCH THE OTHER..."

This is a typical couple who have entered the Masters and Johnson two-week therapy program for men and women with severe sexual problems.

Here is what actually happens when distressed couples from their early twenties to their seventies bare their most intimate secrets, and enter into a radical new reorientation system designed to dramatically improve their sexual performance. Here is a work which may well alter your own ideas about sexual potential from puberty through the so-called "twilight years."

"Robbins and Robbins translate Masters and Johnson's technical verbiage into understandable prose, and summarize a repetitive treatise into an interesting, readable book. They clear up many ambiguities in the original text after interviewing the authors, and one has the impression that the Robbins' popularization is almost the work of four authors."
—Alan F. Guttmacher, M.D.

SIGNET Titles of Special Interest

☐ **AN ANALYSIS OF HUMAN SEXUAL RESPONSE edited by Ruth and Edward Brecher.** A complete explanation for the layman of the controversial Masters-Johnson research on sexual response. Includes commentary by leaders in the study of sexual behavior, as well as prominent social critics. (#Y4054—$1.25)

☐ **PEOPLE IN LOVE: A MODERN GUIDE TO SEX IN MARRIAGE by Claire Rayner.** A marriage manual that covers a life-span of sexual problems, emphasizing the physical, emotional and psychological facets of a sexual relationship, both within and without the framework of marriage. (#Q4330—95¢)

☐ **THE POWER OF SEXUAL SURRENDER by Marie L. Robinson, M.D.** A leading psychiatrist and psychoanalyst tells women how they can overcome frigidity through self-knowledge. (#Q4410—95¢)

☐ **THE CHANGING YEARS by Madeline Gray.** With over 150,000 copies in hard cover THE CHANGING YEARS is the book that doctors recommend concerning the effects of menopause. All matters are discussed and there is a wealth of practical information. (#Q4251—95¢)

☐ **101 INTIMATE SEXUAL PROBLEMS ANSWERED by LeMon Clark, M.D.** Drawing on his years as physician, professor, and editor, LeMon Clark, M.D. provides straightforward answers to the questions men and women ask most about sex. (#T3195—75¢)

THE NEW AMERICAN LIBRARY, INC., P.O. Box 2310, Grand Central Station, New York, New York 10017

Please send me the SIGNET BOOKS I have checked above. I am enclosing $_____(check or money order—no currency or C.O.D.'s). Please include the list price plus 10¢ a copy to cover mailing costs. (New York City residents add 6% Sales Tax. Other New York State residents add 3% plus any local sales or use taxes.)

Name_____

Address_____

City_____State_____Zip Code_____

Allow at least 3 weeks for delivery

AN ANALYSIS OF HUMAN SEXUAL INADEQUACY

JHAN and *JUNE ROBBINS*

A SIGNET BOOK from
NEW AMERICAN LIBRARY
TIMES MIRROR

COPYRIGHT © 1970 BY JHAN AND JUNE ROBBINS

All rights reserved

Acknowledgments and Copyright Notices

The authors wish to thank the following for permission to reprint, in whole or in part, the articles listed:

Little, Brown and Co., Boston, for "The Achievement of William H. Masters and Virginia E. Johnson," from *The Sex Researchers*, by Edward M. Brecher. Copyright © 1969 by Edward M. Brecher.

Pageant Magazine, New York, for "The New Love Techniques We Learned at the Masters and Johnson Sex Clinic," as told to Victoria Pellegrino. Copyright © 1969 by *Pageant Magazine*.

G. P. Putnam's Sons, New York, for "Sexual Shames," from *Marathon 16*, by Martin Shepard and Marjorie Lee. Copyright © 1970 by Martin Shepard and Marjorie Lee.

Little, Brown and Co., Boston, for "Barriers to Sex," from *The Unused Potential of Marriage and Sex*, by Betty Eisner. Copyright © 1970 by Betty Grover Eisner.

Hartman, William E. and Fithian, Marilyn A., for "Desert Retreat."

Chapel Hill, The University of North Carolina Press, for "The Doctor as Marriage Counselor," by Cornelius Lansing, originally appearing as "Sexual Symptoms as a Presenting Complaint" in *Marriage Counseling in Medical Practice*, edited by Nash, Jessner, and Abse. Copyright © 1964 by Chapel Hill, The University of North Carolina Press.

Mead, Margaret for "Sexual Freedom and Culture Change," *Franciscan*, L, No. 1 (Fall, 1967), 8–14.

"Impersonal Sex in Public Places," reprinted from R. A. Laud Humphreys' *Tearoom Trade* (Chicago: Aldine Publishing Co., 1970); copyright © 1970 by R. A. Laud Humphreys.

Rosenberg, Bernard, and Bensman, Joseph, for "Sexual Patterns in Three Ethnic Subcultures of An American Underclass," reprinted from *The Annals of the American Academy of Political and Social Science*, 376:61–76, March 1968.

W. W. Norton and Co., New York, for "Paradoxes of Love and Sex," from *Love and Will*, by Rollo May. Copyright © 1969 by W. W. Norton & Co., Inc., New York.

Greenson, Ralph R., for "On Sexual Apathy in the Male," *Calif Med* 108:275–279, 1968.

SIGNET TRADEMARK REG. U.S. PAT. OFF. AND FOREIGN COUNTRIES
REGISTERED TRADEMARK—MARCA REGISTRADA
HECHO EN CHICAGO, U.S.A.

SIGNET, SIGNET CLASSICS, MENTOR AND PLUME BOOKS
are published by The New American Library, Inc.,
1301 Avenue of the Americas, New York, New York 10019

FIRST PRINTING, OCTOBER, 1970

PRINTED IN THE UNITED STATES OF AMERICA

This book about sexual inadequacy is dedicated to our adequate friends who have used the energetic overflow of their sexual fulfillment to show love for their brothers and sisters all over this world.

Contents

Preface xi

Part I: **Masters' and Johnson's Treatment for Sexual Dysfunction** 13
Jhan and June Robbins

Part II: **The Reproductive Biology Foundation** 103

The Achievement of William H. Masters and Virginia E. Johnson— 105
Edward Brecher

New Love Techniques We Learned at the Masters and Johnson Sex Clinic 116
As told to Victoria Pellegrino

Part III: **Other Sex Therapy** 127

Sexual Shames—Martin Shepard, M.D., and Marjorie Lee 129

Barriers to Sex—Betty Grover Eisner, Ph.D. 147

Desert Retreat—William E. Hartman, Ph.D., and Marilyn A. Fithian 154

The Doctor as Marriage Counselor— Cornelius Lansing, M.D. 161

Part IV: **Young People and Sex** 179

Sexual Freedom and Culture Change— Margaret Mead, Ph.D. 181

The Sexual Hangups of Young Adults— Anonymous 192

Part V: **The Cultural Reflex** 203

Impersonal Sex in Public Places— Laud Humphreys, Ph.D. 205

Sexual Patterns in Three Ethnic Subcultures of an American Underclass— Bernard Rosenberg, Ph.D., and Joseph Bensman, Ph.D. 236

On Sexual Apathy in the Male— Ralph R. Greenson, M.D. 261

Part VI:	A Psychoanalytic View	271
	Paradoxes of Sex and Love—Rollo May	273
	The Psychiatrists vs. Masters and Johnson—Vivian Cadden	299
	Bibliography of The Reproductive Biology Foundation	308

Illustrations

1.	The Penile Squeeze Technique	56
2.	Training Position For Ejaculatory Control	57
3.	The Female Superior Position	59
4.	The Lateral Position	61
5.	Training Position for Nonorgasmic Woman	90

Preface

"There is more delight in sex for a couple who have learned it and each other, as there is more delight in the cello for someone who has learned to play it." The comment was made by Harold Loukes, a much-respected contemporary English Quaker. The recent report by Dr. William Masters and Mrs. Virginia Johnson on "Human Sexual Inadequacy" * communicates the same thought.

The Masters and Johnson volume is a medical text intended for professionals. Since its terminology, precise for physicians, is often difficult for the layman to comprehend, we present this book as an exposition of that work, and include with it the writings of other competent persons who are concerned with sexual problems.

Part I is a summary of *Human Sexual Inadequacy*. Part II consists of biographies of its authors and a review of the previous work of these world famous researchers. It also presents the step-by-step experience of a couple who enrolled as patients in the Reproductive Biology Clinic because they feared that sexual inadequacy was about to destroy their marriage.

Part III describes some of the other important sex therapy being used today. In Part IV Dr. Margaret Mead talks about the new sexual freedom and how it affects the young. This section also contains a roundtable discussion of five young adults who talk freely about their sexual hangups and discuss their experience in the light of their parents' generation.

Other aspects of the subject, seen from a cultural point of view, appear in Part V: in an article on the homosexual subculture; a study of the sex mores in three American ghettos; and an essay that explores why the American male is becoming increasingly apathetic about sex.

The last section, Part VI, contains a penetrating study by Dr. Rollo May that carries the theme of inadequacy beyond the physical to confront the modern dichotomy between

---

* William H. Masters and Virginia Johnson, *Human Sexual Inadequacy*. Boston: Little, Brown and Company, 1970.

love and sex. In summary, there is a report by journalist Vivian Cadden that reflects the differing opinions of prominent psychiatrists regarding the work of Masters and Johnson.

Many people helped us with this book. Special thanks go to editor Jean Read of the New American Library and to Edward Brecher, a leading author in the field of sex research, who read our manuscript and made valuable suggestions. And thanks are due also to our daughter, Penny, and son, Tom for their patient and critical editorial assistance. We greatly enjoyed meeting and were inspired by talking to Dr. William H. Masters and Mrs. Virginia E. Johnson.

JHAN AND JUNE ROBBINS
Roxbury, Connecticut

PART I

Masters' and Johnson's Treatment for Sexual Dysfunction

by Jhan and June Robbins

What Masters and Johnson Are Doing About Sex Inadequacy

A man and a woman lie in a bed facing each other. They are in a motel bedroom. They are nude. The door is locked. The metal blinds are flipped shut. The small lights by the bedside are on. They look straight on for a moment—eyes to eyes. It is perhaps the first calm, direct visual contact the two have made in a long time. One mouth softens with receptivity, the other hardens with determination.

He says, "Did we say you first?"

She says, "No, you first!"

They are about six inches apart. They turn toward each other. He reaches his hands awkwardly and haltingly toward her face. His fingertips stroke her cheek, brush her mouth, touch her eyelids and her forehead, run through her hair.

"Now, you," he says.

She clasps his hand, puts her palm under his chin, strokes his ear and the back of his neck. Her foot reaches out to touch his foot. She strokes his back and shoulders. Then they stop. They get out of bed. In all it has taken about ten minutes. She puts on her nightgown. He puts on his pajamas. They get into their separate beds, turn out the lights, and try to go to sleep. It's called building *sensate focus*.

They're in sexual therapy. They've been married seven years. He thinks she's frigid. She says he doesn't satisfy her. It's a common complaint. They have paid $2,500, taken two weeks off, and driven 700 miles hoping they can learn what's needed to have a good sex life. They are patients at the Reproductive Biology Research Foundation in St. Louis where Dr. William H. Masters and Mrs.

Virginia E. Johnson are having remarkable success treating couples who are distressed because they are sexually inadequate. Although Dr. Masters and Mrs. Johnson are very cautious in their claims, eight out of ten men and women patients have shown immediate ability to overcome their problems. Meticulous follow-ups over a period of five years confirm their statistics.

Dr. Masters and Mrs. Johnson feel that much of the success they have had in treating sexually inadequate patients has been due to their "dual sex therapy team" approach.

"The team should consist of male and female co-therapists," Dr. Masters said. "A man can never truly understand a woman's sexual feelings."

Mrs. Johnson added, "And a woman can never know how it feels to be a man."

They also believe that the female therapist is usually best equipped to explain a wife's problem to her husband while the male therapist does the same for the husband. Each partner, in their unique therapy program, has "a friend in court."

There is no doubt that since its establishment in 1959 the Reproductive Biology Research Foundation has done the most important work, qualitatively and quantitatively, in the field of physiological sex therapy that has yet been achieved or even attempted. Dr. Masters and Mrs. Johnson have helped patients achieve cures for sexual distress and dysfunction that have heretofore been regarded as incurable. The impact of their work is international.

Over a period of months we have talked to Dr. Masters, to Mrs. Johnson, to other physiologists concerned with sex patterns in our society and, perhaps even more important, to couples who have passed through the project as patients. Of the 790 patients, 89 have been physicians; 43 have been psychiatrists.

Dr. Masters estimates that 50 percent of all married couples in the United States are sexually unfulfilled and feeling acutely unhappy about it. He and Mrs. Johnson say that a sexually inadequate person is a man or woman who has not achieved sexual communication in marriage or who doesn't feel good and secure about whatever sexual communication he or she has got.

Large numbers have sense enough to look for help. But

help, for the most part, is unavailing. Couples turn to priests, ministers, or rabbis who often counsel prayer and patience. Others go to social workers—psychiatrically trained marriage counselors—who tend to believe that if you adjust the conflicts in personal relationships, sex will take care of itself. Some go to their family doctors who may miss physical symptoms and assure them, "It's all in your mind." A few are referred to competent psychoanalysts but may spend years on the analytical couch before sexual hang-ups disappear. If ever.

Treatment at the Reproductive Biology Research Foundation is programmed to produce or restore effective sexual response within two weeks. It is plainly called a rapid treatment program.

"Originally," Dr. Masters says, "we stretched it over three weeks but we found that was too long."

It must be noted, however, that patients are seen seven days a week. Dr. Masters points out that in conventional psychotherapy, you must allow time for hello and goodbye and catching up with what happened last week. The patient winds up with a very short hour. The Masters–Johnson treatment schedule is the equivalent in time of many months in conventional psychotherapy.

Dr. Masters and Mrs. Johnson also feel that seeing patients on a seven-day-a-week basis produces an amazing leap forward in treatment progress. It may be compared to taking skiing or tennis lessons every day instead of every Saturday. In seven continuous days you get a great deal further along than you would in seven weeks of once-a-week sessions.

The difference, of course, is that treatment at the Reproductive Biology Research Foundation is not—emphatically not—a how-to-do-it proposition. Sexual techniques are explained, including the famed Masters-and-Johnson-approved side position for intercourse (described on page 61). Dr. Masters and Mrs. Johnson say it is the most effective position their research has found. But the emphasis is on creating permissive, undemanding, fully giving physical relationships in the full confidence that sexual fulfillment comes from giving in order to get.

The episode of touching described earlier usually is directed to occur in the time between the third and fourth day of treatment. The couple are forbidden to touch breast, penis, vulva. They're supposed to run their hands over one another twice within ten or twelve hours. They are not supposed to stimulate each other to acute sexual excitement or to engage in sexual action. That comes later. As one critic has said, "They begin by relearning the gentle art of petting, as it was practiced down by the old mill stream. Except of course they're naked!"

How Well Does It Work?

It's not all that simple. In their medical textbook, *Human Sexual Inadequacy,* Dr. Masters and Mrs. Johnson tell how patients were treated for sexual dysfunction. Women who had never had orgasms became orgasmic. Some women begin to experience several orgasms in a single sexual encounter. Men who had never achieved or sustained an erection found themselves able to do it. Premature ejaculation was cured. Men who had been able to sustain a penetration and erection but not ejaculate solved that problem, too.

Women suffering from vaginismus—an involuntary tightening of the muscles surrounding the entrance to the vagina—were cured. Other women experiencing severe pain in sex activity were found to be suffering from the results of gang-rape or inept hysterectomy. Some were referred for corrective surgery. Men describing pain or other ailments involved with the sex act were helped.

Most important, Dr. Masters and Mrs. Johnson believe, is the work done in treating the sex life of the aging man and woman. Sex activity, Masters and Johnson maintain, is a function as natural as breathing. It begins at birth and ends only when the aging process involves very poor health. A healthy man or woman can expect to achieve and enjoy lifelong sexual activity. The oldest patient that passed through the Foundation clinic during its present 11-year record was a 76-year-old man.

Dr. Masters reminds us: "We don't know how many couples are in sexual difficulties—but one thing is sure, we all get old! Few know what to anticipate in regard to aging sex. When we find things changing, we think, 'Good God, it's all ending!' And we panic—and we paralyze ourselves."

Young or old, you can't get into the Masters-Johnson clinic by just knocking at the door. You have to be referred by a medical or other authority reputably known to the Reproductive Biology Research Foundation. Many applicants are screened out. The two leading reasons for rejection are uncontrolled alcoholism and major mental illness. Psychoneurotics are accepted but not psychotics. The Foundation doesn't go for tranquilizers or other kinds of medication. Masters and Johnson believe tranquilizers can be a depressant to sexual function.

Even those who are admitted must undergo a long waiting period before treatment begins. Only a few couples can be treated during each two-week period. It all moves slowly, and some couples waiting for admission are so distraught by anxiety that they give up or split up before the doors open.

It's acknowledged that the Foundation has had its failures. Some insincere prospects have messed up the statistics by conning their way through the admissions procedure. One case history tells of a woman who was so determined to humiliate her husband that she deliberately disobeyed instructions, needlessly causing him to prematurely ejaculate, even though they had come for treatment of that symptom. It took several days for puzzled Foundation therapists to catch on.

Faced with her sabotage, the wife admitted she wanted no further part of the marriage. Treatment was ended, as was the marriage, but not before Foundation therapists had managed to convince the husband that premature ejaculation could be corrected. They divorced. He remarried and during a long weekend at the Foundation with his new wife they became sexually responsive.

The first wife—the vengeful one—also remarried but was divorced from her second husband in six months. "She was a person who needed help, and we couldn't reach her," Dr. Masters said regretfully. "We flopped. So did her psychotherapist. A zero on the charts."

Among the men and women treated over a period of eleven years there have been other zeros. The highest number of failures—40.6 percent—occurred in the attempt to treat 32 cases of primary impotence—that is, men who have never had an erection that has lasted long enough for intromission. Masters and Johnson frankly refer to it as their disaster area.

It should be noted, however, that they are getting better at it as time goes on. Of the first 16 men treated, there were nine failures. In the second group of 16 men there were only four failures.

Actually any kind of treatment of primary impotence is regarded by most experts as a very doubtful venture. Dr. Dr. Donald W. Hastings, professor of psychiatry and chairman of the department of psychiatry and neurology at the University of Minnesota Medical School, who commented on Masters' and Johnson's earlier work on human sexual response, said, "No training procedure, so far as I know, has as yet been published for the treatment of impotence."

In *Human Sexual Inadequacy* Masters and Johnson do tell how they helped 19 men—59.4 percent of their male patients who had never had a useful erection—to become normally acting males.

About treatment of secondary impotence—men who once were potent but can no longer reliably perform the sex act—the Masters and Johnson report is that of 213 patients treated, 56 failed to regain sexual competence. Nevertheless, 157 did! On impotence, Masters says frankly, "There's still a lot to learn."

Most successful cases in treatment of male dysfunction has been in premature ejaculation. *Only 2.2 percent of 186 patients failed to respond to therapy—97.8 percent succeeded!* At the Reproductive Biology Research Foundation a simple physical method was introduced that enables any man who can achieve an erection to maintain it virtually as long as he and his female partner wish to do so. (It is described on page 56.)

Dr. Masters predicts that within the next decade premature ejaculation will be brought fully under control and cease to exist as a sexual complaint. All that remains, Dr. Masters says, is to train doctors and other therapists to teach the simple "squeeze play."

Critics have said, however, that the soon-to-be-famous squeeze technique is not a cure but a prop, as a steel brace supports a lame leg. Dr. Masters and Mrs. Johnson are unperturbed by such remarks and consider them uninformed.

One hundred percent cure is reported for vaginismus, the convulsive muscular closing of the outer third of the vagina, usually due to hysteria caused by some kind of bad experience. Twenty-nine female patients were seen for this disorder and all were promptly corrected. Unfortunately all or most of them turned out to have additional sexual disorders.

Women reporting inability to have an orgasm—the convulsive, highly pleasurable throbbing of the genital areas— numbered 342. Of these 276 reported several orgasmic experiences before they left the Reproductive Biology Research Foundation and said they were greatly helped or cured. Some of these women, like the impotent men, had never before had an orgasm. Others had enjoyed orgasms with other partners but not their husbands. Most complained of infrequent orgasm with their present partners. Still more could achieve orgasm by hand masturbation of their genitals but not from contact with a penis.

Of those who previously couldn't even reliably masturbate, 90.9 percent became sexually adequate. Of those who'd seldom or never enjoyed an orgasm, 80.2 percent got there. Of women who complained that they didn't achieve it often enough, 62.5 percent reported satisfactory improvement.

In the group of aging men and women—48 men and 27 women—69.4 percent regained sexual adequacy. Notable, however, is that things apparently went better for the men than the women. This may be because the men who came in for treatment tended to bring along younger wives. Masters and Johnson do not say this. At any rate, 75 percent of the aging men but only 59.3 percent of the aging women reported substantial improvement.

The official summary of the clinical experiment tells us of an overall success rate of 80 percent. It sounds like good news, especially to the sexually inadequate, unfulfilled or unhappy person who is thinking about spending $2,500 to get his or her sex life repaired. But it depends on what you're suffering from. Vaginismus and premature ejaculation apparently yield readily to treatment. If your trouble is male impotence or female lack of orgasm, the outlook is not all that bright.

The Intake Interview

Masters and Johnson say frankly they prefer to treat patients who are not living in St. Louis. It's nothing against their home town. They feel achievement or recovery prospects are heightened if the couple can get away from crying babies and away from the boss with his critical thumb on the monthly sales chart. Couples who do live in St. Louis are given three weeks of treatment instead of two. This is out of consideration that they are operating from home base.

One aspect of the therapy St. Louis couples avoid, however, is how to explain to their friends why they are going to St. Louis for two weeks. Many out-of-towners say the wife is suffering from a gynecological problem and are going to consult the experts in the famed Washington University Medical Center.

In addition to trying to screen out serious psychos and drunks the Masters and Johnson admission procedure tries to find out whether the applying couple really wish to cooperate with each other in a truthful and earnest effort. More than one set of applicants have been told bluntly, "You don't need us—you need a lawyer!"

A couple that applies for treatment must agree to a five-year-long follow-up study of their case. Then there is a discreet question about finances. The Reproductive Biology Research Foundation burns up an annual budget of $500,000. If all distressed marital units paid the conventional $2,500 sum it would help make their budget, but many couples don't. The usual sliding scale applied to other kinds of tuition and medical treatment is brought out and discussed. Some couples have been treated for no fee at all. Like all other research projects, Masters and Johnson are involved not only with therapy and research but with the imperative need to pass the hat. Support has come from, among other sources, Hugh Hefner's Playboy Foundation, derived from Hefner's personal fortune and sales of *Playboy* magazine.

Once through the gates there is a prolonged history-taking interview. Masters and Johnson are interested in what Dr. Masters calls "the whole medical and psychosocial bag." They want to know what the patient's sexual value system is like. It takes two days to find out.

Couples on the intake interviews are seen separately. They are immediately told that all conversations are taped. The tapes, never transcribed, are guarded like the British crown jewels for five years and then destroyed. Couples are also told not to discuss with each other the answers they give to the interviewers' questions.

At a press interview we attended Mrs. Johnson was asked, "You put all these questions to these nervous incoming couples—what's the question they are most likely to ask you?"

Mrs. Johnson, one of the most attractive middle-aged brunettes on the public scene ("A 'Happy' Rockefeller type" one woman reporter scribbled), laughed and said, "They all want to be assured they won't have to perform sexually under observation."

Dr. Masters added, "We tell them if you're all that worried about it, you wouldn't be eligible anyway!"

Couples are instructed not to have sex relations after they enter therapy until they are given permission. The reason for this is to remove the pressures of pride and compulsion. It is better to go to bed saying, "Well, we'd like to do it but Masters and Johnson won't let us," than to encounter the same old failure.

A battery of questions rains down on the incoming couple, but Masters and Johnson emphasize that the questioning is not rigidly structured. It is directed in as easygoing and spontaneous a manner as possible. The first set of questions, a who-when-what-and-where sort of thing is called a preliminary baseline. The word "baseline" is one of Virginia Johnson's favorite words. If you ask her a question she says, "I'll give you a baseline on this." You lean forward expecting to hear a definitive five-word sentence and you get a 15-minute-long torrent of comment. As one male reporter said, "It's painless, because she's so easy to look at."

Other areas about which the couple is quizzed are childhood, adolescence, premarital adulthood, marriage, and a special group of inquiries concerned with awareness and response to sensual stimuli—touch, taste, and smell. Some of the questions are more provoking than others. They usually begin with something like, "Well, what seems to be the trouble there?" and the married partners pour forth their mutual complaints.

The couple is gently but firmly reminded that in a problem of sexual inadequacy there is no such thing as a single offender or an uninvolved partner. They are told it is the marital unit that is being treated and not the two individuals. Charges of "It's his fault" and "It's her fault" are skillfully turned off.

Then they get down to the brass tacks on the brass bed. They ask such questions as:

TO THE WIFE: Have you ever had an orgasm? Describe the circumstances. Tell how it feels.

TO THE HUSBAND: Do you think your wife has ever been orgasmic? Tell where and when.

TO THE WIFE: Have you ever noticed that your husband has trouble geting an erection or ejaculating? What were the circumstances?

TO THE HUSBAND: If you've ever had erective or ejaculatory trouble, describe it.

Prospective therapists are warned, ". . . these questions should be evaluated on a basis of maximum professional expertise . . ."

This is a polite way of saying that in Masters' and Johnson's experience patients are not unlikely to tell lies at this point, before they have learned to trust and cooperate with the therapists. In Masters' and Johnson's experience, patients who have previously been through the mill—and "flunked out"—of other treatments such as marital counseling and psychotherapy are more glib and more devious and more self-destructive than those who are seeking help for the first time.

The intake interview at the Foundation is however not the time for expressions of indignation. Whatever is "confessed" or revealed is received sympathetically and un-

AN ANALYSIS OF HUMAN SEXUAL INADEQUACY

critically. The setting is that of a doctor's consulting office with the patient and one of the therapists sitting around a workmanlike desk.

QUESTIONS SIMILAR TO THESE ARE ASKED IN INFORMAL CONVERSATIONS:

Other than conventional intercourse, have you tried other ways to bring sexual pleasure to your partner? If so, what did you do?

Did he (she) appear to like it? What has he (she) done to pleasure you? Did you like it?

Tell about sex experiences with your husband (wife) before marriage. How did you feel?

Tell about your first sex experience after marriage.

How much, if any, adultery has there been on your part in your marriage? Does your partner know about it?

Did you play "doctor" or other sex games when you were a child and if so were you ever scolded or punished for it?*

Have you ever watched anyone else performing the sex act? When and where?

When did you first start trying to masturbate and how often do you do that now? What do you think about when you masturbate?

As an adolescent, when and how did you learn the "facts of life"? Did you pet, neck, or "make out" on dates? Describe your first sexual intercourse.

Were you ever engaged or seriously involved with other persons before marriage? Were any of these homosexual contacts? Why did these relationships break up?

Tell how you met and married. What attracted you most about your partner at that time?

How often did you have sex relations the first month you were married? The first year? Did this schedule live up

---

*The question brings to mind the story of the mother who wrote Dr. Spock: "Doctor, I have discovered that my daughter, aged three, and the boy next door—her own age—are playing sex games. I have read your book and I know that this is normal and right for their age group. But how can I put a stop to it?"

to your expectations? Are sex activities now scheduled or spontaneous?

What emotional or physical situation most often influences the desire for sexual intercourse? What time of the day or night does it usually occur? Do you tell your partner what sexual actions stimulate or please you most? What does he (she) do that turns you on fast? What does he (she) do that turns you off?

Recall and describe the most memorable erotic experiences of your life.

Do you like to be touched, stroked, petted? Does your partner? Do you pet or cuddle your children or dogs?

Do you ever find touching embarrassing or irritating? Do you rub each other's backs or necks when you're tired or strained?

Do you like to lie in your partner's arms after sexual intercourse?

Do you think smells are associated with sex? If so, do you prefer commercial perfumes or fresh sweat? Are you turned off by mouth odors such as garlic or gin or chocolate?

About music, do you and your partner have one or more musical associations that go with sex? Do you like to dance to relieve tension? To generate sexual feelings?

Have you ever been involved in illegitimate pregnancy? Abortion? Rape? Incest?

That's the end of the first two days. An exhaustive medical history and physical examination takes up half of the third day. Dr. Masters and Mrs. Johnson emphasize that patients who come from out of town are encouraged to take advantage of the cultural opportunities in St. Louis. There is a magnificent art museum to be appreciated; also the sculpture of Carl Milles, the soaring arch of Saarinen, a large symphony, a small symphony, and Busch Stadium where the Cardinals play baseball. But it's difficult to see how any patients have time to do so. Those who have friends and relatives in the city are strictly warned off. This is no time to visit cousins. (St. Louis is a conservative city. Even its intellectual element is a bit embarrassed by the Masters and Johnson identification.)

The last half of the third day in therapy is a four-way roundtable discussion that sums up and evaluates what has been said and learned. At this point fibs and fantasies, if they have been told, are thrashed out. Both partners feel a lot better. "A lot cleaner," said one.

The exception occurs when a husband or wife has confided to the therapist something that he or she emphatically does not wish to be revealed to the married partner. Examples are men who have had homosexual love affairs, women who have been gang-raped or seduced by members of their families, or men who have been sexually approached by their mothers.

In one case in which a couple came for treatment of an unresponsive wife, the husband remorsefully said something like, "It's all my fault. She was an innocent—a virgin." Actually, the wife was hysterically rejecting her husband because she had spent seven years in sexual relationship with her father.

If the treatment team agree that the man and woman can't be sexually reconciled without revealing important confidential material, treatment is broken up then and there. In the case above, the couple was sent home. In such instances every effort, Masters and Johnson say, is made to tactfully conceal from the other partner the private reason they have been discharged from the Foundation treatment program.

What's Wrong?
It Can Be Just Physical

It may also happen at this time that male or female physical problems are revealed by the grueling going-over that each submit to. A gynecological or urogenital overhaul is no fun. Sometimes, by the end of day number three, it results in a diagnosis of *dyspareunia*.

When you read *dyspareunia* in a study of sexual dysfunction just read *pain*. Coitus hurts, if you have dyspareunia, no matter whom you do it with. The size of the genitals is irrelevant. It happens to men as well as women. Sometimes even more so.

It seems to us and to other observers of the Masters–Johnson work that the two chapters they devote to what are actually physically observable problems—problems as plain to look at as a sagging roof line on a house or a thin tire on an automobile—are none-too-subtle indictments of the diagnostic capabilities of the medical profession. Should you have to apply to the Masters–Johnson clinic, stand in line until you get there, and get up all that money only to be told that you need a circumcision or that your obstetrician has done a lousy job? In the cases that have passed through the Foundation, apparently often the answer is yes.

The concise and informative material in the Masters and Johnson text that deals with physiological disorders and sex hygiene will, we hope, be widely read by family doctors, obstetricians, and others who are likely to be first on the scene in recognizing and treating such problems. That such problems should be passed over or misunderstood by competent authorities is scandalous.

It certainly does not make cheerful reading. A 50-year-old male, a veteran of World War II, reacted this way: "That part of the Masters and Johnson book reminded me of those venereal disease films they made us look at in the Army. Remember, there were big strong guys fainting on the floor from looking at those pictures?"

The Masters–Johnson findings are briefly summarized as follows:

Male Dyspareunia: A man complains of irritation or even severe pain at the end of the penis after ejaculation. He can't stand to have his penis touched—he can't even bear to leave it in the vagina. He says, "It hurts!" It shames him to say so! It sounds so sissy. But although his wife asks him to retain his penis in her vagina for a moment while they are tapering off, or she might like to gently play with it after withdrawal, he cannot. He is in pain.

If the man is uncircumcised, the problem may be that he has too tight a foreskin or he may not be able to pull it back or the foreskin may be stuck to the penile shaft by a collection of decaying bacteriological matter. Or there may be infection underneath the foreskin. (Men who protest, "But I shower every day!" are often not washing their genitals thoroughly.)

Soap and water solved some of these problems. Circumcision solved others. But some men, it has turned out, would have done better to go uncircumcised. Some men need the protective sheath to fend off a peeling-skin reaction to the acid-alkaline balance of the vagina. Some turn out to be violently allergic to various rubber products, creams, jellies, foams, or perfumed sprays used as contraceptives or supposedly to enhance sexual pleasure.

Other disasters can befall the penis and its associated parts. One is dull, throbbing pain in the testicles which is frequently experienced by men who spend a good deal of time reading pornography and do not afterwards masturbate to ejaculation or men who maintain an erection during intercourse that lasts for 45 minutes or longer. Usually it's a young man's ailment. Aging men who experience pain in the testicles, pelvic area, or inner thighs during ejaculation should ask their doctors to check them out for prostate trouble.

Deformity of the penis—bending sharply upwards or downwards—or sharply left or right—can make penetration of the vagina difficult or impossible and penile thrusting painful to both partners. It can be caused by the scars and deformities of gonorrhea but also by accident.

Four cases were seen by Masters and Johnson in which men were injured in the course of the sex act. Two were struck sharply on the penis by angry women. Two others were rapidly mounted by highly excited female partners who sat straight down very vigorously on the erect penis. All four said the same thing: "I heard something snap."

Surgery, Dr. Masters says, rarely can correct angular deformities of the penis. (An angry woman, who may nevertheless have a continuing interest in the male, would do well to control herself sufficiently to remember to kick him in the shins or stamp on his toes instead of attacking the genitals.)

Masters and Johnson say the woman in the superior mounting position should never sit straight down on the penis but lean forward, insert the penis and slide back.

Female Dyspareunia: Women who came to the clinic stating that they experienced severe pain or great difficulty in accommodating the penis presented an even wider range of undiagnosed or undealt with physical problems. There were a number of cases of vaginismus, the convulsive closing of the lower third of the vagina. Most of the women didn't know they had it. Almost none of the husbands knew their wives had it. It took a simple pelvic examination to reveal it. The cause is said to be from what old-fashioned doctors used to call hysteria.

Twelve cases were attributed or at least traced to the antisexual rigidity of orthodox religion. One woman recalled that as a girl she was repeatedly told never to look at her breasts in a mirror lest it should lead to feelings of pleasure in the pelvis.

Vaginismus is relatively easily cured. Dr. Masters, with the cooperation of husband and wife, used a purely mechanical approach, gradually dilating the vaginal opening with the use of vaginal dilators. Then the wife was ready to be schooled or reschooled to responsive sex. The husband was usually greatly relieved to discover the problem had nothing to do with his ability to make a penile thrust. However, some found that their humiliating inability to penetrate their wives had caused them to lose their own sexual powers. That, too, had to be treated.

Vaginismus begins, but far from ends, woman's complaints about pain associated with the entry of the penis into the vagina. Perhaps Masters and Johnson deal with it first because a well-trained gynecologist finds it so easy to diagnose and demonstrate.

Other problems can be more difficult. The exclamation of the impatient neighborhood doctor, "It's all in your mind!" becomes more understandable. Is a woman complaining of pain being really objective? Is she experiencing real pain translated by the nervous system as surely as a broken leg? Or is she experiencing subjective pain, merely expressing her fear, resentment, and objection to the whole sex thing?

The doctor has to decide. If he can't find anything, he puts his patient down as an antisexual, frigid woman. He may wink at her dismayed husband and say something like, "Try a little harder."

Virginia Johnson is concerned that the overwhelming proportion of literature on sexual response has been written by men who have not bothered to consult women. In literature, the pleasure-pain principle is emphasized in descriptions of sex activities and, realistically, some women feel reassured when they are kissed until it hurts and, in love-making, knocked around a little. Some men like it, too. "It's fun making love to her, she bites near climax."

So what is the bewildered doctor to do? Knowing all this, he is presented with a woman who tries to avoid the insertion of her husband's penis, pulls away from his abdomen while he is thrusting, sobs or screams when he gets in deep, cries when he is finished, and gives him hell for hours afterwards? That's the way Dr. Masters and Mrs. Johnson describe many cases that turn up at the Foundation. They mildly recommend that the doctor should figure that in any consistent complaint of pain something is probably wrong. If he can't find it, he should look again!

Women can have foreskin problems just like men. In our culture women are rarely circumcised. (Among some primitive tribes it is done routinely.) The foreskin that covers the clitoris can get gummed up and infected just as in the male. Wives who masturbate frequently or for long periods of time may find the clitoris or foreskin raw and painful when stretched by an entering penis.

Men who read too much and feel too little about being

effective lovers often clumsily manipulate their women to soreness and infection in the clitoris or vulva. They rub the area too hard or too directly—sometimes with unwashed hands. The physician who is consulted by a woman complaining of pain, burning, or itching in the vagina should immediately suspect and thoroughly explore the possibility of an infection.

Dr. Masters and Mrs. Johnson are also critical of vaginal tampons when not used properly. Used according to directions, they are convenient and harmless but many women do not follow directions. A physician who agrees that the packagers of tampons should include more warnings said, "If a woman leaves the tampon in place too long, then the blood cells in the tampon may begin to disintegrate and spoil like a half-used package of chopped chuck. In the process it changes vaginal acidity levels."

Actually, nearly all tampon manufacturers include in their instruction leaflets the reminder that it is important to change tampons often and not forget they are there. What they don't tell is that you might get an infection if you don't! On days of heavy flow manufacturers recommend using two tampons at one time. It is more hygienic to change them more often.

Women suffer frequently from vaginal fungal infections —a kind of athlete's foot of the vagina. They are also allergic to some kinds of contraceptives. (A representative of one of the major companies manufacturing a number of different kinds of contraceptive devices admitted that there has been little research on the subject of allergy reactions to contraceptives.)

Dr. Masters and Mrs. Johnson view with regret the current and fashionable reemergence of vaginal douching. A generation of gynecologists patiently taught women who are now in their fifties to stop douching. Now their daughters, who are exploring wider horizons of sexual experience, are douching again. Many of these douches seem to be causative agents in cases of vaginal discharge and inflammation.

The vagina, Masters and Johnson explain, protects itself, normally, from irritation and infection by maintaining a high acidity level. Douches sweep it away and the vagina is temporarily defenseless until the acidity is reestablished.

We asked Dr. Masters, "Are you against douching?" He answered that he deplored it but doubted ad-conscious women would give it up. Dr. Masters and Mrs. Johnson recently turned down $10,000 for an endorsement of a vulva spray.

The vagina naturally trends from acidity to alkalinity during the menstrual period. If the desire for sexual intercourse impulsively occurs at this time, the impulse should perhaps be restrained long enough to achieve scrupulous soap-and-water cleanliness of the hands and exterior genitals of both partners. Although this is the time when a woman may feel she most wants to douche, it is most inadvisable. Masters and Johnson do not say there should be no intercourse during menstrual periods—only that the vagina is probably more susceptible to infection at this time.

They report soberly and uncritically on another sexual habit that often causes severe vaginal area infection and resultant pain in intercourse. It is rectal coitus. It causes far more trouble than it need do because, for one thing, it is improperly performed and, also, women—even Dr. Masters' and Mrs. Johnson's patients—are reluctant to say that they do it even when the lab tests point to no other explanation.

Dr. Masters has, after extensive experience in the Foundation clinic, been able to tell doctors that an examining finger inserted in the rectum of a woman who is accustomed to and enjoying rectal coitus will tell the story. The rectum gives itself away, with a cooperative, relaxed accommodation of the doctor's examining finger. It is quite different from the continuous, indignant-seeming spastic reaction that the sexually unstimulated rectum usually makes to expel the finger.

Even then, women embarrassedly continue to deny it but are told that lab reports show they are suffering from coliform vaginitus—an infection of the vagina that can almost only come from contamination from the rectum. Some timidly suggest it might have come from an improper use of toilet tissue. Masters and Johnson say that coition in the rectum and coition in the vagina may each be pleasurable but require thorough washing in between. Not to do so risks infection

Eleven women came to the clinic complaining of pain

in intercourse with accompanying symptoms of what might be called "tired housewife's syndrome." This includes frequent exhaustion, especially after a day spent standing on the feet; back pain; pain in menstruating and "a feeling that everything is falling out inside." Five of these women came with assurance from their referral sources that there was no physical reason for their complaints. It was "all in their minds."

Dr. Masters and Mrs. Johnson found that all of these women had deep cuts or tears in the broad ligaments that support a woman's uterus and pelvic structure. Five of these women, apparently victims of difficult childbirths and inept postchildbirth care, were sent for corrective surgery. The other six were suffering from the effects of criminal abortion or rape. None of these were considered by Masters and Johnson to be primarily sexually inadequate. They were referred for gynecological help, surgery, and psychotherapy.

The Roundtable—
Talking It Out

In the afternoon of the third day at the Reproductive Biology Research Foundation the couple meet together with the cotherapists—Dr. Masters and Mrs. Johnson—in a roundtable discussion. The setting is that of a conventional doctor's consulting room. In Mrs. Johnson's words, "It isn't living-roomy."

The two therapists sit on one side of a large desk, the husband and wife on the other. The therapists begin a joint summary of all that's been said and observed. If medical problems have been discovered which were not previously known, these are explained. In such cases, the treatment team must say frankly that until the physical problems are dealt with, it can't be said with any certainty whether the marriage is troubled with sexual inadequacy or not. Obviously a marriage that has been distorted with physical problems may have got snarled up in other aspects of the sex relationship.

Next, the therapists sum up the facts that have been learned—personal, marital, social—about the two patients. The patients are encouraged to expand, amend, or correct the information as it is reeled out. They usually have to be told several times that it's all right to dispute "the doctor."

Answers given in the interviews are scrutinized for content of sexual myth. Couples who come for treatment often do not have accurate ideas of how sex works—even those who have college degrees. The most common misconceptions are about the size of the male sexual organ. The Masters and Johnson research offers well nigh indisputable evidence that virility and sexual competence are not to be associated with a large penis. They say there is no such thing as a large or small penis; that is, when in action—which is clearly all that matters. The large penis adds about one-third of its length in erection. The smaller penis doubles or even triples in length. And women can't tell the difference anyway. That has been proved by early Reproductive Biology Research Foundation experiments with artificial male organs. Dr. Harvey E. Kaye, supervising psychoanalyst at New York Medical College, agrees with Dr. Masters and Mrs. Johnson. He feels that the myths and superstitions regarding penis size have caused a great deal of feeling of inadequacy. "The difference in penile size," he says emphatically, "means nothing in terms of sexual performance or capability."

Mrs. Johnson said the Foundation gets four or five letters a week asking what can be done about the size of a penis. One man wanted to know if silicone treatments to pad it out would help. Dr. Masters wrote back, "If you have no concern about perpetual erection, be my guest." He smiled as he recalled the incident and added, "Can you imagine trying to get your pants on?"

Other unrealistic sexual ideas, as revealed in the patients' "complaints" are factually disposed of. If there is an unusual degree of conflicting information there is a discussion on the importance of frank communication. Dr. Masters says one of the most damaging sexual fallacies of our time is the notion that a man instinctively knows what a woman wants and when she wants it.

Thus, in discussion, prejudices, anxieties, and inadequacies are held up to what Masters and Johnson call "a mirror."

Repeatedly it's emphasized that the marriage is what the treatment is about and not the individuals concerned. *The marriage is the patient.* It's up to the two partners and the two therapists to make the marriage sexually functional.

It is not psychoanalysis. Dr. Masters and Mrs. Johnson find that people who have been in analysis or psychotherapy often present more problems than those who haven't. The individual who is a psychotherapy dropout sometimes tends to make active, emotional bids for special attention to his or her own particular problems. These persons are politely turned off and brought back to focus on the distressed married relationship, which is the problem all four are hopefully trying to deal with.

Self-justification is also ruled out. Openness is stressed. There is an unashamed and therapy-protected exchange of vulnerabilities: "This is what I like!" and "This is what I don't like!" The roundtable is not a vehicle for a court trial. The information developed changes from day to day in terms of the therapy. Patients gain courage and become less angry and anxious as they go along.

Each patient—the man and the woman—has a partner of the same sex in therapy. A sexually distressed woman can say to Mrs. Johnson, "You know what I mean?" and she does. A male can say to Dr. Masters, "You know, this is how it can go!" And Dr. Masters understands.

Husbands and wives may come to one another's defense: "You're blaming yourself too much. I played a part in that!" They become loyal to one another and often unite and defend the marriage.

Dr. Masters and Mrs. Johnson carefully explain their "spectator" theory. They believe that failure builds upon failure as success builds on success, and they have discovered that sexual failure creates a kind of sexual stage fright. Anxiety—apprehension—enters the bedroom. Sex ceases to be a natural, responsive process. The fun goes out of it.

The wife and husband both worry. Will he get an erection? All the way? How long will it last? Long enough to satisfy his wife? Will she respond? Is she doing all she should? Is she doing it right? Can she herself let go and come? How long will it take her? Can he last that long?

Mentally, each partner gets out a stopwatch, a camera, and a tape recorder. Anxiety mounts to unbearable tension. Each makes an imperious demand on the other. And on himself—or herself. The result is disaster.

A mutually satisfying sexual experience can be wished for but it cannot be willed. One former male patient who had been a college athlete compared the sex act to a free throw in basketball: "You know the whole game may depend on it but that's the thing you have to forget. You've got to have the skills—where to put your feet and hands and eyes. You put in your mind a vision of that ball going in the basket. Then you relax and just do it."

Couples, sometimes literally, cry out, "Why did this happen to us? Why should we be sexually inadequate?" Their protest is that when younger they were obedient kids, polite to their elders, well behaved, ate their Wheaties, did their homework, helped Mom and Dad with the household chores, brushed their teeth, earned their merit badges —so why?

Building Penile and Pelvic Response

Masters and Johnson suggest, let's go on to building sensate focus. The two words, "sensate focus" may well be the sophisticated phrase of the coming year. Six months from now you may go into a shadowy, cool, kindly saloon, order a dark beer and say, "I need to restore my sensate focus." Or you may stretch out on the beach and watch a full moon rise over Acapulco or Coney Island and say, "How's that for restoring sensate focus?"

Sensate focus means zeroing in to the buildup of a very strong sensual feeling. An intense emotional experience conveyed by sight, touch, taste, sound, and smell. Sensate focus is what healthily adjusted couples naturally initiate to build sexual excitement.

"They're playing our song!" Depending on your generation it may mean dancing cheek to cheek, skinny-dipping at midnight, drinking champagne out of golden slippers, or licking champagne off erogenous zones.

One married couple, wedded for twenty-five years, testify that an Italian pop song, "Un Bacio" (translation "One more smothering kiss"), played on their hi-fi is enough to give the husband an immediate erection and the wife a lubricated, swollen vulva—both ready for immediate sexual contact. Their explanation is that when they were somewhat younger they were once separated for a period of eighteen days while he was on a trip to Europe. When he returned he brought her an expensive dress and coat, a beaded evening bag—and a record of "Un Bacio." The record was playing as they tumbled happily into bed in an ecstatic reunion, and the rather inconsequential music and even more absurd lyric has ever since been a part of their sensate focus. When a sophisticated friend skeptically asked, "If you respond to erotic music why not try Ravel or Wagner?" They answered, "But 'Un Bacio' is our song!"

People who can do it have a hard time understanding people who can't. And what happens when one who can do it marries one who can't? This question occurs very often in the roundtable sessions at the Reproductive Biology Research Foundation. A woman defensively says (having been encouraged to reveal her sexual history) "I had a lover before I was married. I was easily able to do it with him!" And the husband says something of the same, usually claiming even wider and more impressive sexual exploits.

There is a major hang-up between the sexes, however. A woman can blandly lie and say, "I had orgasms with my former lover," and no one can dispute her. Who except herself knows if she is orgasmic? A *man can't lie*—certainly not to his present partner—about an erection or an ejaculation or the length of time that ensues between each action.

On building sensate focus Dr. Masters and Mrs. Johnson think that clothing—even alluring black chiffon—distracts from the wish of two people to have a preorgasmic experience. The male and female partners have been told repeatedly that "you have to give to get" and that the way to start is by a gentle trial-and-error method that involves rubbing, kissing, stroking, and otherwise caressing.

They call this "pleasuring" and "being pleasured."

Dr. Masters and Mrs. Johnson tell their patients that in building sensate focus or "pleasuring" each one has a single responsibility—that is, to keep the other from accidentally doing something annoying. There are some people who like having their necks nibbled and others who literally find it a pain in the neck. As stated before, body areas known to be directly sexually responsive must be carefully avoided. That's according to directions.

Hopefully, a warm, tender, expectant glow will be generated within a day or two. If not, roundtable discussions will talk more about what does turn the couple on. Do they like holding hands? A double bed? Perfume? What kind of art? What kind of smelling, touching, or feeling experiences do they enjoy—or dislike? Sand between toes? Muddy-bottomed swimming holes? Wine? Going barefoot?

How much privacy do they ideally wish to have? Separate bedrooms? Separate dressing rooms? Bathroom separate from the rest of the family? Do you kiss each other when separating for the daily tasks? How do you react to good news—do you cry and say "Thank God!" or jump up and down and shout "Hallelujah!" How do you take bad news? Stiff upper lip? Or fall apart?

It is hoped that what Masters and Johnson call "the dimension of touch and smell and sight" will rebuild natural sexual response. This doesn't mean looking at dirty pictures or reading pornography but a series of sensate exercises as described in the opening chapter of this book. Those who recoil from touching or being touched are introduced to "smelly" experiences. One hundred marital units were chosen for the experiment. Masters and Johnson think of fragrance as a possible first line of attack on the problem of sexual response.

They didn't just pour Arpège or Chanel No. 5 on everybody. A special moisturizing lotion was produced on order —not unlike old fashioned Jergen's Lotion or Italian Balm. Both scented and unscented lotions were offered. The scented lotions consisted of four generally thought to be "feminine"—floral, mossy, woody, and oriental. In addition, "masculine" odors were incorporated—lavender, lemon-lime, pine.

The partners were directed to apply the lotion to one another's bodies. "It was just an experimental idea" on the part of Masters and Johnson, but it paid surprising dividends. Patients who frankly had described themselves as nauseated by the odor of seminal fluid or the lubricant that is produced in the vagina of a sexually excited woman found that problem solved.

More significant, men and women who had previously never handled their partner's genitals were now, with the medical authority telling them to apply the lotion, able to do so. It was permissible. The doctor told them to do it. And they found it was fun. They moved quickly to bypassing the bottled lotion and feeling comfortable—for the first time in their lives—with the warm, slippery, viscous feeling of seminal fluid and vaginal lubrication.

Of the one hundred couples, eighteen rejected the use of the lotion. They described it variously as meaningless, undignified, or juvenile. Genital-area moisturizers are not an overwhelming success but seem to be worth trying.

Thus the first three days at the Foundation are devoted to reception, history-taking, medical examinations, preliminary interviews, and the initial experiments in building sensate focus. Daily roundtable discussions analyze and summarize the development of the case.

For most couples, day number four involves discussion of what happened on day number three. After the first three days, however, there is no rigidly scheduled program. By the end of 72 hours the medical examinations have been completed, the social and emotional histories recorded, and treatment is individualized. Day number four usually involves discussion of what happened on day number three. It is hoped that the couples will report that they were able to give and receive physical pleasure. They are reminded to help each other out. Now they are not only charged with the responsibility of protecting themselves from unwelcome gestures but guiding each other toward the welcome ones. Each partner is instructed to place his or her hand gently on top of the other and guide the lover toward the good experiences. The guiding hand is also instructed to indicate changes in pressure or to signal to go more swiftly or more slowly.

Medical direction still strictly limits what is going on. There is a careful lecture on the subject of pelvic anatomy. It's quite amazing to learn that even couples who have been married for years and had children don't have a very clear idea of what really goes on down there. Many don't even know what they themselves really look like! Amazingly, many men who have for years felt and fingered female genitals have actually never seen them.

The close of the fourth day usually marks permission for husband and wife to talk to each other about their sensual experiences. The husband or wife can say, "I liked what you did to me." They are directed to spend longer periods of time "pleasuring" each other. When the patients ask, "Like how long?" they are told, "As long as it's pleasant." There is no clock and no checklist. Dalliance is the order of that day.

In the experiments of building sensate focus through touch and smell Masters and Johnson hope some sexual excitement appears. It is inquired into casually, at the daily roundtable, as though it didn't matter much. The idea is not to provoke anxiety.

"By the way, was there any sign of an erection last night when you were caressing one another?" Except in cases of primary impotence—men who have never had an erection—the answer is nearly always, "Yes," or "I think so."

Men who are in treatment at the clinic for premature ejaculation nearly always report at least a partial erection. *During the two weeks at the clinic they are honor bound not to attempt sexual intercourse or relief through masturbation except at medical direction.* There may be some who cheat, but they don't confess it. The idea, as Masters and Johnson keep telling them, is to create a playful, relaxed, undemanding sexual response. "You aren't necessarily going anywhere." "Take it easy."

There is also a clinical difficulty (that's a technical phrase meaning that the doctors themselves can't really be sure) in defining a premature ejaculator. A man who ejaculates before he thrusts his penis into the vagina is most definitely a premature ejaculator. But if, before ejaculating, the erect penis makes a penetrating thrust or two into the vagina—enough thrusts to accommodate the entire penis in the barrel of the vagina he is a functioning male. His ejaculation occurs in the vagina and his sperm, if united with an egg cell, can potentially create a child.

Such a man is a premature ejaculator only if his wife says so. He has enjoyed his stimulation, erection, penetration, and ejaculation. As far as he's concerned there's nothing to complain about. He may wistfully think, "Well, I wish it could have lasted longer" but he has had a complete experience. His wife, however, tells him that she hasn't, and that it's his fault. He hasn't "lasted long enough!"

The husband feels inadequate because he hasn't delivered any joy. Actually the idea of the prolonged penetration and multiple penile thrusts has its inconsistencies. The late Dr. Alfred Kinsey was convinced that men who can ejaculate within a few moments of penetration are by far the most proficient of human males. When Armageddon or something like it—the Johnstown flood or mother-in-law pounding on the door—abruptly interrupts the sex act, it is the male who can get the ejaculation done in a hurry who will succeed in reproducing his kind. So Kinsey—metaphorically—pins a medal on him. And Masters and Johnson say, "Man, you need help."

Treatment of Premature Ejaculation

In past decades—or even centuries back—so-called sex consultants and medical personnel, to say nothing of theologians and politicians, have attempted to state and legislate what is and isn't competent and proper sexual expression. The Bible tells us that God gets angry when a man practices preejaculatory withdrawal—spills his seed upon the ground. But the Bible in the Song of Solomon gives us some rather useful and explicit coaching in the building of sensate focus. Later on in the New Testament St. Paul reverses the field and tells us that it's probably better to live without sex but that since most of us can't it's better to be married.

Recently a number of philosophically oriented psychiatrists have proposed the idea that orgasmic experience is a relatively new sensation for women. They say women got along for centuries without ever experiencing orgasmic response or worrying about it. They say all women have historically wanted is married status, a home, and the joys of childrearing—that those few women who did experience orgasm were surprised and pleased but thought of it not as an expectation or a right but as a treat. Don't believe it!

Mrs. Johnson is disturbed that most of these remarks are made by men about women. She says, "How do they know?" There is a large body of evidence in literature, history, and the word-of-mouth personal experience passed from mother to daughter that persuades the student of female sexuality that women have been orgasmic since Eve. Other women who were presumably sexually satisfied come to mind: the Queen of Sheba, Helen of Troy, Ulysses' Penelope, Romeo's Juliet. . . .

Queen Victoria, who is often accused of being entirely responsible for sexual repression in the English-speaking world of the past century, is revealed by some biographers as having been more than satisfied by Prince Albert. And on a more private basis there are many records of warm, devoted, emotionally fulfilled love affairs and marriages that could only have come from reciprocal sex.

The problem of premature ejaculation, therefore, is not something thought up in the last few months by the women's liberation movement.

Where it exists, it can be a great source of frustration to the couple involved. There are some men who get so nervous or excited that they ejaculate before they can get the penis into the vagina. There are others who can penetrate but ejaculate before the wife has had an orgasm. The Masters and Johnson research and clinical experience seem to put these "inadequate" males in the same category. We would not presume to argue with these experts but we might presume to ask a man which kind of a premature ejaculator he'd rather be: One who can't perform the complete sex act and therefore cannot normally father a child and repeatedly subjects himself to humiliation? Or one who can perform and be a father but has to contend with a disappointed and angry wife?

The question arises: whose fault is premature ejaculation? The man's—or what the priest, minister, rabbi, or his parents may have told him—or his wife's slow response? Or is it their mutually clumsy and inept lovemaking? Is there a need for development of more sensate focus?

Dr. Masters and Mrs. Johnson tell their patients that good sex is anything that is sexually satisfactory to man and wife. They become markedly impatient with definitions that say a man must "hold out" for a certain number of minutes before he can qualify as a virile lover. One "authority" says "at least twelve minutes." "Nonsense!" say Masters and Johnson.

Experienced lovers can manipulate one another to accommodate almost any chosen time schedule. The time schedule of lovemaking can also be influenced by environment. A national organization concerned with birth control once sent a researcher into a small Midwestern town to find out why the citizens had such an astonishingly high birth rate. After weeks of interviewing the sociologist reported soberly, "The trouble seems to be with the railroad. You see the freight train goes through town at six-fifteen in the morning—too early to get up and too late to get back to sleep!"

Dr. Masters told a class of medical students at Washington University that a female can respond orgasmically 30 seconds after penetration if she has been stimulated to be "wildly ready." Looking around the nearly all-male class we saw a mass reaction of surprise and relief. They seemed glad to have the word from authority. There's no doubt that lots of men think they are premature ejaculators and inadequate lovers when nothing is wrong except that they aren't in rhythm with their partners.

Misconceptions excepted, however, there *are* premature ejaculators, and there are men who, with their wives, would like to spend a longer time in pelvic thrusting than they are now doing. Dr. Masters and Mrs. Johnson feel that a male has a premature ejaculation problem if he's unable to satisfy his partner at least 50 percent of the time. *Providing, that is, the female partner is capable of being satisfied.*

They also say the premature ejaculation often reflects sociocultural orientation. Dr. Masters and Mrs. Johnson state (and their statistical research confirms it) that males of lesser education, lesser income, and lesser socioeconomic groups are less likely to care about whether their female partners are orgasmic. This includes their wives, not only their casual sexual partners. Working-class couples have more frequent sexual contacts—Dr. Masters said, ". . . they take it for granted nearly every night like washing the dishes." The men don't concern themselves with their wives' response. If they do, fine; if they don't, it's none of their concern. Under such conditions it's amazing how many women do manage to grab the brass ring!

"Grabbing the brass ring" is a favorite phrase of Dr. Masters—used as often as Mrs. Johnson's, "Let me give you a baseline." No one, so far as we know, has asked him why he equates satisfactory intercourse with a ride on a merry-go-round. He seems to say that on most occasions it's exhilarating but chancy.

What Mrs. Johnson and Dr. Masters have not tried to explain is why working-class men appear to care less or perhaps are less sensitive to their women's orgasmic response. Are the wives of working-class men not as critical? Or are they generally less expectant and less demanding in all phases of life? Dr. Masters might say, "That's not our bag."

Dr. Masters goes on to say that many working-class men who feel an "obligation" to have sex every night consider rapidity of ejaculation a convenience. "The faster they get it over with, the better!"

Masters and Johnson do not say what happens to the sex habits of the truck driver who saves his money, buys a partnership in the company, and moves to a better neighborhood. That may not be their bag either.

Masters and Johnson feel that all women, regardless of class, clearly have a right to complain about premature ejaculation. It's difficult for a woman to feel sexual tensions elevate during preliminary sex play, approach orgasm during the first few thrusts of penetration, and then get no orgasmic payoff. It makes them angry. It can cause them to be shrewish and cranky for days afterwards.

What factors create a premature ejaculator? Why do some men strike out at the plate or barely manage to reach first base? The athletic metaphor is unfair for Dr. Masters says it has absolutely nothing to do with physical condition—assuming the male partner is in reasonably good health. The halfback on the college team may be a premature ejaculator. The water boy may be "better" in bed.

Sexual histories recorded by Masters and Johnson are consistent in revealing premature ejaculators as culturally conditioned. The circumstances under which most American men have their early sex experiences are at fault.

Men in their forties who went to the Masters–Johnson clinic for help with premature ejaculation frequently turned out to have had their first sex with bored, impatient prostitutes, who have said, "Come on, let's go. I only got a few minutes." If the man—then a lad—was slow or clumsy, she masturbated him, often irritably reminding him that she needed a high turnover to make a decent living.

Here's what a 47-year-old man, who has flunked two marriages because he is a premature ejaculator, told about his first sex experiences:

"I volunteered the day after Pearl Harbor. The Japanese bombed Pearl Harbor on a Sunday if you remember. I had a steady girl. She was at my house that afternoon for Sunday dinner. After church we heard the news.

"I immediately said, 'I'm going!' My girl and my mother cried. My father slapped me on the back. Monday morning at 6 A.M. I was on the steps of the recruiting station along with about fifty other guys.

"I passed the physical and I had three days to spend with my girl. We did some heavy necking. But we parted still virgins. In the Army it was different. They took it for granted that we were all having sexual outlets.

"One night I joined a bunch of guys lined up outside a pretty expensive—ten dollars a throw—whorehouse in a town near our camp. We have to remember that in those days Army privates were getting $28 a month. We were promised something special.

"The problem was the line was very long and I was near the end of it and we all had to be back at the base at midnight. Not only were the prostitutes saying, 'Hurry!' but your own buddies were standing outside there and yelling to hurry it up. So I became a ram-bam, thank-you-ma'am sort of a guy."

Other men have had their first experiences under the fearful shadow of adult authority and the fear of interruption. Policemen flashing floodlights on them as they are trying to make out with their girl in the back seat of the family car. Or being surprised on the living-room couch by parents coming home early because the party was dull or the movie overcrowded.

As far as one's future sex life is concerned Dr. Masters and Mrs. Johnson take a dim view of most advanced forms of adolescent sex play. They believe the female is overstimulated, often without relief. And the male is moved to hasty ejaculation. Virginity is preserved, but such patterns have a way of persisting after marriage when they are no longer necessary or desirable, if indeed they ever were.

Another common sexual practice in which partners shortchange each other is one of the oldest forms of birth control—withdrawal immediately prior to ejaculation. If withdrawal is skillfully practiced, both the male and the female may obtain sexual satisfaction. But the method does not teach the male to control his ejaculation schedule or to be considerate of his partner's orgasmic response. He pulls out in a hurry when he gets the unmistakable physiological signal that he is about to ejaculate. Dr. Masters says this practice not only unhappily "trains" men to be premature ejaculators and therefore poor lovers but is also an inadequate system of birth control as a few drops of seminal fluid loaded with sperm can escape before the warning signal is felt.

Contrary to popular belief, masturbation does not cause a man to be a premature ejaculator. Masturbation has been blamed for everything from insanity to poor grades but it has no known effect on a man's future as an efficient lover.

When asked to estimate the number of premature ejaculating husbands who fail to satisfy their wives, Masters and Johnson are dismayed. They think there are hundreds of thousands of such cases. Many wives suffer without knowing what they are suffering from. (After all they have a house and yard and a fence around it and three nice children and a diamond wristwatch.)

Their ill temper is blamed on everything from menstrual periods to their mothers-in-law.

Those who do come into the Reproductive Biological Research Foundation clinic for consultation about premature ejaculation include husbands who can't be touched on the penis without quickly ejaculating, who ejaculate within moments of looking at a picture of Raquel Welch or reading a semipornographic paragraph in a Norman Mailer novel, or those who ejaculate while engaging in love play.

These are in the minority, however. The majority who seek help at the Foundation are those who ejaculate within the first few thrusts of the penis into the vagina—before the wife has a chance to arrive at orgasm.

Such a patient brings with him a wife who is often attractive, intelligent, informed, and has read most of the sex manuals. She knows her husband has a problem but it hasn't yet occurred to her that as a partner in a marriage she has one, too.

Unfortunately, many married couples with this problem don't get around to seeking treatment for quite a long time. It may be five years after marriage. Or it may be 20 years.

In the interim they don't understand why there is so much quarreling, distraction, and exhaustion. They are diverted by the husband's upward climb in profession or business, the wife's energetic devotion to childrearing, the adventure of establishing a home—until the wife reaches the point where she is ready to split. She may go to a psychiatrist. Yet studies show that psychotherapeutic support for the wife of a premature ejaculator rarely does much good. Technically it's called "palliative" which means something in the nature of a Band-Aid.

Or she may take a lover. Dr. Masters and Mrs. Johnson seldom make nonphysiological judgments; they are only interested in repair jobs. Yet they flatly say the wife who gets involved with other men—be it the milkman or her husband's best friend—is likely to find herself unresponsive with other male partners also. This may be due to guilt (adultery is still socially disapproved and penalized) or perhaps because the other man's sexual efficiency downgrades her own self-confidence. (*"Why couldn't I attract a man as good as that in the first place?"*) Masters and Johnson say some women caught in this bind seek other women for sexual partners.

What happens more often, however, is a period of years of struggle, during which both partners are bewildered and unhappy. The wife knows she's not getting sexual satisfaction. Her husband doesn't know why she is such a bitch.* They have no sensate focus.

In this period, the wife verbalizes and acts out her sexual discontent. Every time she does it, she makes things worse. If you keep telling a person he is no good and he has it demonstrated to him every day, he begins to believe it. It builds up—in Masters' and Johnson's words—a "frightful concern." Pretty soon the husband begins to act like a second-rate person even if he wasn't one before.

Now the married sexual pattern changes. The husband accepts his identity as a sexual *schlemiel* (a vivid Yiddish word that means a worthless do-nothing). The wife goes to visit her mother or her older sister and stays longer than she planned. He goes on lengthy fishing trips. She gets so tired, coping with the laundry and all, that she goes

---

*Dr. J. M. Lewis, Director of Research at the Timberlawn Foundation in Dallas, has met many such couples. He says, "Some men respond by increasing the frequency of sexual attempts, others by withdrawal from all attempts, and still others by finding a sexual partner other than his wife."

to bed early, and—not to disturb her—he sleeps on the sofa. They have sex once or twice a month.

Masters and Johnson say this sexual abstinence is the worst possible thing that can happen to a premature ejaculator. If he seldom has a chance for sexual contact, the more tense and anxious he is about each encounter and the more difficulty he is likely to have.

The woman pays a costly penalty also. The more she beats a man down—the more she makes him feel like two cents worth of nothing—the greater disservice she does to herself. There may be a proletarian pride in wearing a cloth coat instead of mink—but there's no pride in wearing an inadequate man on your arm!

There are two popularly accepted remedies for premature ejaculation. Masters and Johnson say positively that neither of them work. But they're still frequently tried.

The first is the "don't touch" theory. The wife is to do absolutely nothing to stimulate her husband or bring about any "sensate focus." She doesn't even wink, kiss, or wiggle. When her husband has achieved an erection he mounts her as rapidly as he can, each of them hoping he'll last long enough to get inside. The system sometimes works well enough to create a child, but no one has yet reported that it's much fun.

The second is the "think about something else" technique. The husband can achieve an erection and make a vaginal penetration, but after that the idea is to keep his mind on something else. Recently we were told of a 20-year-old boy who lost his girl friend because he was a premature ejaculator. He said, "I was advised to put my mind on a distant problem. So once I got into my girl I used to replay last week's soccer game. I scored last week's winning goal but not the one I was after. She left me for another guy!"

Men older and presumably better informed than this young man say they add up their bank balances, review an argument with a neighbor about a borrowed lawn mower, or count backward from one hundred. Others distract themselves with frantic physical action—biting the lower lip, pulling their hair, pinching themselves, even contracting the rectal sphincter.

None of it helps. The husband comes prematurely. The wife cries or is silent or is furious. They go to the bathroom

—separately—and take an aspirin or a tranquilizer. Maybe they tell each other it will be better next time. The stupid and tragic error is that they have acted to reduce the sensate input rather than enhance it. As Mrs. Johnson says over and over, "You have to give to get!"

Clinical records show that premature ejaculators, faced with repeated failures, often retrogress sexually and become impotent. The transition is clearly marked and alarming. The man may ejaculate when he has half an erection and, later, may ejaculate with no visible erection. Actually, in Masters' and Johnson's words, he just "seeps" seminal fluid and reveals no pressure.

Rapid ejaculators remain that way all their lives unless they go out of their way to learn calculated methods of control. Masters and Johnson are convinced that premature ejaculation can be successfully treated with a simple technique. To hundreds of thousands of couples who suffer because the man "comes" too fast or the woman too slow this simple physiological device can mean a great deal.

How can you describe it? The learned "slow-down" for the man? The learned "speed-up" for the woman? One woman said, "It's like switching from an electric stove to a gas stove." A man compared it to switching from an aluminum tennis racquet back to a wooden one.

A couple that comes to the Reproductive Biology Research Foundation clinic complaining of premature ejaculation are told that at the very instant the ejaculatory experience begins the wife can temporarily retard it by applying what Dr. Masters and Mrs. Johnson call the "squeeze technique." (See figure 1, p. 56). They didn't invent it. They credit it to Dr. James H. Semans, who first described it in "Premature Ejaculation: A New Approach" (*Southern Medical Journal*, 49: 353-357, 1956).

Dr. Masters and Mrs. Johnson tell this wife to begin at once and touch her husband's genitals. She is supposed to fondle him to an erection, with or without lotion. Then they assume a position that is called "training position for ejaculatory control." (See figure 2, p. 57).

In this position the female partner sits up straight, her back braced by the head of the bed, and possibly supported by pillows. She spreads her legs. Her husband lies opposite her on his back, his head in the direction of the end of the

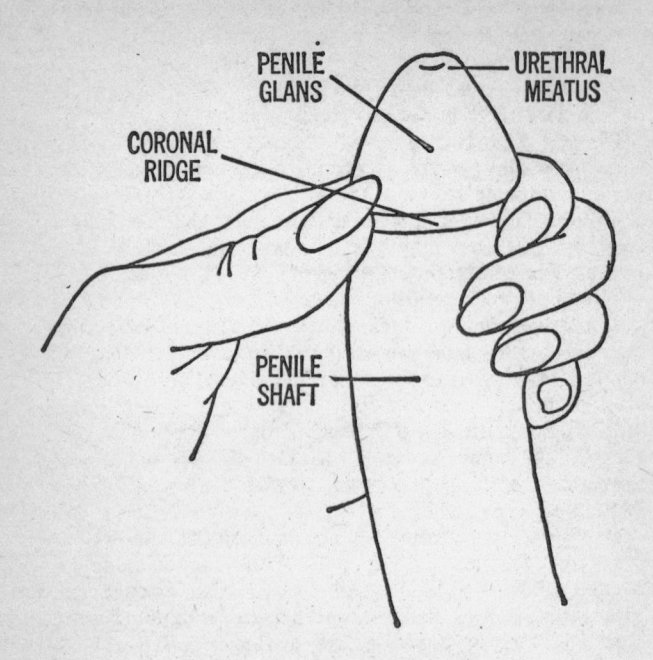

PENILE GLANS — **URETHRAL MEATUS**
CORONAL RIDGE
PENILE SHAFT

1. The Penile Squeeze Technique

bed, and his pelvis placed between her legs. His legs are bent at the knees and placed on either side of her thighs. He is enclosing her with his feet, which are pressing against her buttocks.

Now the wife does freely whatever any sexually cooperative woman would ordinarily do to help excite a penile erection with hands or mouth. Their genitals are close together but not engaged.

When an erection happens she acts to deflate it. She employs the "squeeze technique."

"What?" the authors asked Dr. Masters and Mrs. Johnson, "You mean when the male has an erection the wife acts to put him down?"

"Yes!" they confirmed.

The idea of their treatment is that couples suffering from inadequate ejaculatory control bring themselves to the

2. Training Position For Ejaculatory Control

point of climax—and then reduce their excitement. In repeating the process, hopefully the second response is more intense. Then the reduction is brought about once more. Masters and Johnson only talk about it in terms of re-educating the prematurely ejaculating male but apparently it can be worked both ways.

Here's what Masters and Johnson say in regard to the now famous penile squeeze technique: *When the male reaches a clearly observed erection, the female squeezes his penis, just below the glans. (The glans is that forward-looking, lumpy, and larger part that resembles the head of a jet-prop engine.) With the thumb underneath and the first two fingers on top she squeezes good and hard. (The female is admonished not to be afraid to squeeze firmly—it won't hurt.) The penis should be squeezed for three to four seconds. The erection remains but the immediate need to ejaculate disappears.*

Patients at the Masters-Johnson clinic are shown how to do it with plastic or rubber models. What happens is that a percentage of the husband's penile erection subsides, but he still feels fine and is sexually excited. They resume love play. When he again feels the warning onset of ejaculation, he asks her to squeeze again. There are some wives who just can't bring themselves to squeeze the penis hard enough to make the squeeze play work.

A wife told us, "I squeezed, just as I'd been instructed, but I asked my husband, 'Doesn't it hurt?' He said, 'No, I think you're supposed to squeeze harder.' So I did. But I was still afraid that he was just being brave."

For such hesitants, Dr. Masters and Mrs. Johnson direct that the husband place his fingers over his wife's and show her just how much pressure he can bear.

What happens next is described by Masters and Johnson as "nondemanding intromission." That's their delicate and dignified way of describing a posture for intercourse in which the wife is in command and yet makes no demands on her husband. (See figure 3, p. 59). It is said by historians to have been highly favored and popular among the upper classes in Rome about 2,000 years ago. Seemingly its advantage is that it is the sexual position least tiring for the male.

The "female superior coital position"—or, Roman position—is advocated by Masters and Johnson, like the squeeze play on the penis, as a temporary technique to cure sexual inadequacy. (If, afterwards, it proves pleasant and useful, that's a matter of personal choice.) It is combined, at the direction of the cotherapists of the Reproductive Biology Research Foundation, with the squeeze play, and is usually advocated toward the close of the sixth day of treatment. It is carried out as do all other personal physical encounters in the Masters–Johnson therapy, in the total unrecorded privacy of the married couple's bedroom. Here is how it goes:

Over the past three or four days the couple has learned to do the squeeze. No penetration of the penis into the vagina has yet occurred. It's been strictly against orders. But now they have the green light.

The husband lies supine—that is spine down on the mattress—with his head toward the headboard of the bed. His legs are slightly spread apart. His wife crouches astride him with her bent knees approximately opposite his nipples. She uses all the techniques she has been taught in the past few days—including the massaging lotion—to encourage him to have an erection. She may apply the

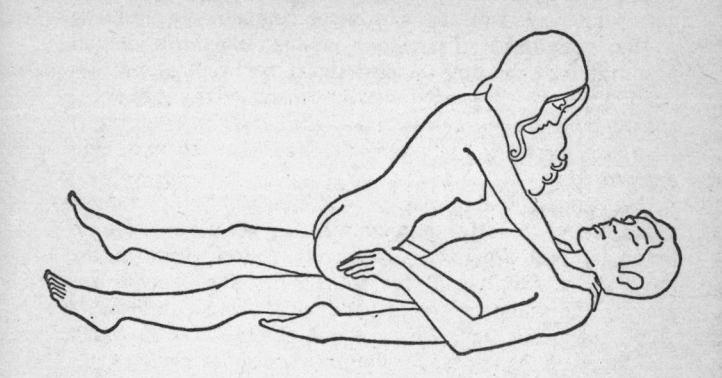

3. The Female Superior Position

squeeze technique several times as her husband's erection and impulse to ejaculate builds and goes away. Then she leans gently forward so that her breasts are dangling over his chest. With her hand she gently guides her husband's penis so that it slips effortlessly into her vagina. His hands support her hips.

Dr. Masters tells medical students that the woman should always guide the penis into the vagina. He says soberly, "Why not? She knows where it goes."

Once the penis is inserted the wife does not move. She doesn't rock back and forth. She must not "sit down" strongly on her husband's hips but remains in the leaning forward position. Her hands may be on his shoulders or on the mattress beside his shoulders. Neither is asking anything of the other at that time except the quiet pleasure of vaginal containment. If the husband tells his wife he feels the onset of an ejaculation she arches her back, permitting the penis to slide out, and firmly performs the squeeze therapy. Then she reinserts the penis as before.

Pelvic thrusting on his or her part is still forbidden. The husband is cautiously given permission to move his penis in and out of her vagina just enough to retain his erection. The wife is under orders to remain motionless.

Couples often ask why the female "superior" position is

advocated. They worry about whether it reinforces the male's already sensitive feelings of inadequacy—to be put flat on his back with his wife in the commanding position. In the roundtable discussions it's all explained. Sexual positions have become bogged down (or "hung up," depending on which generation you belong to) by numerous absurd taboos. *The best sexual position for intercourse is whatever serves at the moment what you both need and want to do.*

One understanding patient commented, "Why not all kinds of positions for intercourse? Do we have one kind of chair? No! We have straight chairs for sitting at the table so we won't spill the soup. We have benches for playing the piano or eating barbecued ribs so our elbows won't get in the way. We have arm chairs for sitting back and thinking. And sofas for flopping and snoozing."

In some states, however, there are archaic laws that prohibit a woman from assuming any position on top of a man.* Yet Masters and Johnson state positively that the most common position for sex in the United States—the man above—is the poorest for male ejaculatory control. Even gravity is against him.

Other questions that arise concern what happens to the crouched, motionless wife while she is entertaining an erected penis that isn't doing anything. The answer is that she is experiencing a slow but sure elevation of her own sexual tension. She is also having the opportunity to think and feel responsively for perhaps the first time in her life. She mustn't demand or coax or pump. Just suspend herself, enjoy the penile intromission, and feel sexual excitation mount.

When the male is able to move with cautious, upward pelvic thrusts and still retain his control, the woman is told to begin to make equally mild responses.

Now they are told to change their position to what Dr. Masters and Mrs. Johnson state is the best position for coitus—that is, the lateral position. (See figure 4, p. 61). They refer to it as a multiple protection system. They state that couples who have tried it and learned how to do

---

*Dr. Masters said "If all the sex laws were enforced, there would be nobody left to be jailers!"

4. The Lateral Position

it use lateral coitional positioning by choice. Here's how it goes:

The couple start in the female superior position described before and begin mild pelvic thrusting. The squeeze play is brought into use if needed. Then they shift to a lateral, face to face position, as follows:

Situation: The husband is lying on his back with his legs spread slightly apart. His wife is crouching over him, with her legs outside his thighs leaning forward over his chest. Now they decide to convert.

Step 1: The husband takes his left hand and lifts his wife's right leg.

Step 2: The husband moves his left leg under her right leg so that his leg is now outside of hers.

Step 3: The husband raises his left leg so that it's bent

at a 40-degree angle and the sole of his foot is resting on the mattress.

Step 4: The wife lengthens out her right leg. Her right leg is now between her husband's legs. Her weight is now leaning on her remaining bent knee—her left knee.

Step 5: She lowers and extends her body so that it is even more parallel—almost chest to chest, although her left leg is still bent and her weight is balanced on that knee.

Step 6: The husband puts his left hand across her shoulders in the middle of her neck and his right hand on her buttocks and uses the strength of his arms to hold them firmly together.

Step 7: Now they roll—he to the left, she to the right. The penis remains in the vagina.

Step 8: They complete the roll. The male is turned on his right flank: The woman is largely lying on her stomach, tipped to her left off her husband's torso. Each may need to be propped in that position by pillows. Her right thigh rests its weight on his left thigh.

Step 9: The woman puts her right arm and the husband puts his left arm around each other's necks. Their other two arms are left free for fondling and love play.

Step 10: The wife bends her right leg upward a bit so that her knee is braced against the bed. Her left leg is thrown over her husband's right hip so her knee is resting on the bed. With these slightly bent knees and her weight thrown to her left, she has leverage for bearing down on the penis at her and his will.

Masters and Johnson admit there may be some difficulty in converting from the female-mounted "superior" position to the lateral position. In their textbook they do not say who blows the whistle. Presumably the idea is mutual or it comes from one partner and is willingly acceded to by the other.

When a couple with a problem of premature ejaculation has learned to use this position they are almost ready for graduation from the Foundation program. They are told that the squeeze technique is not supposed to be a part of their future sex life but should be used, when needed, for the next few months. They are encouraged to have frequent and regular sex. In-between times they are urged to be spontaneous—to do what comes naturally.

Hopefully, when they leave the Foundation they will leave their stopwatches and anxieties behind them. The sense of putting on a performance will also have disappeared. Wives are told that in the early days of their menstrual period, when most couples do not care to have intercourse, they can use their time manually stimulating their husbands and then using the squeeze technique. Masters and Johnson consistently emphasize the role of the wife in pre-ejaculatory problems. To the woman who asks, "Why can't he turn himself off?" they say something like, "He can learn to turn himself off, but it doesn't help to reeducate him alone. When he goes back to you, he would have just as much trouble as ever. However, if you can help to reeducate him, together you can work out this problem."

Sometimes after leaving the Foundation there occurs, for reasons no one knows, a period of impotence. It sends former patients scurrying to the telephone. They are assured not to worry; that's the way it works. Masters' and Johnson's reported success rate—based on cures lasting five years or more—in this most common of male problems is 97.8 percent. But they say repeatedly that it can't be done without a cooperative, involved sex partner. They seem to feel that as the sexual double standard dwindles, and men and women assume a joint and equal responsibility for one another's sexual joy, the anxiety-ridden rapid ejaculation symptom will disappear.

Men Who Cannot Ejaculate

"Ejaculatory incompetence—that should only be my problem!" said one man bitterly. "So you can't have a child—so what? You can get it up. You can get it in. You can do just about everything else you're supposed to do. If you have sense enough to keep your mouth shut, your wife may not even know the difference!"

Masters and Johnson call ejaculatory incompetence the reverse side of the coin of premature ejaculation. One group of men do it too early; the other group just can't do it at all. A woman may scorn or get angry at the premature ejaculator, but she is only puzzled and sometimes frightened by the man who can't ejaculate. It seems so unnatural.

There is one favorable aspect of the problem; these nonejaculatory men carry on active, intravaginal pelvic thrusting for long periods of time and their women are often multiorgasmic. They may not get pregnant, but otherwise they can't complain.

Nevertheless, it's a serious problem in male inadequacy albeit a fairly rare one. Over a period of 11 years, Dr. Masters and Mrs. Johnson encountered only 17 patients with this diagnosis.

Masters and Johnson "blame" many nonejaculation cases on rough "old-time religion." They cite histories such as:

An orthodox Jew who attempted his first sexual experience at age 24. He was persuaded to desist by the young woman who said she was menstruating. Orthodox Judaism strictly forbids intercourse during the menstrual period and for some days thereafter. He took her straight home and never saw her again. Some years later he married, and he and his wife conformed strictly to the Orthodox Jewish rules about menstruation. But the young man developed such a horror of being contaminated by the vagina that he "dried up"—he couldn't ejaculate even when the calendar schedule of his religion gave him permission. He just couldn't mix his body fluid with his wife's.

A 36-year-old Roman Catholic man who told how at age 13 his mother was horrified to discover him masturbating. She told his father who punished the boy severely. Then they took him to a religious adviser. The boy was by this time terrified and nearly in hysterics. He was told his act threatened him with mental illness and that he would never be able to "be a man" if he ever did it again. The boy not only never masturbated, he never even had a nocturnal emission. When he grew up and married, he could not ejaculate. The guilty shock at age 13 had indeed unmanned him.

A son—an only child—trained by a rigidly Protestant mother and father to total physical privacy. No sharing of the family bathroom. No showers at school. No dating until age 18 and then only under conditions that would have exhausted a Spanish duenna. All his father told him about sex was that the seminal fluid was dirty, an insult to a good woman, and that intercourse was only to be resorted to when children were desired. At age 26 the young man married a 27-year-old woman who came from the "right" background. The family minister, shortly before the ceremony, warned him that his bride would be in terrible pain at the first sexual encounter. But on the wedding night the young man found that his penis slid into her vagina quite easily. He was immediately angry and suspicious. He withdrew and started to question her. She broke down and admitted she wasn't a virgin. There was a terrible quarrel. She begged for forgiveness. Although he said he forgave her, he couldn't ejaculate. For the next seven years he spent 45 minutes or more several nights a week in vigorous pelvic thrusting. She became multiorgasmic. But the more sexually responsive his wife became, the more alienated he felt toward her. He was sure her premarital experience was responsible for her sexual pleasure. He subconsciously didn't want to be contaminated by discharging into her vagina. He became a totally nonejaculatory male.

These "freeze-outs" are extreme. To some readers they may also sound outdated. Unfortunately many children are still reared that way.

Masters and Johnson report that other men are non-ejaculatory with their wives simply because they don't like them. How can you argue with that?

They cite the case of a man who was married to a rich and domineering distant cousin. She kept telling him that if it weren't for her father's money he wouldn't amount to anything. So he denied her—subconsciously—his seed.

Another man was secretly homosexual. He married to preserve appearances in his career but really didn't even want to touch a woman. He had a male lover and was able to ejaculate with him but was unable to do so with his wife.

A third patient married a woman who was, unfortunately, ugly. Studies of art and history reveal that women who might be considered "ugly" have nevertheless been sexually attractive to men but not, seemingly, this one. She made the grievous error of insisting on consummating the marriage. The more she demanded, the further her husband retreated. He rarely attempted intercourse and could not ejaculate.

A no less tragic but far more sympathetic case in the Masters–Johnson file involves that of a congenially and happily engaged pair who married—and the bride foolishly chose her wedding night to tell her husband she had been raped by two men when she was a teen-ager. Her husband was emotionally overwhelmed. Not, he insisted, repelled, but unconsciously he was struck with such horror that he could not ejaculate. The marriage lasted six years, then broke up. The husband discovered to his real dismay that he could not ejaculate with any woman! He had rejected the whole intravaginal thing, transferring the recoil of rape from one woman to the next.

Another man was married and doing fine until his children, aged six and eight, suddenly entered the bedroom while he and his wife were having intercourse. The husband, rapidly approaching ejaculation, had passed the point where he could stop. He ejaculated in the presence of his calm but interested children. For the next nine years, even though he put a bolt on the door, he could never ejaculate again.

Still another man entered his bedroom to find the classic confrontation—his wife and his best friend. The two begged forgiveness. The husband said he forgave. But he could never again ejaculate.

Masters and Johnson are masters of understatement. They say nonejaculators are the victims of complex problems. To sum up there are the repressive influences of religious orthodoxies. (The authors of this book don't understand why religion, which is supposed to be an expression and consciousness of man's love of God and the attempt of God to communicate with man, should concern itself with sexual repression. But there it is.) There are men who aren't "straight" sexually. Men who don't like their wives. And men who had undergone severe emotional shock.

The Masters and Johnson treatment for the nonejaculator reverses the routine prescribed for the premature ejaculator. The wife is urged to be demanding, to massage her husband's penis vigorously with the lotion—in whatever fragrances the husband finds acceptable. She is instructed how to force his ejaculation manually.

In treatment, there is a day or two spent in developing increasingly intimate sensate focus (as described on page 41). Then the wife is told to masturbate her husband almost to the point of ejaculation. Then she mounts him in the female superior position and continuing the masturbation, slips his penis into her vagina.

She should move fairly quickly at this point. However, even if she can't—and most of the seminal fluid is spilled outside—if even a few drops enter the vaginal barrel—for some strange reason the mental and physical block against intravaginal ejaculation begins to crumble. Of the seventeen such patients referred to Masters and Johnson there was a success rate of more than 80 percent.

The Reproductive Biology Research Foundation is preparing to do considerably more work in the field of incompetent ejaculation. What they do say at present is that the "cure" depends in large part on the decency, sincerity, and intelligent cooperation of the partner.

The Cure of Impotence

Of the male patients who came to the Reproductive Biology Research Foundation for treatment of impotence, 245 could not get an erection. As noted earlier, Masters and Johnson call their treatment failure rate in this division "a disaster." It seems they are being overcritical of themselves, as they've actually had more success than anybody else who has tried it under clinical conditions.

Masters and Johnson divide impotence into "primary" and "secondary" divisions. A man who is *primarily* impotent has never had an erection that has lasted long enough for intromission. A man who is *secondarily* impotent is one who used to be able to get an erection and achieve an intromission but for one reason or another can't do so now.

Impotence may be due to disease, anxiety, physical or emotional shock, or what Masters and Johnson kindly call "untoward maternal influences." That's a nice way of saying that a domineering mama—whether she dominates with a strident voice, frequent headaches, or subtle sexual seduction—can cause her son to be impotent. It's scarcely a new idea.

Strict religious orthodoxy—there were many Jewish and Roman Catholic patients reporting—also comes under fire once again. Dr. Masters and Mrs. Johnson are plainly worried, medically speaking, about too many "thou shalt nots" and not enough "thou shalts," reinforced by church or synagogue. Unfortunately the research does not state the additional cultural origins of the patients. But Jews and Roman Catholics exist in a fairly wide spread of the globe's geography and add to their theology the other aspects of the culture where they live.*

---

*Anthropologist Dr. Dana Raphael Jacobsen says that Italian youngsters, Roman Catholic though they be, don't grow up with

Dr. Seymour L. Halleck, professor of psychiatry at the University of Wisconsin Medical Center, says, "When a man begins to feel that his partner is dominating him or making inordinate demands upon him, he may also feel that it is absolutely essential to his self-image to be extremely potent. At this point, he is in danger of being impotent."

To a man distressed by impotence, of course, it doesn't immediately matter where the problem came from. It's what to do about it.

Six men who came for treatment said they discovered their impotency when as male virgins in their early twenties they married virginal women. Loss of erection resulted apparently because neither knew how to be cooperative and the husband felt he was a failure. And became a chronic failure!

There is actually a case history in the Foundation files of a mother who insisted on continuing to bathe her teenage son and after scrubbing him to erection and ejaculation, said, "No other girl can please you like mother can!"

Other men were seemingly made impotent by homosexual seduction. They thought once they had performed a homosexual act they were permanently committed to this form of sex.

Many were traumatized by early bad experiences with prostitutes. The Masters and Johnson clinical records pretty well eliminate the fanciful notion that a prostitute has a heart of gold or that a prostitute is a good and patient teacher for a young man having his first try at sex. Most of the prostitutes whose behavior was reported at the Foundation were impatient and, not surprisingly, indifferent women.

Other failures at initial coitus resulted from being drunk, being under the influence of drugs, or just plain tired out from the physical and psychological drain of the marriage festivities. But these don't explain why the men did not rather quickly recover from them. Few men, we would imagine, are gold-medal winners on their first try but most, even after some humiliation and dismay, are able to try

---

sexual hang-ups imposed by their religion. Italy, she says, for the most part has a sensual culture, and the children easily learn sensate focus from their parents. The Italian clergy does not attempt to prohibit sensuality—or, if they ever did, they have long since given up.

again and without too much difficulty learn to succeed—at least for themselves. But apparently for some a disastrous first experience has permanent effects.

Perhaps the most courageous and certainly the most sensational aspect of the Masters and Johnson clinical treatment is the use of surrogate—or "fill-in"—female partners to help out impotent males who are unmarried. The Masters and Johnson view is that you can't achieve a cure for impotence by yourself—you need a partner.

It's too bad that the readers of this book, or the Masters–Johnson textbook, who are curious about this aspect of their work cannot have the engaging experience of talking to the authors about it. They are absolutely unflappable. They talk about it as matter-of-factly as your mother-in-law talks about her recipe for pecan pie.

As Masters and Johnson explain it, the men who were referred to the Foundation for help with impotence badly needed a group of female "sex donors"—women to relate to while the therapy took place. Women whose ease with their own sexuality and sympathy for the male would help cure their impotence.

These female surrogates participate in the roundtable discussions. They take part in the exercise of sensate focus and in the achievement of restoration of erection and intromission. They perform these ministrations as calmly and easily as a nurse.

Dr. Masters and Mrs. Johnson, conservative scientists in a conservative city, admit they sweated out the surrogate problem. However, having decided to go ahead with it they say that it will probably be a continuing policy of the Foundation.

How do they go about recruiting surrogates or wife-replacements for such an undertaking? The patient has no voice in the process. Male patients were matched to unmarried women "volunteers" all of whom were respectable women associated with St. Louis and many with the Washington University community. They are "matched according to age, education, cultural background, etc." A young doctor who studied the Masters–Johnson criteria for matching patients with surrogates broke up laughing and said, "It's like those crazy experiments in dating by computer. You drop in a card that's punched to say you're 19, white, Protestant, and from New England. And they give you three gals just like you—and each date turns out to be a bore!"

The object of the "matching" that goes on at the Reproductive Biology Research Foundation is of course not the same as a punch-card date. The idea is to give a male patient a partner with whom he will feel comfortable and, hopefully, become receptive.

What kind of women volunteer for such a task? It must be kept in mind that these are not women volunteering for a sexy experience. It's not like being asked who'd like to help out with Peter Fonda or his father. These women —who have come in for a lot of criticism—are voluntarily entering into a very intimate, complicated, emotional, and physical relationship with men who freely confess they are "no good as men." The women can't hope to get all that much out of it.

The female volunteers are meticulously screened. Those who have qualified include high school and college graduates and two postgraduates. All but two had been previously married. Nine were mothers.

The surrogate volunteers went through the same grueling physical examinations and psychosocial inquisition as do all the candidates for treatment. Six of these women were already known to the Foundation as they had worked with Dr. Masters and Mrs. Johnson on their earlier work as reported in *Human Sexual Response* (Boston: Little, Brown and Company, 1966).

Asked why they wanted to help out as wife stand-ins in research on inadequate sexuality, nine of the women said they had seen members of their family in that kind of trouble. Three had once been married to sexually inadequate husbands. Of these, one died in military service, one became an alcoholic, one killed himself. One volunteer had seen her sister's sex life destroyed by gang-rape. Another had seen her brother turn homosexual because he couldn't make it straight.

Three said honestly they welcomed participation in the experiment as a way of relieving sexual desire. Another was a woman physician who was frankly just curious—a female. She made valuable suggestions that the Foundation has adopted.

How did it work out? Forty-one unmarried men were assigned surrogate partners. Their recovery score from their various ailments of inadequacy was as good as those who came to the clinic with cooperative wives. Thirty-two of the unmarried males had their symptoms of sex dysfunction reversed, and 24 of the 32 have since successfully married. Only one of the 24 newly married men has reported that his inadequacy has returned. No one has run off with a surrogate.

Women patients were not allowed to have surrogates. Dr. Masters and Mrs. Johnson firmly believe that in our present culture in the United States surrogate partners for women wouldn't work. Not that they are against it for moral reasons but they feel that women must have deep emotional relationships with their sex partners.

Undoubtedly many men who are alarmed to find themselves impotent would like very much to be admitted to a medical examining room and told it comes from having the mumps. It takes the load off. Masters and Johnson list many physiological reasons that may cause secondary impotence. They carefully explain that they didn't get all these cases in their clinic but state that any physical dysfunction that lowers the body functions can be a cause of sexual inadequacy.

Actually, a few such cases—only seven of 213 men—referred to the Foundation turned out to be impotent because of physiologic dysfunction. It is hoped that doctors the country over are alert to these causes. But unfortunately some are not.

Masters and Johnson divide the physical causes for impotence into 10 categories. Most of them are incomprehensible to nonmedically trained readers—the full list is in the Masters and Johnson textbook *Human Sexual Inadequacy* and intended for the guidance of doctors. Familiar to many of us, however, are: congenital deformities, various kinds of heart trouble, addictive drugs, alcohol, amphetamines (what the kids call "speed"), reserpine (used in many mental hospitals to produce tranquility and docility), nicotine, digitalis (for halting heart attacks). Endocrine problems are part of the physiologic inadequacy picture. Also, Addison's disease, castration (seems likely), a type of diabetes, ingestion of female hormones (estrogen), and obesity (getting too fat).

Masters and Johnson list in the genito-urinary field, prostatitis, and in the field of diseases of the blood, leukemia and anemia. Among infectious illnesses they include genital tuberculosis, and gonorrhea. *Most startling among the neurologic disturbances is the indictment of electric shock therapy used in psychiatric treatment.*

Patients who undergo surgery for prostate cancer should also be made aware that impotence can and often does result. Dr. Masters and Mrs. Johnson say flatly and rather indignantly that it is cruel not to prepare man and wife for the fact that removal of the prostate gland threatens potency.

The "authoritative put-down" was also blamed for inadequate treatment of impotence. Patients related how they had come to the doctor and been firmly told there was nothing that could be done.

Almost anyone will recognize that it takes a lot of nerve in the first place to come into your doctor's office and say, "Uh-ah-doc—I have this problem . . ." These patients—21 males ranging in age from 42 to 68 years of age—were told by their doctors before they reached the Foundation that they were getting old and that they and their wives just had to resign themselves to it.

Two other males were told their impotence was the result of admitted adultery. Another married couple was told the husband's impotence was the result of his having agreed to his wife's having an abortion before they were married.

And the last couple were promised by the clergyman they consulted that if they became faithful church attenders (including committee meetings and church suppers) their problem would end. Two years later it hadn't.

In fact, what happened in most of the cases was that things got worse instead of better as soon as the patients got a "thumbs down" or scolding reaction from authority figures.

Dr. Masters, both in his writing and his response to questions, often retreats gravely and dignifiedly into five-syllable words. But no one can read Dr. Masters and Mrs. Johnson's analysis of secondary impotence without getting the impression that if they weren't highly professional people there are other professionals of whom they take a dim view. But they make do with the subtle professional critique, such as ". . . the iatrogenic influence as an etiological agent in onset of symptoms of secondary impotence . . ." Which means, to put it crudely, that the doctor did it. Or at least heavily influenced it.

Dr. Masters and Mrs. Johnson believe very strongly that the onset of many sexual problems is the result of other impacts. Your boss bawls you out or fires you. Your neighbor upstages you—he buys a Pontiac and leaves you behind with your Volkswagen. Your neighbor's kid gets a better report card than your kid. You can't pay your mortgage. Your daughter is dating a really wrong guy. Then the initial failure is reinforced by panic and more failure and becomes a permanent problem.

The contribution of the domineering mother as a cause of impotence has been so well documented in plays, stories, and psychoanalytic literature that it scarcely needs reenforcing here, although Masters and Johnson present some rather chilling case histories.

However, five cases of men who came for treatment of secondary impotence turned out to be suffering from the effects of domineering fathers. Since this hasn't been very well spelled out in the literature it is worth describing the history of such a case which Masters and Johnson present in *Human Sexual Inadequacy*.

Mr. C., 39 years old and his wife, 37, had been married 13 years when they came to the Foundation for treatment. They had three children. Mr. C. had been brought up in a family in which the mother was overwhelmed and subdued by her demanding and autocratic husband who made no secret of his frequent affairs with other women. Mr. C. recalls that he was disturbed as a youngster when he learned of his father's infidelities.

The father demanded excellence of performance from his son in academics and athletics. The son did his best to deliver, often feeling that he was doing more than he really could.

Mr. C. began to masturbate at age 13 and had casual, rather meaningless coital connections with this girl or that until he graduated from college. Then he met a girl—apparently the right kind of girl—and married. Three children were born during the first six years. Mr. C. was unhappy and unsuccessful at a number of jobs. In some he was plainly incompetent; in others he just quit. He got to feeling pretty up tight at home. He spent less time with his children and took to the bottle. He was chronically tired and irritable in the evening. His sex relations with his wife diminished.

Then he went to work for his father. He didn't like it although he was doing his job well. He was panicky at the idea of what his father would do to him if he failed. Then he did fail. A simple mistake of judgment made an important customer furious. The father turned on his son and bawled him out—reviewing all the failures of his son's childhood—as he would never have done to an ordinary employee or business associate. Mr. C. felt he lacked the guts that another employee would have had—to tell his father to stick his head in a bucket and walk out.

Masters and Johnson say, "His session with his father left him with a feeling of total inadequacy."

Like many a man who has been clobbered in the office rat race, Mr. C. came home that night, probably had more than was wise to drink, strode angrily around the house, and finally took his wife to bed with the idea of restoring his ego. At least he could do the primeval thing. But as he mounted her, his mind was boiling with his father's angry reproaches. In bed, he achieved an erection but couldn't make it into the vagina.

He was impotent for three months. One night, however, he woke up—possibly after an erotic dream—and found that he had an erection. He quickly rolled onto his wife and made her pregnant.

The pregnancy distressed her. It was unplanned, and her husband insisted that because she was pregnant they should not have intercourse. After the child was born they attempted to resume their sex life but his impotency—seemingly triggered by his error in business—was repeatedly confirmed. So eventually the couple made their way to the Foundation's front door.

In their chapter on secondary impotence Masters and Johnson say a great many calm, balanced, but ultimately harsh words about the sexual damage that is done to a child when there is a single, strong parent or when there is no parent at all or one who is not more than a shadow. A boy is equally harmed by too little or too much father. He may have had a mother who was boss and a father who was little more than a dishrag, or a father who drove his sons on to jump almost impossible hurdles with the admonition that it does no good to finish second.

In each situation, *clinical records create the impression that it tends to create secondary impotence to be forced to finish first.*

You may be wondering if there aren't some men who are born "crippled"—so to speak—who have no hope of a normal sex life because of anatomical or irreversible chemical reasons. Masters and Johnson would say hesitatingly, "Yes," but quickly add that such cases are so rare they should be disregarded except by the diagnostic specialists. They are genetic misfortunates, about as common as Siamese twins.

They note, however, that there is no patient who comes into the Foundation hanging his head so low as the impotent male. He is convinced that nothing can be done for him. Yet, inwardly, he believes he is or could soon again be a properly functioning male if it weren't for his wife. She, on the other hand, keeps asking for assurances —"You can see it's not my fault!"

The wife may not have caused it but she has sometimes reinforced it by hinting about her husband's inadequacy.

In some cases when a wife complains to her best friend that "My husband can't make it in bed!" the friend may say sweetly, "Gee, honey, what's wrong with *you?*"

What's wrong is likely to be that she doesn't give enough of what Masters and Johnson describe as "psycho-sexual input." She responds "like a wooden Indian." Between the partners sexual input is blocked from both directions.

At the initial interviews, she has to examine her egocentric attitude and understand why she is equally involved in her husband's impotence. If she really wants it cured, she'll have to agree to work on herself, too. Her accusations have got to be reversed just as surely as her husband's fears.

It is also emphasized that the only way an impotent man can begin to recover his potency is to concentrate on making love with a woman. By acting as a lover, he rescues himself.

The impotent husband and his wife—by now hopefully made anger-free and cooperative by roundtable discussions

AN ANALYSIS OF HUMAN SEXUAL INADEQUACY 77

at the Foundation—participate first of all in pleasuring the wife.

Pleasuring the wife? "Hey, isn't this all mixed up?" asked one reporter at the authors' press conference in Boston. "If he's impotent, *he*'s the one that needs working on, not her!"

But Dr. Masters and Mrs. Johnson patiently explain their unique idea that male impotence is cured by getting the impotent male to excite a female.

The impotent male is under medical orders not to try to "will" an erection. He's supposed to let things go as far as they seem to want to go and then let them taper off and not worry about it. It may take several days but eventually—in those cases which are ultimately successfully treated—an erection of the penis appears while the man and wife are pleasuring. Even in instances where the phenomenon hasn't appeared in years or never, the couple is supposed to regard it casually. Neither cheers, nor are grateful tears in order. And absolutely no attempt at intromission. Just an optimistic report at the roundtable discussion on the following day. "Take it easy" is the rule.

Although "teasing" is among sexually functioning persons supposed to be unethical and a breach of contract, the Masters and Johnson system teaches women to use "teasing" techniques to bring an impotent male partner to a functioning pitch. It's a difficult lesson to learn. When the first erection appears, both husband and wife think, "If we waste this one, who knows if we'll ever have another chance?" But Masters and Johnson keep a firm hold on the reins. The wife is told to be calm and confident even as the erection disappears and then, after the lapse of fifteen minutes to half an hour, return to sex play and confidently anticipate another erection. If it happens once, it nearly always happens again.

The wives involved in the "teasing" phase report that they enjoy it. They are stimulated by the recurring penile erections. (Masters and Johnson commented, "This thought has seldom occurred to the husband.")

On about the fifth day (it may be sooner) the wife is instructed to take the "superior coital position"—that is, crouching across her husband's hips—before they begin the sex play which both of them now securely know will lead to erection.

When the erection occurs, the wife's role is crucial. She is instructed to appear pleased, yet detached—as though it happened every day. Moving slowly she leans forward and carefully slips the penis into her vagina. As she does so, she continues to use manual "teasing" techniques of stimulation.

Sometimes, at this point, the erection collapses. The couple are under orders not to get upset. One couple told us that they laughed when this happened. That's hard to believe, but it's better than crying. Patiently, tenderly, they try again. Or put it off until tomorrow.

If the intromission is successful, the wife begins moving back and forth, casually sliding along the penis. If the erection holds, she then quiets herself, and the husband begins to thrust, also undemandingly.

It's obviously difficult for sexually adequate readers to imagine mutual pelvic and responsive penile thrusting that doesn't instantly gather steam and result very soon in an orgasmic crescendo. But these student lovers are told to concentrate only on enjoying pelvic pleasuring and not to worry about anything, not even one another. The atmosphere is supposed to be dreamy and tender, like lovers lingering under an oak tree after a picnic of cheese and bread and wine. The relationship goes where it goes and stops where it stops, and at the next picnic things proceed further. Eventually, everything begins, progresses, and results as it should.

Masters and Johnson have a moving paragraph in their text in praise of the wives of the impotent male patients. They point out that many of these women arrive at the Foundation frustrated, seeking revenge, and bitterly angry. Some are still quietly devoted to their husbands but feel helpless. More than 90 percent have been able to cooperate with the therapists' instruction and have "made all the difference" in success and failure.

Female Orgasmic Dysfunction

Masters and Johnson believe that cultural bias against women has held back research in female sex response. Until very recently there's been no knowledge of the biophysics of female sex and there isn't an awful lot known even now. Those who've done research haven't had the money or facilities to compare their efforts and arrive at useful agreement as to how women function as sexual beings. And few lab reports that have been turned in by gynecologists and obstetricians have been correlated with the observations of psychiatrists and marriage counselors.

Men have the permission—indeed, the expectation and encouragement of society—to develop their sexuality in a natural context. Women, still, are not so permitted. Growing girls are taught to repress or romanticize their sexual expressions, and the hope is expressed that they will be "good" girls—that is, not have any active sexual feelings or sex activity until they marry. How, then, can a young married woman proceed to do effectively what all her life she has been taught not to do? How, having held her boy friends at arms length for six or seven years, can she suddenly permit herself to be responsive?

Even the vocabulary used by sympathetic and "modern" parents in discussing sexuality with their daughters is unintentionally repressive. "I hope you won't, but if you . . ." Female virginity is still a moral virtue and even a commercial asset. "Yielding to temptation . . ." is still heard in mother-daughter talks. The sex act is still something a man does to a woman and not something they do together!

Not even today, Masters and Johnson point out, is a married woman honored by her capacity for sexual response. A good wife keeps a clean house, has babies (hopefully males), entertains gracefully, and bakes apple pies.

It's a rare man who goes around gratefully remarking that his wife is good in bed—it's considered vulgar and insulting. It also implies that his wife has had a lot of experience—and might tempt his friends to come around scabbing while he's out of town.

Thus women have been forced to inhibit or distort their sexuality to the point where they can't even achieve it honestly in the privacy of the marital bedroom.

Masters and Johnson state, "The human female's facility of physiological response to sexual tensions and her capacity for orgasmic release never have been fully appreciated." *Even more startling, Masters and Johnson suggest that women may have subconsciously consented to having their superior capacity for response repressed in an attempt to balance themselves with their vastly less capable men folk!*

Male readers won't like this notion much but in their first volume, *Human Sexual Response,* Masters and Johnson cite a case history of a couple that engaged in sex play and recurrent coitus for a period of nearly two hours, during which the male had two orgasms and the female experienced seventy-five! It does give one something to think about.

In the volume under analysis, *Human Sexual Inadequacy,* there is a skillful review of what happens to a woman in the process of sexual response. Her muscles become tense. There is a pooling of blood in certain tissues, producing a discernible pink blush in the skin and an increase in breast size. Her vagina produces a lubricant, logically a device for easing the entrance of the penis. Her vagina expands or "tents," ready to accommodate the penis. The clitoris—the sexually sensitive organ located in the female vulva and often condescendingly described as a "little penis"—erects and flattens out, ready to respond to contact with the male penis. (Is the penis perhaps a "gross clitoris"?)

The uterus itself actually gets bigger and when orgasm occurs the outer third of the vagina and the uterus both begin to throb and undergo contractions that are accompanied by a high level of sensual pleasure. Immediately afterward there is a rapid letdown of both muscle tension and blood congestion. The woman who has been stimulated to the point of orgasm and not achieved it takes a lot longer to relax and get muscles and blood cells back to normal.

Masters and Johnson maintain that every woman, whether or not she has an active sex life, receives periodic "demands" from her body for coition. The vasocongestion or pooling of blood in the tissues give her a warm, swollen, throbbing, and itchy feeling in the genital area.

They say that occasionally menstrual periods, which also produce blood congestion in the vulva and sensitive nerve reactions, may stimulate sex desire. Yet some religions and most custom prohibits sex relations while a woman is menstruating. Women who have responded to sex urges while menstruating say that while they experience orgasms as intense as any they know about, they feel apologetic about "messing up" their husbands with bloody discharge.

But Masters and Johnson are concerned here with orgasmic dysfunction. They have before them a woman who is suffering because she has either never known sexual fulfillment or she has had the ability and lost it.

What's to be done for her? A nonorgasmic woman can conceive a child—many children—and never know the joy of sensate copulation.

Masters and Johnson do not say how many of the women who presented themselves at the Foundation for treatment of orgasmic dysfunction have had children, but one can't help but sympathize with the woman who has been impregnated, delivered, and raised a child and never or almost never experienced a sexual incentive or reward. Is the pleasure and dignity of motherhood supposed to compensate? One is tempted to cry, "Unfair!"

Dr. Masters and Mrs. Johnson discovered that some women develop considerable pride in their ability to accept sexual disappointment in a dignified way. Thus you get the turn-of-the-century upper-class New England spinster in her dark silk dress, drinking tea out of Limoges cups and having an emotional relationship only with her cat—spayed, of course.

Or her modern counterpart, the perennial P.-T.A. chairman who dispenses with sex about as briskly as she would a subcommitee meeting. Her husband just happens to be part of the family.

The foregoing comments—the authors' own—are not meant to say that P.-T.A. presidents tend to be sexually unresponsive. (Some of our best friends are P.-T.A. presidents.) On the contrary, it might be equally strongly argued that the energetic woman who flings herself into community activity is a very sexy dame indeed who has got more sex output going for her than she or anyone else knows what to do with!

Orgasmic dysfunction is not confined to older women. An 18-year-old coed may bed down with numerous boy friends but once she gets one to the altar—and finishes writing "thank you" notes for the wedding presents—she stops pretending it was all that great. Because, for her, it never was.

Two vital features separate the complaining female from the complaining male.

1. The competent male can usually satisfy himself sexually regardless of whether he has a sexually responsive female for a partner or not. All she has to do—vulgarly speaking—is spread her legs and be compliant. He may have a better experience with a responsive female, but he can do it anyway. The female is dependent on a sexually competent partner.

2. The female is usually captive to the age-old idea that it's her duty, primarily, to satisfy her partner. She rarely feels free to say, "Never mind what you want. This is what I want." Many women have said they get a bigger sexual charge out of cunnilingus than penile intromission—indeed, advance hints of the Masters and Johnson forthcoming volume on homosexuality say that homosexuals experience stronger and better orgasms than heterosexuals. But what woman feels free to blueprint a sexual encounter? Yet few men hesitate to say, "Do this" or "Do that."

So Masters and Johnson get some fairly angry women at the Foundation. These women feel they've been subjected to discrimination and shortchanged. Some are the complainers and some are the complained against.

Dr. Masters and Mrs. Johnson include in their report on orgasmic dysfunction one more lengthy indictment of religious orthodoxy and its ill effects on sexual responsiveness. It is summarized as follows:

Mrs. A. was reared in a strict Protestant home with Sundays totally devoted to church and church activities, weekly prayer meetings, and the like. At home everyone was always dressed "proper" as the parents conceived it, and Mrs. A. said she never remembers seeing any member of her family or anyone else in an undressed state. Sex was never mentioned in the family; books were evaluated for their purity and radio programs censored.

When Mrs. A. first menstruated she was totally unprepared. She thought she was dying. She ran home from school. Her mother reacted coldly and told her young daughter she must suffer the curse of Eve all her life until old age and must be prepared for monthly pains in the stomach. She went to a church-sponsored college that was coed but the school had what was called the 18-inch rule. It meant boys and girls were forbidden to hold hands and had to keep 18 inches between them at all times.

At graduation she went to work for a publisher who specialized in religious material. She met and fell in love with a young man of similar background. They kissed three times before their wedding. It was the only time she'd ever been kissed by a man. Her father, she said, had never kissed her.

The day before she was married her mother told her she must allow her husband certain physical privileges. These were not defined, but she was assured it would hurt. On her wedding night her husband tried to find the proper place to insert his penis. He failed. Nine years later, the marriage was not yet consummated. Fortunately the couple was referred to the Foundation for treatment.

Another history cited by Masters and Johnson warns of what happens when there is no dominant influence in the home. Students of psychology and related fields know what happens when there is an absent parent or when one parent rules to the exclusion of another but it is less well known that when both parents sweetly agree all the time that can make trouble, too.

Mrs. B. was an only child, a fragile, curly-haired, exquisite "doll baby." Her parents dressed her in white kid shoes and pink ruffled dresses and hardly ever picked her up or cuddled her—maybe for fear of wrinkling the ruffles. She was supposed to be a walking china doll. She felt she was disregarded emotionally—that her parents didn't care if she was sad or happy, just that she look pretty.

When she was a junior in college she made what she

remembers as the one major decision of her life. She got engaged and married to a man seven years older who promptly took her parents' place and made all the decisions. At first, Mrs. B. was complacent and undemanding about sex. The case history doesn't say how or why it happened, but she apparently decided she was missing something. She wanted to give more and get more.

The B's came to the Foundation. The result was ironic. Encouraged through the use of the Masters and Johnson lotion on his body the husband developed into a much more adept lover. He began to enjoy himself and respond as he never had before—or even dreamed of doing. But she remained "sensately anesthetized." Neither the lotion nor the sensate exercises nor the roundtable discussions nor the prescribed sexual relations did much to increase her response. The therapists view this case with mixed reaction. While the male partner improved beyond his wildest expectations, the wife's symptoms were not successfully treated.

Women are still traumatized by being jilted. (That means they get really upset.) Some just never get over it. There was the case of Mrs. C. who was a "good girl." She said she enjoyed "petting" but decided to remain a virgin until marriage. She fell in love with a "nice boy"—that is, one who was sociologically well suited. The engagement was approved by everyone. During the engagement period she still with difficulty resisted coitus but hand manipulated her fiancé to ejaculation quite regularly.

Three weeks before the scheduled marriage, her fiancé went on a business trip, met, and one week later married a divorcée who had two children.

The jilted girl was humiliated. "Crushed" is the word Masters and Johnson use. Six months later she married a man she described as kind and considerate. Although she said she'd been highly stimulated by her former fiancé, she couldn't respond to her husband. She had an affair with another man who stimulated her to the high pre-orgasmic level she had enjoyed with her fiancé but she didn't get satisfaction with him, either.

Mr. and Mrs. C. came to the Foundation for much-needed first aid. Mrs. C. was helped only when she was made to see her husband as a valuable individual in his own right and not as a humiliating substitute for the lover who had jilted her.

When a woman patient comes to the Reproductive Biology Research Foundation complaining that she is nonorgasmic she, like her male counterparts in adequacy problems, gets classified.

Class 1 includes the woman who can't masturbate or be successfully manipulated by hand or mouth but can and does reach orgasm during ordinary sexual connection—that is, with the male penis in her vagina. *It may come as a shock to quite a large number of women that if you can have an orgasm while in coitus with your husband but can't achieve it from connection with hand or mouth you've got an inadequacy rating.*

Class 2 includes women who have never experienced orgasm from the work of a penis, but who can and do—with or without a partner (male or female)—reach orgasm with other kinds of stimulating techniques. It includes the female homosexual (the word "Lesbian" like the word "frigidity" is not in the Masters–Johnson vocabulary).

Class 3 rounds up women who have infrequent and unpredictable orgasms, whether by conventional connections or others. What bothers them—and sends them in for conference—is that they aren't confident. They can't tell when they go to bed and begin sex play if they will have an orgasm or not. Either way, they don't know why.

Masters and Johnson present a rather appalling case history in which a woman was made nonorgasmic by her emotional reaction to the state of her husband's bank account. Our great-grandmother had a saying, "When poverty knocks at the door, love flies out of the window." Here's how it happened to one modern couple:

Mr. and Mrs. E. grew up, met, courted, and married in a most conventional mid-twentieth century way. Each had masturbated as teen-agers and had several love affairs before they met. Their marriage was almost instantly and mutually orgasmic and for twelve years they were sexually and socially happy. Then, through no apparent fault of his own, Mr. E. was fired. He was out of a job for eighteen months. He began for the first time in his life to drink heavily.

Their sex life was painfully derailed. Sometimes Mrs. E. rejected and taunted her husband or reproached him. In turn, he made unreasonable demands on her—presumably because he felt financially inadequate and needed to feel sexually more than adequate. His wife slammed the bedroom door on him. It was a bad time for both.

Then Mr. E. got a new job. He stopped drinking. There was money in the bank. His wife reopened the bedroom door—and found to her amazement, distress, and horror that she could no longer respond to him, no matter what kind of sexual approach he employed.

Masters and Johnson speak repeatedly of how easily a sex relationship is distorted or used as the focus for a nonsexual problem. This wife paid a high price for equating sex with money, status, and sobriety.*

As with males, early experiences in woman-to-woman homosexual relationships make an imprint that is difficult to reverse. Masters and Johnson take homosexuality pretty calmly. They point out that it has been an integral part of every known culture, and there is no point in expecting it to disappear or even to worry about whether it's bad. We asked Dr. Masters and Mrs. Johnson whether they considered homosexuals to be sexually inadequate. Dr. Masters said not if they're adequate. That is, the homosexual, per se, is not inadequate. Just different.

Since homosexual relations don't lead to babies, it's safe to assume that a majority of women will continue to prefer heterosexual—man-to-woman—living. The problem arises when a thoughtful homosexual woman decides she wants to switch. She wants to get married and have babies. She often finds that she can't respond to her husband. She is afraid to tell her husband that her early introduction to sex was homosexual. Guilt-ridden, she is unresponsive. In such cases, therapy of the Masters and Johnson format is indicated. Professionally unguided "confession" will only make things worse.

Other problems the Foundation deals with in regard to orgasmic dysfunction are those of low sexual tension—females who cannot achieve orgasm either in coitus or manual

---

*Dr. Seymour L. Halleck of the University of Wisconsin Medical Center says, "The sex act is more than a mere physical fulfillment of sexual needs. Sex can be used to relieve tension, to gain status, to obtain reassurance, to flatter one's vanity, to express love, and to gain a certain amount of control over the behavior of others. In short, it is not only a loving act but can also be a vehicle for establishing one's sense of power."

manipulation—but such cases are considered rare, at least at the Foundation.

We have been told that such a woman may have been a lively teen-ager with plenty of casual dates but no serious commitments. She often doesn't ever remember masturbating or experiencing pleasurable pelvic sensations with either bath towels or fantasies about sex. The dates who made passes at her she turned off for the simple reason that she herself wasn't turned on. She saved her money, bought attractive but not seductive clothes, took herself to pleasant, fairly conservative vacation resorts. Bermuda rather than Acapulco.

The type of woman who had nothing wrong with her but low sexual tension is described in another instance by Masters and Johnson. Here, all went well until the woman's husband became depressed over the fact that while his wife was totally cooperative when it came to sex—she never said no—it was plain she just wasn't much involved. One of the few high points of their sex life occurred one night when they had been celebrating a successful business deal. That night, she was orgasmic by manipulation.

The other problem Masters and Johnson discuss is that of a woman who is successfully and responsively orgasmic through penile intromission but can't masturbate—or be masturbated—successfully either by hand or mouth. The researchers conclude that these women had severe "no-no's" repeatedly imposed on them in childhood or else they have tried masturbation a few times—failed—and thought, "Who needs it?"

Masters and Johnson feel that a sexually adequate woman is one who can masturbate successfully *as well as* respond to her husband. The single, the widowed, and the divorced also need to be able to relieve sexual tension for themselves, and to feel free to do so. Masters and Johnson believe that masturbation helps to keep you healthy and sexually tuned.

Treatment of Female Orgasmic Dysfunction

In interviews with Masters and Johnson the nonorgasmic wife talks frankly about what she and her husband are currently doing in sexual interchange. She tells what sends her and what doesn't and what she accepts but really doesn't like at all.

The wife talks freely about past sex experiences, if any, with other partners. Often she faces the fact that she has been lying to herself or living with absurd fantasy. The guy she had an affair with in her junior year of college wasn't really all that great. Or she may have been badly heartbroken and rejected and not want her husband to do any of the things her rejecting lover did. But how can the poor guy know?

All this is talked out at the roundtable discussions. Clearly a woman arrives at an erotic arousal and an orgasmic giving and receiving response when she is getting those physical attentions her lifelong experience has taught her to value. Some women have rape fantasies and dream of being overwhelmed. Some fiercely resent overaggressive lovemaking and want to be treated tenderly all the way through it.

Dr. Masters and Mrs. Johnson hazard the fascinating idea that just as the trigger mechanism that sends women into labor is unknown, so is the mechanical system—probably a combination of brain imprints, nerves, and chemistry—that sends a woman into orgasm unknown. They speculate that the two may be set off by the same or closely related mechanism. It is a common old wives' tale that many women become more responsive sex partners after childbirth.

The couple reporting orgasmic dysfunction get the same

prescription for the first few days as all the other patients. They answer questions and get physical exams and instructions in developing sensate focus.

Dr. Masters and Mrs. Johnson emphasize that the sexually dysfunctional woman needs an additional element in the prescription. She needs to be "given permission." She needs to be told that it's all right. She needs to learn to honor—*honor* is the word they use—her privilege to enjoy sex.

If she has been faking, she has to stop. If she has been cheerfully accommodating, she has to stop that, also. The sex partners have got to be helped to adopt the "give to get" concept and behave toward one another with honesty.

Women—at least those who have passed under Masters' and Johnson's observation—seem to be focused on or hung-up on the need to make a sincere and idealistic commitment. The male's commitment may be something really naïve like, "Sure, honey, I know you're not a tramp. Not you! This is something special. Between you and I forever." And forget the grammar. For generations, men have lied to women, and women have provoked men to lie merely to unleash the conscientious permission that a woman in our culture needs to respond.

The Masters and Johnson theory, as we have noted before, largely enjoins silence when man and wife are trying to repair their sex life. It's a good idea. The verbalized anxieties that emerge in coitus, even among people who describe themselves as well adjusted, are really amazing. We asked twelve couples ranging in age from 22 to 53 to say what they most commonly recalled saying in coitus.

Here's the summation of the run down:

HE: Tell me you like it, baby!
SHE: Do you love me?

When the practice in sensate focus has reached the point where the nonorgasmic woman and her partner are granted therapeutic permission to indulge in active coitus, the couple is instructed in assuming a position that is designed to be nondemanding for the male and educational for the nonorgasmic female. (See Figure 5, p. 90). As a position for sexual intercourse it is unfamiliar to common practice in the United States. But it's not unknown. Last year it was rather casually sketched in a Sunday edition of the *New York Times* and provoked no comment, or at least

5. Training Position for Non-Orgasmic Woman

only a few wrinkled brows. The *Times* called it the bride's position. It's recommended as a good one for first intromission. Some couples that we've talked to have tried it and say it seems rather remote. Others say it's great.

Anyway, Masters and Johnson only recommend it as a troubleshooting position for the nonorgasmic woman. Here's how it goes:

Step 1: The husband sits up against the headboard of the bed. Unless the headboard is padded, he will probably wish to pad his back with pillows.

Step 2: The husband spreads his legs and his wife, with her back against his chest, sits between his legs. Her back is resting against his chest. His arms are around her waist and clasped over her stomach. Her hands are under his thighs, holding on to the backs of his knees.

Step 3: The husband waits for her request to insert his penis. He can stimulate her breasts, kiss her neck. The position means that the male is unlikely to directly touch the woman's clitoris in a manner that hurts or irritates her. Some women indicate that they like to have the clitoris directly stimulated. Most don't. For many it's painful. For many others it's just plain annoying. Explained one outspoken young matron, "It brings things on too fast. I can't keep up."

When both are sitting upright with the female's back resting on the male's chest it's up to the male to do the teasing. The wife should be coming on at this time with vaginal lubricant. The husband's fingers will gently but suggestively spread the natural lubricant over the entire vulva area.

Step 4: The penis gently, undemandingly, is thrust into the vagina.

The husband at this stage is supposed to be warm, tender, altogether giving. Masters and Johnson recommend that he should let his wife drift along and learn to feel good about the vaginally contained penis without any obligation to pay back the borrowed ecstasy.

If ecstasy—orgasmic release—doesn't occur for her the session at the next day's Foundation roundtable discussion will emphasize that it's surely building up. It should happen when they do it again tomorrow or the next day. The couple is encouraged to believe that they'll get there. Each experience is a step forward, even the failures. When serious failures occur, the couple goes back to the beginning and starts over with the early exercises of sensate focus.

About 80 percent of them finally make it. The day after success with the "male undemanding position" the female turns around and she assumes the "superior coital position" (the male lying on his back, the woman crouched over his hips) and then they roll over to the Masters and Johnson recommended lateral position. This still leaves the female in the driver's seat, but apparently it's the love posture of the future.

Husbands have asked Dr. Masters and Mrs. Johnson, "But suppose at that point I feel like ejaculating?" The cotherapists tell him that he'll be happier and have a better time if he doesn't. He can signal his wife to use the squeeze play. If ejaculation occurs anyway it is reported, discussed, and the next sexual contact is redesigned as follows:

The wife who is trying to become orgasmic is told, "The penis belongs to you just as much as your vagina belongs to him!" She is instructed to withdraw if she's not ready. Many women need this kind of reassurance. In bed (Masters and Johnson tell such women) masochism gets you nowhere. But the husband is not left outside the design. He is told that his wife should manipulate him to ejaculation at least as often as he wants it. *And every fourth day is declared a vacation from any kind of sexual activity.* That's the day they go to the art museum or to see the Cardinals play baseball or a ride on a Mississippi riverboat.

Of 342 women patients who were treated for orgasmic dysfunction, there were 66 failures and 276 successes. The cooperation of the husbands was considered a vital factor. Wives who were lucky enough to have concerned, loving, and helpful husbands were the ones who made it. A few managed to "break through" without husband help, but not many.

Clearly, Dr. Masters and Mrs. Johnson consider women's orgasmic problems more complicated than men's. That is to say, more complicated because society admires a sexually functional male—"a good swordsman"—even if he is also associated with immoral behavior. But a superbly functioning female—even if she only functions with her husband—is supposed to keep it a secret and keep the shades drawn.

Here's the testimony of a woman who finally experienced orgasm. The speaker has been married five years and has two children. She's describing orgasmic sex:

"What's it like? There are no right words. I asked my neighbor—a real swinger—and she laughed and said it's like swallowing LSD and jumping into a washing machine.

"I understand what my neighbor means—that it really blows your mind and your body at the same time. But she leaves out the spirit. You feel yourself getting so close to your husband and so absolutely right with him and yourself. I don't care what they say about masturbation, there's got to be another person that you care about that's going with you. As my neighbor says, 'What's the fun of going to the circus alone?' "

"You begin wrestling around and he puts his hands all over you and pretty soon you get this crazy, zapped-up feeling that you're driven upward by a pulsation in your body. If you're underneath him, you arch your back and beg for it. If you're on top, you bear down and go for it. Then suddenly you're both up and over for a little moment and in some kind of earthly heaven!"

Sexuality and the Aging Person

Dr. Masters and Mrs. Johnson have said that they regard the last section in their book—the one on sexual inadequacy in aging persons—as the most important in their work. They feel it's very desirable from a psychosociological point of view to keep healthy people, regardless of their age, happily and effectively making love. They strongly emphasize that there should be no age turnoff for sex—that you can keep on having responsive intercourse as long as you can find somebody to do it with you.

When a couple comes to the Foundation and presents a complaint of middle-aged sexual letdown, they get, in addition to all the other intake procedures, a series of questions designed to illuminate the situation. The questions begin blandly enough. What is the current state of your marriage? Do you still like your husband (or wife)? Do you think your mate is kind and affectionate and understanding toward you? Are you interested in the same things? Do you spend your spare time together?

The quiz goes on:

Has your attitude toward sex been changed in recent years? As you've observed your friends growing old along with you, do you think their attitudes have changed? What, for example, have you observed?

How often, now, do you have intercourse? Are there any difficulties? Has your responsivity altered—is the orgasmic reaction the same or less intense? How about your mate?

Have you and your mate changed your political or religious view or otherwise altered your social viewpoints? Do you give more or fewer dinner parties?

Are one or both of you working? What kind of job?

What else do you do outside the home—clubs, sports, and so forth?

If you have children, have they grown and flown, or are they still living with you?

Are you baby-sitting your grandchildren?

How about your physical history. Any surgery? Sex hormone replacement? Do you regularly take any other form of medicine?

Regarding medication to ease the aging process, Dr. Masters and Mrs. Johnson are in favor of steroid hormone treatment in women—and against it for males. They explain their point of view but first insist on talking to their patients about the physiological and psychosexual aging process for both sexes.

Thus the roundtable interviews involve an exchange of additional information to which the younger couples are not exposed. Dr. Masters, when he becomes angry, glares until his blue-gray eyes seem ready to start from his brow. His face never changes. He doesn't scowl. His voice doesn't change. You just get those emphatic eyes right between your own eyes like intellectually scornful bullets.

What really riles him is the suggestion that sex is a youthful prerogative. He says males and females often turn off sex in their fifties because they've been told to do so. He says it's a terrible, tragic waste.

Panic, apparently, is what ends sex at middle age. Especially for men. The sexual response changes. A man finds out he can't do at 60 what he was doing at 30. So he thinks, "I'm finished!" He quits. When, actually, sex experiences just as good or better, if perhaps a little different, are awaiting him.

Dr. Masters explains that you can't run down the road at 60 as fast as you can at 30. But you can take more time to observe the wildflowers and you know more about them.

What difference does it make, after all, if it takes you 30 seconds or three minutes to get a sensate reaction to a sexual overture? So they're playing your song—just play it a little longer! It's "September Song," with Walter Houston. Or The Fantasticks singing, "Do You Remember?" It seems that songwriters have understood aging sex long before the sexologists.

For the aging male in addition to slower reaction time, there will be other changes. The little drops of pre-ejaculatory fluid that appear in the eager penis tips of younger men may be absent.

The older man can usually maintain an erection after intromission and continue to thrust for much longer periods of time than younger men. Many a middle-aged wife is astonished to find herself at age 46 multiorgasmic because her older husband keeps at it for such a long time. The ejaculation, when it does occur, is likely to have less seminal fluid and less semen than that of a younger man. If the older man is married to a younger woman who wishes to have children, this factor must be taken into consideration.

The orgasm of the older male is usually of shorter duration (while the older woman's orgasm may be much extended). He doesn't get that early-warning reaction, but ejaculates all at once without any premonition. This may be due to a low testosterone production or to an abnormally long period spent with the penis in the vagina.

Dr. Masters and Mrs. Johnson, who have vigorously opposed stopwatch sex, nevertheless offer clinical details such as, in the aging male, the "expulsive contractions of the penile uretha are onset at 0.8-second intervals . . ." and the aging man can only cast his seminal fluid from three to 12 inches.

The older man also gets a rapid relapse in his erection —often within a few seconds. And he can't usually achieve a second erection, intromission, and ejaculation the way he could when he was twenty years old. Both the aging male and his wife are counseled to recognize that these are variants which occur with maturity and are not to be thought of as failures.

Unfortunately what happens is that when an aging man finds his flaccid penis slipping out of the vagina immediately after ejaculation he worries: "I'm getting to where I can't do it the way I used to! Maybe the next time I won't be able to do it at all?" If he worries often enough, his fears may come true.

Wives, equally worried, can also splinter the aging sex scene. They get very upset if their husbands don't ejaculate at every coital connection. Dr. Masters, Mrs. Johnson, and other sex researchers and counselors reassure worried partners that a man doesn't necessarily have to ejaculate every time he has intercourse. For an aging man, three or four sex experiences may be required for one ejaculation. The male should feel free to "ejaculate on his demand schedule" as Masters and Johnson recommend.

With that kind of understanding, a healthy married couple should be able to function sexually well into the 80-year age group.

Although it may be a little difficult to think about a couple—male age 66 and female age 62—coming into therapy for sex failure, it is indisputably their right to be concerned. Masters and Johnson detail such a case:

Mr. and Mrs. A. had been married 39 years. They had three children, the youngest 23 years old. All of the children were married and living away from home. They said they'd had a good sex life with both of them regularly orgasmic until they saved up their money and took a trip abroad.

Many young couples report that their high moments of sexual encounter took place abroad or on a vacation when they were separated from domestic and job-holding responsibilities. For this aging couple, however, the rigidly scheduled pace of their vacation in Europe, far from turning them on, knocked them out. Racing from sightseeing bus to funicular railway to train to airplane and bedding down every few nights in a different hotel or inn completely exhausted the couple and disrupted their ordinary sex habits. Mr. A. found he was in trouble. He took longer and longer to achieve an erection and, just before they returned home, he found he couldn't do it at all.

He went to his doctor who pointed out that after all he was in his sixties and there was nothing that could be done. The couple, as Masters and Johnson put it, "accepted their fate." For four years. Then they got themselves referred to the Foundation, and shortly afterwards their competence returned. Now at late 60 and early 70 they have intercourse once or twice a week.

What's the lesson? To resist those travel posters if you're over 65? No. Just get educated as to what to expect from sex if you're over 65. The trauma of Mr. A's sudden sexual changeover had nothing to do with the change in time flying over the Atlantic or the garlic and truffles in

French food. It could have come from the exhaustion of a trip from Chicago to Moline—or putting up the storm windows—or plowing the north 40. It could happen to a much younger man. It's just that aging men—and their aging wives—are more prone to this kind of panic. The panic knocks them out and it's hard to recover both confidence and competence.

Older couples come to the Foundation because they just can't accept what other authorities have told them—that sex ends at female menopause. Masters and Johnson detail a wry case history that involved a woman patient who was nonorgasmic until she was in her mid-fifties.

This woman married at age 30 and had three sons and a daughter but she was never fully orgasmic. She reached what Dr. Masters and Mrs. Johnson call plateau level of sexual excitement but could never really make it. Otherwise she and her husband were happy and compatible. They consulted different sex experts to no avail and finally resigned themselves to making the best of it.

Then one of their sons got married. Observing the obvious physical attraction between their son and his bride, they came to the Foundation and said they'd like some help. Their problem was easily resolved. The wife first reached effective manipulative masturbation and went on from there to good sexual responsiveness with her husband. Meanwhile he learned something about ejaculatory control. They were sent to the Foundation by a referral from clergyman and physician. They had wasted nearly a quarter of a century.

Another aging woman patient gave this history: She was brought up in an all-woman family. The father had separated from the mother at an early age. The embittered mother told her three daughters all men were "no-goods!" The younger daughter—who eventually became the Masters and Johnson patient—married a kind, decent guy and had two sons. Her husband was the only man she had ever dated socially.

When the second son married and "emptied out" the home, the wife told her husband she was through with sex and requested separate rooms. Her husband insisted on going to the family clergyman for advice. The clergyman endorsed the wife's point of view. He said no woman her age, having done her wifely and motherly duties, should be expected to "continue in a role that nature had reserved as the responsibility of younger women."

The husband's physician, however, persuaded the wife to accompany the husband in therapy at the Reproductive Biology Research Foundation. The physician told the wife that her husband's mental and physical health was at stake.

The wife came into the Foundation angry, distrustful, and not very cooperative. To her own amazement she soon began to understand the information, to perform in therapy, and very soon became fully responsive sexually. She was 57 years old and her husband 63.

It has been said that the sexual problem of an aging man is the fear that he can't do it and the sexual problem of an aging woman is the feeling that she shouldn't do it. Oddly enough these fears and taboos are reinforced by the attitude of the younger generation—that enlightened group in their teens and twenties who have firmly claimed sexually active freedom for themselves, but deny it to their parents and grandparents.

If mom and dad at age 55 shut the bedroom door it's surely because mom wants to put an electric hot pad on his aching back. It's too bad. Pop shouldn't have attempted to change that tire. If grandma and grandpa do more than just hold hands and rock in front of the fire it's downright embarrassing.

The idea that the postmenopausal woman can't maintain a high sex reaction level is a folk taboo. Mark Twain, in his earthy *Letters from the Earth,* compared man to the candle and woman to the candlestick. He said that although the candle burns down and droops, the candlestick never loses its readiness for receptivity.

But like the response of the aging male, the receptive aging woman comes on a little more slowly. The older woman's vaginal lubrication may take four or five minutes to develop, while ten or fifteen years ago she might have been ready for intromission in fifteen seconds.

It should be said here that young women who undergo radiation treatment for cancer in the pelvic area sometimes develop an "aged" vagina years ahead of time.

In their chapter on the aging woman Dr. Masters and Mrs. Johnson make the fascinating statement that the vagina is a potential rather than actual space. What they mean is that it's deflated and has the potential to expand large enough to accommodate a baby's head or the largest penis in the world. When a young woman is sexually stimulated, her vagina promptly expands to accommodate the penis. The vagina of an older woman becomes smaller and less elastic and may take a little longer to contain the penis. The inside walls of a young woman's vagina are corrugated like a tin roof; the inside walls of an older woman's vagina become thin and smooth. There is a slight reduction in the size of the clitoris but it responds in exactly the same way as in a younger woman.

Women aged 50 to 70 years report that their orgasms change. They have four or five such contractions at orgasm rather than the eight to twelve reported by orgasmic younger women.

Some older women report severe pain in orgasm. Sometimes it's said to be in the lower abdomen or it zooms down the whole length of the vaginal barrel, into the vulva and even down one or both legs. It's called a uterine spasm and Masters and Johnson say many cases can be helped by sex-steroid replacement.

There's a big argument going—well, a vigorous academic discussion—about whether women in menopause should or shouldn't get sex-steroid replacements then and afterwards. Some doctors just give tranquilizers. A favorite is one or another version of aprobarbital, a hypnotic drug used as a sedative.

Dr. Masters and Mrs. Johnson are all for the steroid replacements. They say the hormones help to cope with the hot and cold flushes, emotional instability, headaches and spinal aches, and "that tired feeling."

More important, from Masters' and Johnson's point of view, the sex steroids are apparently helpful in supporting or repairing dysfunction of the aging vagina. Irritability and pain in the bladder and urethra are a common problem with menopausal women, and there is an immediate—sometimes inconvenient—need to urinate directly after coitus. Some women have unhappily told about helplessly voiding while in coitus. Hormones also aid the aging woman who notices a change in the tissue structure over her mons, or pelvic arch. It gets soft and flabby. It has nothing to do with how she diets or exercises.

The medically supervised administration of steroid hormones helps many women to return to a more active sex interest. What puzzles Dr. Masters and Mrs. Johnson is that many women don't need steroid replacement techniques. For reasons no one yet can explain these women, although they stop menstruating in their late forties or early fifties, apparently continue to manufacture their own steroids. Or something else that is as good or better than the replacements a woman is offered by her doctor.

These women are fairly easily identified by their high levels of physical energy and mental alertness. Some of them are married and have sex relations several times a week. Some are widowed and offer no apparent evidence about their sex life. But Masters and Johnson speculate that regularity of sexual activity—with or without a partner—is what keeps up the production of natural hormones.

A number of women in the 50- to 70-year age group report they have stepped up their masturbation. Many of these are married to older men who are invalided or who say, "No sex!" Dr. Masters and Mrs. Johnson feel that society should grant these women freedom to relieve their sexual tensions in any way they see fit as long as it is acceptable to our culture.

The question, of course, is what sex activity is acceptable to and needed by our culture? Other sex mores—if not our sex practices—are changing dizzily for both sexes of all ages. The authors assert that we're progressively becoming more uninhibited and more proficient at sex and that we're enjoying it more. So why is there so long a waiting list for admission to the Reproductive Biology Research Foundation? Those on the waiting list are by no means just old people, and certainly the ones who are middle-aged have young sons and daughters who will have trouble being sexually responsive because they have been reared by troubled parents.

We feel, regretfully, that the Reproductive Biology Research Foundation will be in business for quite a long time to come. That is too bad. There is probably no medical service that would be happier to be forced to close its doors for lack of patients.

PART II

The Reproductive Biology Foundation

The Achievement of William H. Masters and Virginia E. Johnson

by Edward Brecher

EDITORS' NOTE: *Edward Brecher is a distinguished medical journalist whose books and mass media magazine articles have international status. With his late wife, Ruth, he wrote "An Analysis of Human Sexual Response," a brilliant interpretation and critique of the earlier Masters and Johnson work. In the following material from his book,* The Sex Researchers, *he tells about the original Masters and Johnson project, a laboratory-conducted inquiry into what happens to human bodies in the course of erotic stimulation. Mr. Brecher also gives us some interesting biographical notes on the personalities of Dr. Masters and Mrs. Johnson.*

With the publication of their first book, *Human Sexual Response*, in April 1966, Dr. William H. Masters and Mrs. Virginia E. Johnson of the Reproductive Biology Research Foundation in St. Louis became world-renowned almost overnight. Newspapers in many countries carried accounts of their work on the day of publication, plus frequent follow-up stories. More than 300,000 copies of their book, at ten dollars a copy, were sold in the United States. It was translated into nine foreign languages. An additional 500,000 paperback copies of an account of their work by my wife and myself were also sold, and our book was also translated into nine languages. Tens of millions of readers learned of their work through magazine articles; non-readers heard of it through gossip. Not since the Kinsey reports had sex research made such a stir in the world.

The stir was fully warranted. For *Human Sexual Response* described, in scrupulous detail, precisely how the human body responds to erotic stimulation during both masturbation and coitus. Responses of the penis, scrotum, and testes, the breasts, clitoris, labia, vagina, cervix, uterus, and other parts of the body were all presented and explained. The Masters–Johnson study made it possible to follow the entire human sexual cycle from the first stirrings of erotic desire through orgasm to ultimate subsidence as objectively as nineteenth-century physiologists had followed the digestive cycle from mastication to excretion. Their study, moreover, was authoritative; it was not based on speculation or random data but on direct laboratory observation of more than 10,000 male and female orgasms. ...

The role of Masters and Johnson in the history of science, however, is only partly based on this major physiological achievement. Their second book, *Human Sexual Inadequacy*, published in April 1970, represents an equally monumental *therapeutic* achievement—a report on the causes of sexual inadequacy in the male and in the female, and a presentation of precise therapeutic techniques for overcoming sexual dysfunction, based on eleven years of experience. ...

The two Masters–Johnson reports, *Human Sexual Response* (1966) and *Human Sexual Inadequacy* (1970), are related in intimate ways. The former is concerned with a population of sexually very effective men and women, able with ease to experience orgasm even in the laboratory under scientific observation. The latter is concerned with a sexually dysfunctional population, unable to achieve effective sexual response even under favorable circumstances. The earlier book is concerned primarily with physiological response, and fully establishes the principle that the sexual climax in both women and men is the normal physiological outcome of adequate sexual stimulation. The later book is concerned primarily with the psychology of sex—and in particular with the psychosocial factors which block physiological sexual response. Taken together, they present the two sides of the sexual coin. They were made possible by the fact that two remarkable human beings, Bill Masters and Gini Johnson, were able to rise above the sexual perspectives of their time and place, and to view human sexuality with both broad scientific objectivity and deep therapeutic concern....

William Howell Masters was born in Cleveland in 1915, the son of parents in comfortable circumstances. He attended Lawrenceville Preparatory School in Lawrenceville, New Jersey, and secured his bachelor of science degree from Hamilton College in 1938. During his science studies at Hamilton, or perhaps earlier, he acquired a strong dislike of mysteries. If he asked a sensible question, he wanted a sensible answer. If no clear answer was readily forthcoming, he was willing to go to considerable pains to secure one. It was this dislike of mystifications and confidence in rationality, I am convinced, which led him to decide on a career in scientific research and which has held that career on a rigidly successful track ever since.

Following graduation from Hamilton, Masters enrolled in the University of Rochester School of Medicine and Dentistry—not to prepare for the practice of medicine, but as a step toward research in the biological sciences. During his first year at Rochester, he worked in the laboratory of one of the country's foremost anatomists and authorities on the biology of sex, Dr. George Washington Corner—the first major event in the chain which was to lead to the Masters–Johnson reports.

"I remember [Bill Masters] as a very serious and intelligent young man of more independent character than many," Dr. Corner recalled in 1966. He assigned Masters to a problem in sex research—the estrous cycle in the female rabbit, and the ways in which it differs from or resembles the menstrual cycle in the human female. One stumbling block to the rabbit research was the ignorance and misunderstanding which still shrouded the *human* cycle in mystery. It was this laboratory experience, and Dr. Corner's influence generally, which led Bill Masters to narrow his goal from biological research in general to sex research in particular.

Dr. Corner approved this decision, but gave his student three often-quoted *caveats:*

He should wait until he was at least 40 before tackling sex research.

He should first earn a scientific reputation in some other scientific field.

He should wait until he could secure the sponsorship of a major medical school or university.

No doubt that advice was well meant, and was warranted by the conditions of the time. The general prejudice against sex and against any exploration of sexual problems was at least as strong in scientific and academic circles as elsewhere during the 1940s; Puritanism and Victorianism still held sway in an only slightly diluted form. The few researchers who dared to tackle sexual or quasi-sexual research topics hazarded their careers; they were gossiped about and attacked. Financial support was scarce. For an unproved young M.D. to try to barge into so sensitive a field inadequately prepared would have been foolhardy indeed.

In restrospect, however, it is clear that this cautious advice to young Masters—which must also have been given to countless other highly competent young scientists throughout the first half of this century—was (and remains today) a serious stumbling block to sex research progress. Until young men and women of insight and enthusiasm, less hemmed in than their elders by post-Victorian restrictions, are not only welcomed but actively recruited into the field and amply supported in their projects, sex research will continue to lag behind other less important scientific areas.

Dr. Masters married in 1942 and received his M.D. degree in 1943. From 1943 to 1947 he was an intern, and then a resident in obstetrics and gynecology at Barnes Hospital and Maternity Hospital, Washington University School of Medicine, St. Louis. Thereafter he became successively instructor, assistant professor, and associate professor at the medical school. In 1951 he was certified as a specialist by the American Board of Obstetricians and Gynecologists. His two children, a boy and a girl, were born in 1950 and 1951. Along with his medical school assignments he served as associate obstetrician and gynecologist at St. Louis Maternity Hospital and at Barnes Hospital, and as consulting gynecologist at the St. Louis

Infirmary and at Salem Memorial Hospital in Salem, Illinois; and he engaged in the practice of gynecology.

During the six years from 1948 to 1954, Dr. Masters published 25 contributions to the medical literature, covering a variety of obstetrical and gynecological topics. Fourteen of these papers were concerned with a single research project, pursued intensively for seven years—hormone replacement therapy for aging and aged women. The titles of these papers indicate the nature of the research: "Female Sex Hormone Replacement in the Elderly Woman" (1948); "Investigation of Sexual Regeneration in Elderly Women" (1949); "Androgen Administration in the Postmenopausal Woman" (1950); "The Rationale and Technique of Sex Hormone Replacement in the Aged Female" (1951); "Long-Range Steroid Replacement—Target Organ Regeneration" (1953); and "Estrogen-Androgen Substitution Therapy in the Aged Female" (1953).

This geriatric research program was another in the unique chain of events leading to the Masters–Johnson reports, largely through its impact on Dr. Masters's own attitudes. There are many stances or attitudes which a man may take toward sex. One is sheer sensuous enjoyment. Another is recoil in horror. A third is ethical evaluation, and a fourth is aesthetic appreciation. No doubt there are others as well. Dr. Masters's two major accomplishments to date—his studies in the physiology of sexual response and in the therapy of sexual inadequacy—resulted from his ability to set aside, at least in his professional life, all of these common reactions to sexuality, and to substitute for them the kind of attitude that scientists customarily hold toward digestion, circulation, and other physiological phenomena. Studying the effects of sex hormones on women years or even decades past the menopause was an admirable training ground for establishing precisely such an attitude in a young physician still in his thirties. Masters's work in hormone replacement therapy was important in its own right; several million menopausal and postmenopausal women today benefit from hormone replacement therapy. But it was also one more important step in the education of Dr. Masters. (Incidentally, it gave Masters a continuing concern for the long-neglected sexual problems of the aging and aged—a concern which motivates several of the studies he now has under way in St. Louis.)

Dr. Masters, as I have pointed out, hates mysteries and mystifications. Both as a medical student and as a gynecologist, he had found himself constantly hampered by lack of the simplest knowledge concerning normal sexual functions. Efforts to understand and to treat sexual complaints in pathological cases were repeatedly stymied by the mystery which surrounded the responses of normal males and normal females to normal erotic stimuli. Thus, gradually, Masters's decision to engage in sex research narrowed down further to a decision to get to the heart of the matter and study the sex act directly. . . .

It was the predominantly favorable reception accorded the publication of the second Kinsey report in 1953 which gave Dr. Masters the courage to launch his own study the following year. He has often since expressed his indebtedness to Kinsey, whom he never knew personally, for "opening the previously closed doors of our culture to definitive investigation of human sexual response."

By 1954, in short, Dr. Masters was ready to launch his lifework. He had made a reputation for himself with his research in other fields. He had the institutional support of a major university medical center. In only one respect was he lacking Dr. Corner's specifications; he was still two years short of 40.

The 1954 Masters research plan called for a comprehensive study of physiological responses from initial erotic stimulation through orgasm to quiescence, in both masturbation and coitus, in a variety of postures, in both men and women of a wide range of ages, and at various stages in the menstrual cycle, using sophisticated instrumentation as well as direct observation and motion-picture recording on film. As a preliminary to this vast undertaking, Dr. Masters first interviewed at length and in depth 118 female and 27 male prostitutes. Eight of the women prostitutes and three of the men then participated as experimental subjects in a preliminary series of laboratory observations —a sort of "dry run" for the project.

This use of prostitutes became the subject of snide remarks and leers when the Masters studies first became known. The studies were obviously valueless, it was suggested, because prostitutes were involved in them; besides, what self-respecting scientist would demean himself by contacts with prostitutes?

It seems to me, in contrast, that Dr. Masters was either remarkably perceptive or exceedingly lucky in deciding to turn to prostitutes at this preliminary stage. They, after all, are the best-informed experts in the world on human sexual response—or were, prior to the Masters–Johnson studies. During the routine course of her work, a prostitute is typically visited by a man who has eaten too much and drunk too much to be sexually very effective. It is probably long past his bedtime; fatigue further impairs his sexual responsiveness. In some cases, he is assailed by feelings of guilt at fornication, and of shame that he must resort to a prostitute. The surroundings are hardly inspiring. The client has no affection for his partner of the moment, and usually selects her because she happens to be available rather than because of any particular attraction she might have for him. Despite many such obstacles, the prostitute is expected to and in almost all cases succeeds in arousing her client erotically and triggering his orgasm in as short a time as possible—often within a few minutes. Even a moderately competent and intelligent prostitute, after a few hundreds or thousands of such encounters, is surely a worthwhile informant concerning sexual response patterns. The prostitutes he interviewed, Dr. Masters later affirmed, "described many methods for elevating or controlling sexual tensions and demonstrated innumerable variations in stimulative technique. Ultimately many of these techniques have been found to have direct application in therapy of male and female sexual inadequacy and have been integrated into the clinical research programs." It is hardly to Dr. Masters's discredit, but rather to the discredit of his predecessors,* that he tapped and they failed to tap this rich source of clinically valuable data.

For purposes of *physiological* study, however, the St. Louis prostitute population proved to be unsuitable. Many of them were migrants, in St. Louis one month and not to be found the next; an essential feature of the Masters plan was the prolonged observation of responses as they developed through the years in individual subjects. Many

---

*Except Dickinson and Kinsey, who also recognized the value of data available from prostitutes.

of the prostitutes, moreover, exhibited substantial degrees of pelvic pathology—including a condition of chronic congestion of the pelvic region, presumably the result of frequently repeated sexual excitation without orgasmic release. Hence, despite the value of his prostitutional studies in other respects, Dr. Masters was forced to exclude most of his observations of their response patterns from his physiological findings.

The prostitutes themselves, however, provided him with a clue for finding respectable men and women willing to participate in his research project. They cited many examples of sexual activities occurring in the presence of observers. A client might engage two prostitutes, for example, or two clients might engage one or more prostitutes, and other combinations might be arranged. There were both men and women, the prostitutes reported, who enjoyed engaging in sex in the presence of others. Much more important for Dr. Masters's research program, there were respectable men and women who had no strong feeling about privacy either way; they simply lacked, for some reason or other, the strong privacy taboos common in our culture.

Dr. Masters, accordingly, took a gingerly first step toward securing respectable volunteers. He let it be known through the university and medical school community that he was planning a study of human sexual response based on laboratory observations. News such as this spreads quickly along the local grapevine. One medical school professor tells another, who tells his wife, who tells a neighbor. A medical student tells a nurse, who tells her sister-in-law.

The returns from this local gossip were of two kinds. A few of those who heard about the research via the grapevine came to Dr. Masters's office on the medical-school floor of the maternity-hospital building eager to volunteer "for kicks." They were promptly eliminated.

More welcome were visitors who were genuinely concerned with some important human problem which sexual research might solve, and who wanted to help solve it. Some couples were referred by their own physicians; some came because they hoped to learn ways to increase their own satisfaction and enjoyment of sex. Former patients of

Dr. Masters came, and brought their husbands, when they heard he needed volunteers. . . .

It was during the phase of recruiting volunteers that Mrs. Johnson came to work for Dr. Masters. Born Virginia Eshelman in the Missouri Ozarks in 1925, she had studied music at Drury College in Missouri, and later attended Missouri University—where she discovered the world of sociology and psychology. In 1950 she married; in 1952 and 1955 her son and daughter were born. Separated from her husband soon afterward, Mrs. Johnson registered for a job at the Washington University Placement Bureau at a time when Dr. Masters was seeking a woman to assist in research interviewing. For his project he had specified a woman with experience and interest in working with people. The Placement Bureau sent Mrs. Johnson to fill the job, and she has been there ever since.

This was another of the major links in the chain which led to the Masters–Johnson achievement; for by good fortune, Mrs. Johnson proved to be one of those rare human beings who sees the world as it is, undistorted by traditional ways of looking at things. She brought to the Masters–Johnson partnership, in addition to this clarity of vision, a very deep empathy with other people, especially other women. Her contribution was important in the program of laboratory observations; but it proved even more essential when the Masters–Johnson program of therapy for sexual inadequacy was launched a few years later. . . .

Can the Masters–Johnson form of therapy be effectively used by other therapeutic teams?

I was delighted on my most recent visit to St. Louis to learn that the answer is yes.

A second team of therapists has been added to the Masters–Johnson staff—Dr. Richard Spitz, trained originally as a pediatrician, and Dr. Sally Schumacher, a psychologist. Using Masters and Johnson techniques, they are securing comparable results. I see no reason why, within the next few years, this form of therapy should not become available at other centers throughout the country and world.

In both their physiological research and their therapeutic program, it seems to me, Masters and Johnson represent the high point to date in the grand tradition of sex research stemming from Havelock Ellis. That tradition through the decades has been concerned with the disastrous effects of sexual repression—of sexual Puritanism and Victorianism. It has demonstrated the social roots of sexual frustration. It has not only documented these effects, but has insistently sought remedies. Indeed, sex research itself turns out to be the sovereign remedy; for by determining the facts and making them publicly known, it destroys the ignorance on which the Victorian ethic is founded.

At an April 1970 press conference, Masters and Johnson outlined three additional sex research projects now under way.

One concerns the sexual effects of aging and sexual therapy for the aging.

Another, launched in 1965, concerns homosexual response and homosexual inadequacy. The laboratory portion of this project, Dr. Masters indicated, was nearing completion in 1970 and the therapy of female homosexual inadequacy had begun. A report could be expected in the mid-70s.

The third study, concerned with adolescent sexual physiology and inadequacy, was just beginning, with no report scheduled before the end of the 1970s. Thus the rhythm of a major report every five years or so, each report based on ten years or more of research and clinical study, was being projected through the coming decade.

Human Sexual Inadequacy has a crucial message for parents and teachers concerned with sex education and with the prevention of sexual dysfunction. The key concept in prevention as well as in therapy, the Masters–Johnson data clearly indicate, is sensate focus.

Every babe in arms who grows up in a loving environment experiences sensate focus during much of his waking hours. Happy three-year-olds can be observed in a state of sensate focus many times a day. By the onset of puberty in our still quasi-Victorian culture, the experience is much rarer, and in many cases is either gently or ruthlessly repressed. Masters and Johnson, as we have seen, achieve their therapeutic results in large part by helping their patients to reestablish sensate focus. Thus the educational moral fairly leaps from the pages of their report: if we stop inhibiting sensate focus in our children initially, and if we teach them to value it along with the other values we try to instill in them, there should be little need for them to seek to regain in therapy, decades hence, the inviolable birthright of which they should never have been deprived.

New Love Techniques We Learned at the Masters and Johnson Sex Clinic

(As told to Victoria Pellegrino)

EDITORS' NOTE: *Victoria Pellegrino, an alert editor for* Pageant Magazine, *encountered "Beverly" and "Bill" (names changed, of course), who, married six years, had just successfully passed through the two-week therapy program in St. Louis. She persuaded them to talk. Their complaint was the one most commonly presented at the Reproductive Biology Research Foundation: the male is preejaculatory and/or the female is frigid. Both felt they were on the way to divorce until, with a doctor's advice, they were told to go to St. Louis. Now they are a sexually harmonious couple. Beverly and Bill's experience reinforces Dr. Masters' and Mrs. Johnson's contention that in most cases of sexual malfunction the difficulty lies with both partners.*

BEVERLY: Bill and I were married while he was still in college, and the beginning years were very hard for us. We had a child that first year, plus we were both working to pay for Bill's schooling. Yet, we were in love; the hard work was more than worth it.

Naturally, with a new baby and with a husband working days and going to school nights, our sexual relationship was hit and miss. We were too tired, really, too preoccupied. Although our lack of a good sex life worried me, I

Reprinted with permission of *Pageant Magazine*. Copyright © *Pageant Magazine*, 1969.

said to myself that this would change after Bill was out of school. But it didn't.

We made love once or twice a week, and during those six years, I never had an orgasm. At times, I had a small feeling of release; at times, I was very tense. This, in turn, made me feel very inadequate. I reasoned that I could not have an orgasm, therefore I must be frigid. Adding to my unhappiness was the fact that I didn't think Bill cared about me. He was very involved with his new job and when he was home, he'd read the paper or watch television. There never seemed to be anything to say to each other.

I began to feel that I couldn't stand to live the rest of my life making love without enjoying it.

One day, I told Bill I wanted to leave him. He was shocked and very upset—which really surprised me. I hadn't thought he cared, as I've said. So, I agreed to stay and tried very hard to make this marriage a success. After that, we did get along a little better and our sexual life improved somewhat. But things were still not the way I thought they should be.

During this time, I had read about Dr. William Masters and Mrs. Virginia Johnson and their book, *Human Sexual Response*. I knew that they were two of the best-known sex researchers in the country and that they had a clinic in St. Louis, Missouri, called the Reproductive Biology Research Foundation, to which troubled couples went for help. Moreover, I had read about their work with sexual inadequacy, and about the fantastic results they were having.

I decided I wanted to go. It was just a matter of money, for they charged $2,500 for a two-week period. That would be in addition to the motel and eating expenses.

At first, I had a very hard time convincing Bill. I argued that we were going to be making love for the rest of our lives, that this problem wasn't one you could forget about or ignore. When he said no, I again thought he didn't care.

BILL: Although Beverly's sexual dissatisfaction worried me, I told myself that this was her problem, not mine. I now see that I didn't want to admit to myself my own fear of inadequacy and failure.

We had a number of fights before we finally got to St. Louis. For one thing, I didn't have the money. For another, I was afraid people I knew might find out. Mostly, I was afraid to hear what Masters and Johnson might say.

However, as the months passed by, our marriage was one of continuous conflict. I thought it would be on the rocks soon. So, I said to myself that we had to try something. And, I also felt, *Hell, let's see whose problem this is, hers or mine.* St. Louis was really a last desperate measure.

BEVERLY: Once we had decided to go, we had to rake up $2500 plus money for our hotel. I took a part-time secretarial job and we borrowed some money from the bank. For three months, we didn't go to a movie, didn't eat dinner out once. I made casseroles and hamburger patties until they were coming out of our ears. We finally managed to get the money.

I know people will say that $2500 is a lot to spend, but I felt that the treatment was important and worthwhile. People wouldn't get upset about spending money on an expensive car or a trip to Europe—so why balk at spending money on something that will affect your entire marriage?

We made several calls to St. Louis and talked to the receptionist there. Our doctor, whom we had spoken to, also called Masters and Johnson, since they insisted upon having a doctor's recommendation. Finally, we set up an appointment and arranged to have my mother take care of of our children and drove to St. Louis.

With some trepidation, we went in to the clinic's receptionist. She was a wonderful person with a friendly, enormous smile. She gave us advice on what to do, where to eat, what to see while in town. She emphasized that we were on a vacation and that we should have a good time and be very happy, that we were completely cut off from all our worries and cares. She even gave us a great picnic basket with all the things we would need during our stay there: plates and cups and utensils and irons, pots and pans, everything. Then, we said goodbye and settled into our comfortable, luxurious suite in a motel across the street—they'd made the arrangements—and then went out to dinner and to a movie.

Our first interview on Tuesday was with both Dr. Masters and Mrs. Johnson. Dr. Masters is extremely imposing looking and dominates any scene. Mrs. Johnson is a very pretty woman, but not glamorous, and wears little or no makeup. The doctor looks like a statue, and his eyes seemed to go in two different directions at the same time. Their personalities seemed to complement each other.

That first day, Dr. Masters nearly made me fall out of my chair. He said, "I can see you're having your period." I was speechless. Mrs. Johnson started laughing and said, "Oh, he can always tell." He said, "Well, reproductive biology is my business." She then told me that he can tell when a woman is three-weeks pregnant—just by watching her walk!

They explained to us how the next two weeks would work: We would see them during the day for about an hour, and then we'd be given homework to do that night. Everything we said would be taped. They also emphasized that during the first two days, we couldn't talk to each other about anything that was said in their offices. The purpose of this was to wall up communication so that we would be eager to talk on the third day. They also didn't want us to plan what we would say to them—and thus ruin the spontaneity and purpose of the therapy. They also explained that different couples receive different treatments—naturally—and that ours would depend upon our particular problems and our response to treatment.

Then I went with Mrs. Johnson to her office. It was comfortable, with dark paneling and furniture. I noticed that on one table she had a beautiful wooden sculpture of a couple lying facing each other. In a very feminine, yet efficient way, she asked me questions about my childhood and adolescence: How did my mother feel about sex, as far as I knew; how did my father feel; what were my early impressions and experiences with sex?

I told her that my childhood had not been happy, that my parents were constantly bickering, and hadn't seemed to care about me. I was left on my own and soon learned that the only person I could depend upon was myself. I never had had any sexual experiences until after I graduated from high school. I said that I enjoyed sex with my husband in the beginning, but that I was having a harder and harder time responding because he didn't satisfy me. I confessed to her that I thought I was frigid.

BILL: From that first day on, I felt full confidence in Dr. Masters. I admired his wry sense of humor and felt at ease with him—as much as I could under the circumstances, anyway. I told him that my mother had died giving birth to my younger brother and that we had been raised by three old-maid aunts. My father had remarried and gone off somewhere, and I remembered being always lonely as a child.

I said that I had picked up a few girls for one-night stands in college and had made love in the back seats of jalopies, that sort of thing. However, I never had had a close relationship with anyone before my wife. As he listened to me, the doctor seemed interested and encouraging.

The next day, I saw Mrs. Johnson, and Beverly saw Dr. Masters. They asked each of us to describe our marriage. They also asked what pleased us in sex, and what turned us off, that type of question. After these two interviews, our fears about the clinic had, to a large degree, subsided. We made up our minds to enjoy ourselves, and that night I took Beverly to a Greek restaurant and later to a movie.

BEVERLY: The third day, Bill and I had complete physicals and blood tests. Then all four of us got together. Dr. Masters said our sexual problems stemmed from two things: (a) We had poor models as parents (they rarely showed affection or exhibited healthy attitudes toward sex), and (b) we were both very inexperienced in sexual matters. He said he did not advocate that everyone should have premarital experience. However, Dr. Masters said it was Bill's responsibility, early in the marriage, to have done something about satisfying me. And, he said that I should not have assumed that Bill didn't care and that he was sexually satisfied just because he had an orgasm. Both of us puzzled over that for a while. What Dr. Masters meant was that it's very easy for a male to have an orgasm, but that this is not necessarily a total experience. It may be a physical release, but not emotionally involving or satisfying to him.

They gave us our first assignment that night. Our "homework" was to touch each other all over, except for the breasts and the genitals. We were not "allowed" to make love that night—or for several nights thereafter. They gave us body lotions to give back rubs to each other.

They stressed that one person should touch at a time: One is the giver, the other the taker. For example, Bill was supposed to spend twenty minutes tracing the lines of my face, then rubbing, touching, and caressing me. During that time I was to do nothing, just to receive, to think about how it felt. Later, I was to do the same for him. Both give and both get. This exercise was very hard to carry out. I felt so guilty at first, as if I should immediately return this affection. However, once you do this, it's distracting and ruins the whole mood and feeling. It's impossible to give at the same time that you're getting. So you take turns at this sensate awareness, and the whole thing works beautifully.

BILL: When we walked in on the fourth day, we were both relaxed and felt the experiences of the night before had been pleasurable.

Then, Dr. Masters hit me with something that I'd dreaded to hear: I was a premature ejaculator. They explained that I should not get alarmed, that all this meant was that I didn't sustain myself long enough to satisfy my partner.

However, before I had time to sink into despair, they confided they had a technique to cure this problem. The woman takes the male apparatus, the thumb is on one side below the ridge, while the other two fingers are on the opposite side, one finger above the ridge, one below it. The woman gives a firm, hard squeeze for about the count of ten. This makes the man lose his sense of urgency, the need for him to ejaculate.

This technique is naturally a little awkward in the beginning and may cause some people embarrassment. However, the point is that it works. It becomes a habit. The squeeze is like a programming device. After a short time, you can create the same feelings without it.

Now, we haven't used this technique for months. It isn't necessary anymore. Before, intercourse lasted only about five to ten minutes. Now, I can make love to my wife for an hour or longer. I believe that, with this simple technique, Masters and Johnson claim 100 percent success with premature ejaculation.

This technique is naturally very different from what most marriage manuals tell you. They usually instruct a man to think about "something else" to put off ejaculation. Dr. Masters says this is bad—and anyway, most men know it doesn't work!

That night, we practiced the technique and everything else we had learned up until that point.

BEVERLY: A very funny thing began to happen to me on the fifth day. I, who was always in control of situations, couldn't handle this one at all. Bill was progressing with this new technique, but I was almost frozen with fear that I wouldn't be able to have an orgasm during intercourse. If I didn't, I would have failed, and I was very much afraid of failure. This fear was the biggest obstacle I had to overcome.

Masters and Johnson tried to calm me by saying that I shouldn't worry, that I *would* be able to overcome my six years of lack of success. This session with them was very short: Our assignment that night was to (1) continue practicing the technique, and (2) stimulate all areas of the body without making love.

They stressed that both partners should touch each other very lightly. They said rubbing anesthetizes the nerve endings, while light caresses stimulate the nerve endings.

The sixth day, I talked to Mrs. Johnson for a long time about my feelings of inadequacy and my relationship with my husband. Then, they saw both Bill and me on the seventh day. They said so many important things that day.

They said if you don't communicate in any other area or at any other time of the day, communicate in bed. Let this be your own area, like a little island, where you express your love feelings for each other. If you want to ignore each other the rest of the time (although this is not suggested), okay, but keep the rest of the world out of the bedroom. They said communicate by touching, communicate through your senses. Mrs. Johnson was constantly saying, "Give to get."

Dr. Masters also said that a person shouldn't watch himself in bed. For, if one partner thinks about what is going on, he detaches himself from the situation. You have to be relaxed and involved, so totally involved that you're not able to look on as an observer. The doctor told me that if I did this, an orgasm would just come to me by surprise. However, he said the goal of intercourse should be not orgasm but enjoyment.

Fantasizing was something else we discussed. Dr. Masters said this was all right—if anything enhances sex for you, do it. He said that now we needed everything we could to help us. Later, after we had built up more and more successful experiences, we wouldn't need this help. So, a person could fantasize about anything—that he was at a party, that this was the first time he'd ever made love, anything at all.

The assignment that night was to assume intercourse position, with the woman superior, but with little or no movement. We did this the next night also and found it stimulating for us both.

On the eighth day, I saw Dr. Masters alone and he talked about himself and his work. He said he works about eighty hours a week and sometimes goes a whole week without going home. I asked, "Doesn't your wife mind?" He said, "I don't know, I'm not there often enough for her to tell me whether she does or not." He said his work was the most important thing to him, although, he added, one always wonders about the correctness of a decision.

That night, Bill and I had our first big fight. I told him that I resented him for having let me think I was frigid all those years when it was really partially his fault. I felt as though he had put all the burden and feelings of inadequacy on my shoulders, rather than admit to himself that he wasn't the perfect lover. Naturally, that night I was frozen with anger, and we did not accomplish much.

The ninth day in therapy, we talked about our fight. Both Dr. Masters and Mrs. Johnson told me that I had to forgive Bill and forget my resentment if I expected to be successful. I thought that was easy to say but hard to do, and said I didn't know whether I could forget the whole thing that easily. They then told me that in my present state of mind, I couldn't possibly be open to new suggestions, so they instructed me to spend the night working out my feelings. I remember that the more I thought, the more confused I became, so we ended up going to a nightclub to see a show.

BILL: By the next day, Beverly had relaxed a little, although she was still frightened and somewhat resentful of me. That day, Dr. Masters showed us a technique, a new position, that would cause deep penetration for the woman and would allow the maximum freedom of movement for both parties. To illustrate, they used little wooden dolls. They said this would be difficult to adjust to.

To get into this position, the man lies flat on his back with a pillow behind his head. The woman is on top; she leans forward, puts her cheek against his, straightens her right leg between his two, and moves the top of her body slightly to the right. The other leg is bent outside his body. This means that she is at about a 45-degree angle to him, her head several inches away from his. She may put a pillow under her torso, which allows no strain for either person. Dr. Masters said that many couples found this position so comfortable that they talked for hours—or went to sleep—in that position.

After explaining this technique, he went on to say a few more things about marriage manuals. He disputed their usual contention that partners should have intercourse a certain number of times a week. Rather, he said, there should be kept up a *level* of sexual contact day after day. He said that every night there should be some touching without the commitment to consummation. Moreover, he said, couples should not aim for simultaneous orgasm. He said that sex should never be contrived, and that whenever you try to obtain an orgasm, it's too contrived, and you may lose it. So many things he said differed from the marriage manuals.

At first, all of the new advice was hard to put into action. I think what eventually made the treatment effective was the fact that there was this constant sexual buildup. Practically every night, a little more would be added. Moreover, in St. Louis, there were no phones, no children, no job. There was nothing to think about but ourselves and our goal: sexual happiness.

BEVERLY: Dr. Masters, up until this time, had been extremely satisfied with Bill's progress. However, he was not happy with me, and said so. He told me I was keeping myself detached from what was going on, that I wasn't "joining the party." "You've got to relax and get involved in this," he said. He told me I was sulking and feeling sorry for myself, that I had a poor attitude and must forget the "I-me" and think in terms of "us." He said I should stop worrying about whether I could have an orgasm.

I went back to the suite that day very upset, and I remember we both had a few more drinks than usual. It seemed to me that I was trying to do what they said—yet obviously I wasn't getting the message. In my desperation and panic, I looked to my husband for comfort. This may seem natural to many women, but it was a big step for me, since I had always thought of myself as extremely self-sufficient. That night, my husband and I became closer than we had been in years. Slowly, my defenses were crumbling.

BILL: On the twelfth day, Dr. Masters and Mrs. Johnson emphasized that a man is supposed to take directions from the woman as to what pleases her most. The woman should not be shy about this, they said. Dr. Masters also told Beverly that eventually she would become multiorgasmic—as he believes most women can be. He said women are capable of having climaxes during foreplay, intercourse, and afterplay.

BEVERLY: That night, when we made love, we were both relaxed and happy. I was just enjoying and feeling what was happening, and all of a sudden I realized that I had reached the plateau stage and I could achieve a climax. I guess it was the point of inevitability: It came upon me effortlessly. I thought: *I'm going to have an orgasm.* Then, I thought: *Don't panic, don't force yourself, or you'll lose it. Just relax, and if it doesn't come, don't be upset.* It just came over me very naturally, wavelike convulsions that went through my entire body. As Dr. Masters had implied, it came to me by surprise.

No trumpets heralded this triumph, but who needed them? I went to sleep with a small smile on my face. I felt I had, at last, become a "real woman."

BILL: The next day, I suppose we were both so pleased it showed as soon as we walked into their offices. Beverly confided what had happened—and both Masters and Johnson were obviously happy. We promised to call them every two weeks for a while and to keep in contact, at longer intervals, for a period of five years.

On the way home from St. Louis, we were both very

peaceful. Beverly had relied on me, and I was building up a new confidence in myself.

Now, as a result, I think we both feel we are more adequate individuals. We don't have to feel this shame, or wonder if other people have happier sex lives. We are confident that we do have a happy sex life, and that's important.

BEVERLY: Many women go to therapy for years and still never overcome their sexual problems. And, the reason is that their therapy never involves the husband. You have to get the husband in on it. If a woman is going to a psychiatrist for a frigidity problem and her husband isn't involved, it may not work. Critics of Masters and Johnson say that if you don't treat the woman's neurosis, you still have a neurotic woman. But Masters and Johnson say, fine—would a man rather have a neurotic wife who couldn't have an orgasm or a neurotic wife who could!?

I had a problem, and Bill had a problem: I was non-orgasmic; he had premature ejaculation. With his problem corrected with their new technique and new position, I was able to correct mine. Now, we know how to communicate love and affection with our bodies. There is some caressing every day, and this brings us closer together.

BILL: I really think that a good marriage is not possible without good sex.

When our troubles came to a head, I was extremely concerned about Beverly finding another man who could satisfy her. This would have been a terrible blow to me—and, as I said, I was desperate to do something about it.

Now, when Beverly and I make love, I know without a doubt that the ability is there on my part. We don't have that problem to worry about anymore.

In St. Louis, I also learned that two free individuals must love, care for, and respect each other. A woman has to show a man she needs him. A man will then respond. If their sexual problems are worked out, they are both way, way ahead of the game. I can't say that our marriage changed from nothing to everything by going to Masters and Johnson. But I can say—and I think I speak for Beverly, too—that we both are much happier and contented today—we have a much better marriage.

PART III

Other Sex Therapy

Sexual Shames

by Martin Shepard, M.D., and Marjorie Lee

EDITORS' NOTE: *One of the boldest concepts in psychotherapy today is the marathon encounter. In this new version of group therapy men and women with psychological problems meet with a psychiatrist in informal surroundings and act out or verbalize their difficulties. Often these difficulties are linked to sexual inadequacy.*

Here's the story, extracted from the book Marathon 16, *of ten such people who recently spent sixteen consecutive hours in one room. No one left except to go to the bathroom. Each of them criticized, expressed actual hostility or friendliness, spoke out ruthlessly and candidly about themselves and each other. The participants, each of whom chose an alias which was used throughout the session, are listed below.*

PARTICIPANTS:
"M" (DR. MARTIN SHEPARD): *A 34-year-old psychiatrist who was leader of the marathon.*
SARAH: *An attractive woman of 39 whose voice and appearance reflect "breeding."*
LITTLE PRINCE: *A female flower child of 21, with long red-blonde hair and a husky voice.*
YAEL: *A small 41-year-old woman, half bird, half gremlin, who is highly intelligent and acutely conscious of her identity as a German Jewess.*
JANE: *A conventionally pretty girl of 28.*
KARI: *A statuesque Norwegian girl of 29*
SHERSHONSKY: *A quiet man of 39.*

BOB: *An equally quiet man of 27.*
ROBERT LEA: *A not so quiet man of 35.*
PHILIP: *An 18-year-old hippie.*
BERNARD: *A strong man of 35, built for wrestling.*
MARJORIE (MARJORIE LEE): *A woman of 48, co-author and observer; pre-ordained non-participant.*
Time: *From 10 a.m., June 21, 1969 through 2 a.m., June 22, 1969.*
Place: *The office of Dr. Shepard, 12 West 96th Street, New York City. It is a rather small room, one belonging to an apartment of other offices. The furniture is modern Danish. There is no evidence at all of framed medical and psychiatric degrees. It is a room in which one is encouraged to feel free and very much at ease.*

Dr. Shepard is consulting psychiatrist to the New York City Department of Correction at Rikers Island, and has a private practice in Manhattan. He was attending physician in the Group Therapy Clinic at New York's Mount Sinai Hospital.

He and Marjorie Lee are co-authors of Marathon 16 *and* Games Analysts Play. *The following is from their book,* Marathon 16.

M: I'd like you to think of something else now: the thing you're most ashamed of.
LITTLE PRINCE (*moaning*): Oh, God . . .
KARI: Oh, shit.

The atmosphere is one of silent tenseness. People look into their laps or off into space. Little Prince seems the most agitated.

BERNARD (*finally*): In what area?
M: Your own area.
SARAH (*laughing*): I'll be darned if I can think of anything!
BOB: Um . . . the thing that I'm most ashamed of in my life is, um . . . almost a sort of rerun of *Portnoy's Complaint*. . . . It's pretty much ended now, but, well, from the time I was twelve or thirteen on, I masturbated with a great deal of frequency and was very, very ashamed of it . . . and worried that I was doing damage to myself. . . . Uh . . . um . . .

M suggests that all the men sit down on the floor

with Bob in order to share this common experience.

BOB: You know . . . I would mess around, you know . . . when I could have been doing more constructive things. A number of times, especially as I got older, I would say, "Now it's time to stop, this is kid stuff." But yet, like I was going back to it. . . .

M: You dirty old fox. (*Laughter.*)

BOB: I was married, uh, about a month ago, but it's still something which, you know . . . which stays in my mind. . . .

SHERSHONSKY: Did you like it better than screwing?

BOB: No.

SHERSHONSKY: Well, what's to be ashamed of?

PHILIP: It's just supposed to be bad.

BOB: Right. That's it.

ROBERT LEA: It's a dirty thing to do, isn't it? Terribly dirty and filthy! It's really a *groove!* (*He laughs.*)

M: Can you loosen your belt, slip your hand into your pants, and talk to us while you're touching your cock?
Bob is taken aback, but he follows M's instructions. His hand is now on his penis, and his speech is wavering, confused, hard to follow. The group attention paid to this act is deliberately strong, seeming to be forced, particularly among the women, who retain their seats outside the circle of men.

BOB: Yes . . . um . . . I don't . . . uh . . . I did feel ashamed then, in the past . . . I think, I guess . . .

ROBERT LEA: Well, experiment now and see if you feel the same.

BOB: Yeah . . . uh . . . (*He continues to touch himself.*)

M: How do you feel, sitting there that way?

BOB: Uh . . . no reaction.

M: *None?* (*There is sudden uproarious laughter from the men.*)

BOB: I feel as if there is no reaction. . . .

M: Does your hand feel your penis, or does your penis feel your hand, or both, or neither, or what?

BOB: My hand feels the penis.

M: See if you can let the penis feel the hand.

BOB (*after a pause*): To a certain extent, it can.

M: Let's all join him. (*He puts his hand inside his pants.*)

BERNARD (*shouting quickly*): I don't feel like it myself!
M: Okay, you don't have to.
Shershonsky tries the experiment, but the others refrain.
PHILIP (*to Bob*): You're accustomed to sleeping with your wife every night?
BOB: Yeah.
PHILIP: What if she took a vacation? Would you be tempted to masturbate?
BOB: Uh, I . . . I probably would be.
BERNARD: What do you think's wrong with it? Your Jewish upbringing?
BOB: Yeah, uh, probably . . . I mean . . .
M: What do you think we all think of you so far? Tell each of us.
BOB: I don't know. Nobody else put their hands in their pants, you know, and I think—
M: Shershonksy did, briefly, and I did. What does that mean to you?
BOB: I think, uh, you may all share the same kind of things, at least to a certain extent. You know, in part we've all gone through it. . . . It's not unique. But that doesn't lessen in any real sense the . . . the feeling of shame I had, and have. . . .
M: Let's all tell him a story about masturbation. The person who speaks, sit in front of him and tell it.
ROBERT LEA: Uh, I felt the same way you do until I realized what goes on in my head goes on in everyone's head. Yesterday, after I couldn't consummate a relationship with this beautiful, young thing, I went home and masturbated. And I do whenever the spirit grabs me. Every day, every other day. I like doing it!
BERNARD: Do you prefer that to intercourse?
ROBERT LEA: Well, I . . . I equate it with it. I'm not partial to it.
M: I was playing around when I was a kid around eleven or twelve, and all of a sudden this thing got hard, and then, suddenly, fluid shot out. I ran downstairs, was sure my parents knew what I was doing, and I felt very uncomfortable. Then I went through years of locking the bathroom door. I also felt it was a pretty funny, special, creepy thing to do because no one talked about it. I still can enjoy masturbation—probably because I've

been a sperm donor since I was in medical school, and every now and then a gynecologist calls up and says, "Hey, send us down some right now. (*Laughter from the women.*) So I pick out all the juicy females I know—patients, my wife, my friends' wives, other people—and have them to my heart's content. Another story that comes to mind—why I don't know—occurred about two summers ago. I was out sailing alone in the middle of Peconic Bay, and the sun was coming down, you know, and I had on a bathing suit, and the sun was just pouring on me, and suddenly I had the feeling, "My God, what a gassy thing it would be to drop my pants and masturbate on the spot." And I did. It was kind of a wild experience. But I can't put into words what it was about. The sun, the sailing, being out there in the middle of the bay, with people off in the distance not knowing what the pretty sailboat was doing, but it was nice.

PHILIP: Actually, I have never masturbated. I've played with myself fairly frequently, but coming to orgasm by self-manipulation . . . I won't do it, no matter how horny I get.

ROBERT LEA: What is there you don't like about it?

PHILIP: It's the nature of . . . of what it is in society. . . .

SHERSHONSKY: You won't even, uh, touch your cock now?

PHILIP: Well, I'd probably be embarrassed. . . .

M: Try it anyway.

PHILIP: I know it's there.

M: We know you have it.

Philip complies. He says that it feels all right, that he is not ashamed of it, but that he would never manipulate to orgasm. Bernard states that he supports Philip in this view and could not consider masturbation when there is an availability of women. It strikes him as "abnormal."

ROBERT LEA: Do you feel it's "dirty"?

BERNARD: I didn't say that. I just simply do not find myself stimulated by it.

M: I'm struck by the similarity between the approach to your cock, and your approach to people. There's an aversion to using your hands.

BERNARD: Yeah, uh . . . and yet I consider myself more lecherous than maybe 90 percent of the men in this world.

M: All the more surprising. It's almost as though touching sets up an inhibition process.

BERNARD: A touch, by me, cannot do it. It can't be another man, and it can't be myself.

ROBERT LEA: If you can't dig this part of yourself, how can you expect someone else to?

BERNARD: I don't think that necessarily follows. (*He is becoming slightly, but perceptibly, annoyed and turns to the group for affirmation of his sexual stand.*)

M: Shershonsky, sit in front of Bernard and tell him a story about masturbation.

SHERSHONSKY: Yeah. Well, uh, I have masturbated, and do, and will. For a while I felt a little guilty about it, but then I did some reading and talking to people, and it, uh, never, uh, was really a hang-up. . . .

He then tells a story about a beautiful young girl who stood on a balcony when he and his Army buddies were marching by. She seemed to be flaunting her sexuality at them, and later he masturbated successfully, using her in his fantasy. He says he finds it harder to talk about it than to do it; and adds that he would not want his children to feel defensive about it.

M: Bob, how do you feel about yourself now?

BOB: Well, it's good to know that people don't only pass through it, but they—

ROBERT LEA: But they remain in it.

BOB: They remain in it. That's right! (*Bob and Robert Lea begin to laugh.*)

JANE: Can I say something from a woman's point of view?
Jane says that she is amazed that men are ashamed of masturbation; that every man she has ever known does it, including the man she lives with.

YAEL: But would it bother you if he would have intercourse with other women?

JANE: Yeah, it has.

M (*to Yael*): Would it bother you if your husband did?

YAEL: It's . . . it's inconceivable. But yes, it would bother me.

LITTLE PRINCE: I'm just wondering if any of you have ever considered the idea of whether or not women masturbate.

BOB: I know they do.

M: How do you know?
BOB: From reading. (*Much general laughter.*)
M: Ask each one of them individually. Start with Yael.
YAEL: Start with somebody else for a change!

The laughter which ensues in this period is less tense than it was earlier. It is now less an expression of individual anxiety, and more one of camaraderie.

SARAH: Actually, I don't remember masturbating very much.
M: Have you ever?
SARAH: Hhmmnn. Yeah, I have. But I've never been able to bring myself to climax that way. But, uh, most women do. It's sort of unnatural not to.
JANE: I masturbated all through high school, and in fact, uh, I frequently brought myself to climax. But when I started fucking, I stopped masturbating.

Little Prince relates how she masturbated when she was young, told her mother about it, and was considered to be a sinner, thereafter being forced to go to confession. Later she read a book by Albert Ellis and decided to beat her guilt. At present she masturbates successfully whenever her lover is away.

KARI: I never remember masturbating when I was a child, but I remember seeing my mother now. And, uh, my children . . .
M: How about you, though?
KARI: I don't remember! I just complete, uh, a cutoff! I've tried and I cannot come to a climax masturbating! (*She is suddenly high-pitched and shouting.*)
M: How do you do it?
KARI: With the finger.
M: Where?
KARI: In my vagina. The clitoral . . . uh, you know. I, uh, become excited, and at a certain point the feelings just turn off, completely off! And when I can't remember from children, I know something's wrong. It smells rotten. . . .
BERNARD (*interposing quickly*): The *story* smells wrong.
M: How about the secretions. Did you ever sniff them?
KARI: Yeah. Uh, it doesn't smell bad.

BERNARD (*playing Kari's alter ego*): "Why does my story smell rotten? I'm not telling the truth."

M: Yael?

YAEL: I thought you were going to forget about me!

Yael tells of a boy she knew at an orphanage where she was put as a child. They played with each other sexually, which saved her from masturbation. At present, however, she does it and can come to orgasm; but she prefers to be "held by a man." She adds that she wishes she had known earlier that it is "normal."

KARI: My father used to be a masturbator . . . plus being a religious fanatic at the same time. It was quite hard to—

BERNARD: How did you know he was a masturbator?

KARI: Well, because, uh, I would come into a room and there my father would be, and, uh, the bed would be going, and then of course he would stop abruptly, and put his hand up, and then he was left hanging in the air. And that made fights with my mother, so then, of course, it got clarified . . . the omen on masturbation, the guilt . . . When you have these guys masturbating on the roofs . . . we happen to have one across from us, and it can just . . . just drive me crazy!

M: Like Daddy?

KARI: Uh-huh, like Daddy. It just used to drive me crazy. And I mean I caught this guy at it. . . . I hate . . . all that shit . . . and I'd scream! Aaaaaauuuuggghhh! (*It is a real scream and seems to be for the moment as well as for the past.*)

M: You can just keep on feeling guilty about this forever, if you like, or—

LITTLE PRINCE: Yeah, it's such a habit—feeling guilty.

YAEL: That's very interesting, that it's a habit. Will the next generation be completely sexually free?

LITTLE PRINCE: After three more generations.

YAEL: You really think it will come?

LITTLE PRINCE: Yeah. Oh, god, yeah. It certainly will.

PHILIP: It's very near.

YAEL: I know that in the kibbutz the original idea was free sex, and it just didn't work.

LITTLE PRINCE: What I'm hoping for is that there will be enough *I Am Curious (Yellow)*'s, and enough masturbation, and enough orgies, and enough wife-swapping so that it will all get into its perspective. It won't be the Almighty Cock anymore. It'll just *be*.

JANE: Beautiful!

SHERSHONSKY: I'd just like to dump one thing, if you're all listening. When I was a kid a man took me up to his apartment to give me joke books and some candy. And, uh, he started to fondle me and show me all sorts of pictures with all kinds of sex in them. And then he made me, uh, jerk him off. And I was sort of crying, you know . . . and well, he came, and I was very sick, really shook up, and there was nobody to tell it to. Things were rather bad between me and my father then, and I couldn't tell anyone. And then this caused another funny situation. I was going to a Jewish religious school for kids, and there was this young teacher there, and he used to put his arm around me, and one day he showed me some dirty matchbook covers and he pinched me a little. And this got me very unhappy, and I set fire to the school. I made this tremendous stink bomb with a strip of film, and set fire to it outside his door, and they had to let all the kids out of school. And then they kicked me out. They called up my home and they said, you know . . . I'm a degenerate and they don't want me there anymore. . . .

M: What made it so hard for you to tell this before?

SHERSHONSKY: Well, I was kind of locked up. I had a rigid father and I just couldn't talk to him. He'd have beaten me. . . .

YAEL: What about your mother?

SHERSHONSKY: Well, the same thing. But it was very disturbing, because it was the guy that showed me the pictures and pinched me that called up my house in such great indignity, and you know . . . The Voice of School . . . Your son . . . I have to bring this to your attention, Mrs. ———. You have a very dangerous, sick son there. He set fire, and we're gonna have to kick him out." It just seemed like such a big injustice, and I couldn't tell anyone. . . .

M (*sitting behind Shershonsky and playing his alter ego*): "I didn't talk about it because I thought maybe there was something funny about me, that I was giving off funny signals that would *make* the schoolteacher and the other guy try these things with me. I was so ashamed people would see *me* as a pervert that I kept it in."

SHERSHONSKY: Uh-huh. That could be. . . .

ROBERT LEA: You just had an orgasm, Shershonsky.

SHERSHONSKY: What?

ROBERT LEA: A mental orgasm. You just got rid of this massive load.

SHERSHONSKY: Yeah. That's out now. It's nice to have it out.

M: You don't know what to do with a thing like that as a kid.

SHERSHONSKY: No.

M: I had this thing happen in a movie house when I was about twelve. My younger cousin and my parents went to a movie, and some older guy came in and said, "Hey, I came in late. Will you tell me what the movie was about?" So I said, "Yes, I will." And he said, "Is it all right if I put my hand on your knee? I'm nervous." So I said, "Okay." But then he started to go like this. . . . (*M demonstrates the man's hand moving up M's leg.*) You know, I started to feel a little bit uncomfortable. So I put my hand in my pocket and jammed it over my testicles. And he kept going up, and twisting my hand, and I said to my cousin, "Let's walk to the back or something." We walked to the back, and I still didn't know what to do. And when we came back, I thought, "I know what I'll do. I'll put my cousin onto him." (*General laughter.*) And this guy had the effrontery to say to my cousin, "Switch seats with that kid." (*More laughter.*) And I didn't know what to do, so I switched seats back. And again the whole thing started off. Shit! That thing kept up for about an hour or so, and then (*M laughs*) he finally got discouraged and left. I *could* talk to my father, but I didn't know what I was telling him, except I said, "Hey, you know something funny was happening with this man who kept touching me, and he said he was nervous, and I tried to change seats with Michael." And my father said at this point, "Ahhah . . . that man is a strange degenerate, and if it ever happens again, you better tell me." But it was interesting because I didn't know what to do with it. I didn't know what to do.

Shershonsky and Yael tell M he was lucky that he could tell his father.

SARAH: I can remember when I was that age and there would be a guy trying to feel me up, and I didn't really know exactly what was going on. I sort of knew, but I didn't. And I didn't want to be rude. (*Much general laughter.*)

Yael recalls having been seen sitting in a man's lap in the park, and being spanked unjustly for it by her parents. Later, in another country, an unmarried uncle made advances to her from time to time.

M: If we're talking about shame, let's get into what's most current, because—

YAEL: M, do you have a bathroom?

M (*pointing the way*): Sure.

BERNARD: I have a very strange sexual hang-up that I've never confessed to anyone before, and I've always been curious as to what people's reactions would be to it.

M: Whose reaction would you be most curious about?

BERNARD: Partly in Sarah's, because she's the, you know, closest to the norm here.

M: Okay. Sit directly facing Sarah.

BERNARD: I'd rather not. I can tell it better spontaneously.

M: Give it a chance.

BERNARD (*facing Sarah*): When I was about seven or eight there was a girl in my class who was much taller than the boys, including myself. And what gave me a charge was the fact that she was so physically larger than myself. I didn't know about sexual relations until about fifth grade, but I had strong sexual feelings. I would occasionally play with her, get on top of her, and this fantasy never left me. Obviously, it was just the beginning, and . . . uh, um, uh . . . and if anything, it increased as I grew older. And I've always had a great sexual interest in women larger than myself. But I don't very often meet women larger than myself, so I have to fantasize it about large women with small men. I was, uh, at a summer camp a few years ago and one of the campers was a very little boy who always got hung up on the big girls. He would walk with these girls, and, uh, I got tremendously aroused by this, um, fantasy.

M: What fantasy?

BERNARD: The fantasy is of getting a male sort of phagocytized by this large woman, and being made helpless by her.

SARAH: What are your theories about it?

ROBERT LEA: It seems to me you consider yourself a big prick, and you want to get entirely into this, uh, into this womb...

M (*to Bernard*): Can you lie down on the floor, on your back, and close your eyes? Then go into the fantasy bit.

BERNARD (*lying down*): The typical fantasy I have is making love to an enormous black woman who sort of lifts me up, and, uh, I can't even reach her breasts from where I stand, so she has to lift me up. And then I suckle them, and then she lifts me higher and I'm able to kiss her. She is the one who is totally in control of the sexual situation. If she wanted to allow me to penetrate her, she would have to lift me up to do it. She's much too strong for me to, uh... to try to penetrate.

M: Keep your eyes closed. Is there anyone here like that woman?

BERNARD: I suppose Kari comes closest, but doesn't completely fulfill this.

M: It all takes place standing up?

BERNARD: No. I have a variety of, uh, variations.

> Bernard explains that in one of his variations the woman lies on top of him. M suggests that all the women lie on top of Bernard in order to simulate the weight and bulk of a 300-pound Negress. Kari, Little Prince, Jane, and Sarah comply. Yael does not join them. Bernard describes the stimulation he feels and begins to have an erection. He speaks of all this in a blushing, self-conscious, and intellectualized style. The women heaped upon him are genuinely moved by his story and are eager to be of help. After acknowledging the erection, he states that it makes him uncomfortable and that he wishes to know what the others think about it.

M: Who in particular?

> Bernard, still beneath the pile of women, eyes closed, claps his hands to Little Prince's back.

LITTLE PRINCE: It's a groovy fantasy. Beautiful! Enjoy it.

BERNARD: I can understand a little guy who wants to be a

big guy, but for a fairly big guy to have a fantasy about being a little guy, sexually, is really perverse....

JANE: Are you ever passive in bed?

BERNARD: Never.

JANE: Would you like to be?

BERNARD: No. I'd be ashamed of being passive in bed. I'm afraid that, uh, all the men would feel that I'm not a good lover if I tried to, uh, be passive....

JANE: I think you have to allow yourself to do whatever you feel like doing.

SARAH: I enjoy it a lot in bed if a guy sort of relaxes and lets me be active for a while.

JANE: Yeah. I often get turned off when a guy is so active he doesn't give me a chance.

LITTLE PRINCE: Yeah. It makes me feel like all I'm doing is being passive.

BERNARD: You like to be more active?

LITTLE PRINCE: I like to be both. I like to lay back and enjoy it and then when I'm ready, get on top of him and do it. I dig seeing him do nothing, just breathing and groaning.... Do women *make* you be active?

BERNARD: Yes.

LITTLE PRINCE: They won't allow you sometimes to—?

SARAH: Gee, it's nice sometimes just to feel helpless ... but I guess it's hard for a guy to be that way.

BERNARD: Yeah. You're not allowed to.

M: You're allowed to. We just allowed you to.

JANE: Yeah.

BERNARD: Well, my own interpretation of this has been, it's, uh, an infantile drive.... My mother must have been this anonymous woman suckling me ... with whom I'm totally helpless....

M: That's your whole big put-down on things that are less mature, and less manly and tough and strong. Sex is a combination of infantile-exfantile ... all sorts of "tiles."

LITTLE PRINCE: You feel what we just did is not normal?

BERNARD: Uh, it doesn't hang me up. It increases my sexuality.

M: How can you play it out at home?

KARI (*giggling*): How about masturbation for a start?

BERNARD: I can't.

M (*mockingly*): That's right. That's an infantile fantasy, isn't it? I mean, kids do that before they have women.

ROBERT LEA: And men do it after they have women. (*Laughter.*)

M: Close your eyes and tell me the most passive thing you can think of doing with your wife.

BERNARD: I suppose my greatest fantasy would be to be totally paralyzed, lying in bed, getting an enormous erection. And my partner, at her will, would insert it and bring me to orgasm. I would be totally incapacitated.

M: Have you ever asked your wife to do something like that?

BERNARD: No. I wouldn't dare.

LITTLE PRINCE: Why?

BERNARD: Oh, I would never admit this to her.

LITTLE PRINCE: But why?

BERNARD: I would be terribly ashamed.

JANE: What do you think she would do about it?

M: She'd probably like it.

LITTLE PRINCE: Yeah.

ROBERT LEA: She might be overawed.

LITTLE PRINCE: What could happen that would be so awful? She might not think that you're a man? You'd lose your masculinity?

BERNARD: I would never want my wife to think I had any sexual hang-ups.

LITTLE PRINCE: *What?*

BERNARD: Because it's . . . um . . . uh . . .

PHILIP: It's not a hang-up.

BERNARD: I keep calling it a hang-up, don't I . . .

JANE: If you just said to her one night, "I want to be completely passive, and just have you fuck me."

ROBERT LEA: Tell her you're tired. (*Much laughter.*)

M now suggests that Bernard play two roles: that of himself, speaking to his wife, and that of his wife, answering. When Bernard finds this too difficult, M shows him how by playing Bernard's role, using Little Prince as the wife.

M (*to Little Prince*): "Look, when we go to bed tonight, I want to lie back perfectly helplessly, not move a muscle. That would really turn me on."

BERNARD: No, no! I don't really want to do this with my wife! My wife actually *is* a very sexually aggressive wom-

AN ANALYSIS OF HUMAN SEXUAL INADEQUACY 143

an, but it doesn't turn me on. The reason is, I suppose, that—

M: Forget the analysis. Is there a woman in your present life you'd like to do it with?

BERNARD: Oh, yes.

M: Someone else you're making it with?

BERNARD: I'm not, but I'd like to be.

M: Is she someone you could approach in the next few days and ask her?

BERNARD: She'd probably slug me.

M: Try it with your wife, then. (*The women laugh.*) Play it out.

BERNARD: Who . . . who do you want to have play my wife?

M: Someone you're screwing. You can't do it with someone you're not screwing.

BERNARD: Well, one of my fantasies is making it with this Russian shot-putter. What's her name? Olga Something. I always follow how far she's putting the shot. And, uh . . . I identify with the shot. (*He tries to laugh.*)

M: First it was a Negress; second, it was a shot putter. You want to be overpowered, right?

BERNARD: But I don't want to do it with my wife!

M: All right, all right—afterwards you can do it with someone else. But now I want you to pretend it's your wife. You're going to go home and tell her you want this thing, but that you were always afraid to ask her because you thought she'd think you weren't enough of a man.

BERNARD (*to an imaginary wife*): "I think what we might try sometime is, I'll come home, and you can give me a spinal, a low spinal, and then I can act out this role of being . . . uh, of being a paraplegic."

Little Prince bursts into laughter.

BERNARD (*extremely distressed*): You see? She thinks it's really perverse!

M: Is your wife equipped to give you a low spinal?

BERNARD: Uh . . . no.

ROBERT LEA (*with several others*): What's a low spinal? What is that?

M: It's an anesthetic. It paralyzes you.

ROBERT LEA: Oh, that's wild! I would dig that!

BERNARD (*to his wife again*): "I think this would be a very, very wild thing. We could then, uh, make furious love."

M: "*You* could make furious love with *me!*" (*An explosion of laughter.*)

YAEL: Uh, isn't a certain part of your body also paralyzed when you . . . ?

BERNARD: She'd give it to me low enough so that—

M: For God's sake, will you play it straight?

BERNARD (*trying again*): "Would you be interested in . . . ?"

M: "NO!" (*Much laughter.*)

LITTLE PRINCE (*as the wife; gently*): "Tell me what you want, Bernard."

BERNARD: "I would like, tonight, for a change—something new: to have you give me a low spinal."

M (*now playing alter ego to Little Prince's wife role*): "You know I don't give low spinals!" (*Much laughter.*)

LITTLE PRINCE: "Tell me what you want, what you really want. . . ."

BERNARD: I want you to paralyze both of my lower legs, and just, uh, lay me on my back, and, uh, manipulate me, and bring me to orgasm inside of you."

LITTLE PRINCE: "You mean you'd like me to make you come? I don't see why I have to paralyze your legs."

M (*to Bernard*): Shift seats now. Be your own wife, and talk to me. I'm Bernard.

BERNARD (*speaking as his wife*): "Well, this is really absurd! What's wrong with the way we've been doing it? This could be a very dangerous thing, and moreover— I'm not even sure I'd like it this way."

M: Now switch back. Be you, talking to your wife.

BERNARD: "Well, if you really like me and you really want to give me some pleasure, I think you could put aside your own feelings of . . . uh . . . uh . . . repugnance about this. I can assure you it's not dangerous, and, uh, nobody has to know about it. . . ."

M: Now be your wife again.

BERNARD: "Well, okay. We'll try it once. Now, how do you give a low spinal?" (*Laughter.*)

YAEL: Why does he have to say it with words? Why can't he just lean back and try it?

BERNARD (*eager to stop*): Who's next?

M: Are you going to do it?

BERNARD: I'll . . . I'll try it tonight. Yeah.

BOB: Why do you think you said first that the three-hundred-pound woman should be black?

BERNARD: It's better that way. It makes her more savage, more—

ROBERT LEA: Primitive.

BERNARD: Right. That's the word.

PHILIP: And you think all this is very uncommon?

BERNARD: Yes, I do think so.

PHILIP: Eldridge Cleaver has this theory about how the effete white man turns to the Amazon black woman ...

BERNARD: Let me ask the men here. Has anybody else had this sort of a fantasy?

ROBERT LEA: Oh, yes.

BOB: Certainly not in that much detail. But I've had similar thoughts....

BERNARD: Let me ask the women. Have you ever wanted a very small, passive mate as a sort of kick?

LITTLE PRINCE: I don't think size matters.

BERNARD: It's very important!

LITTLE PRINCE: I think you made her so overpowering because even in your fantasies you weren't allowing yourself to "do it." In some of my fantasies, I've had to be overpowered. It had to be a huge person with a knife all the time.

JANE: Yeah. You have to make it absurd. I feel the way she does. It has nothing to do with size. It's just that sometimes you want to be passive.

LITTLE PRINCE: To have someone be awful and really overpower you.

M: I dig a woman coming on strong and me just lying back. Of course, it makes hassles because your wife wants the same thing sometimes. (*Laughter.*)

YAEL: Why-why-why does Bernard have to *live* it out?

JANE: Because he considers it a hang-up.

YAEL: But let's suppose that he would be convinced from today that it's not a hang-up.

BERNARD: Well, I must say I'm really relieved to find out it's not such a way-out thing.

M: If a fantasy gives you pleasure, and it's not hurting anybody, and it's not making you crazy or growing hair on your palms, then why not enjoy it?

YAEL: Well, I agree, but why should he live it out? Why can't it stay a fantasy?

M: Often fantasy is an expression of what we would like to do, but don't have the courage to do, because we're embarrassed or ashamed. But if you want to live your life more adventuresomely, you can try doing more things. If you've been through a Freudian analysis, you're not supposed to *do* anything—just *understand* everything. So if you want to, you can just sit back there and say, "I know . . . it's related to my mother!" (*Several people laugh softly.*) . . .

Barriers to Sex

by Betty Grover Eisner, Ph.D.

EDITORS' NOTE: *Dr. Eisner was involved in the first research project on the West Coast investigating the therapeutic effects of an as yet unknown drug, LSD. She has lectured on the results of this research and is the author of many articles on drug therapy. She is presently at work on a new book built around her experience in group therapy for the emotionally disturbed. In* Barriers To Sex *she deals with how sexuality is turned off in childhood and adolescence and how adults can turn on again. Her article reinforces the Masters and Johnson work in the development of sensate focus. It is reprinted from her book,* The Unused Potential of Marriage and Sex.

It is interesting that any major problem which arises in sexual interaction—outside of traumatic sexual experiences in youth—is almost without fail a problem of defect of feeling or of adequacy—not of sex. Contrary to general available information the most important site for the opening of sexuality lies not in the genitals but in the solar plexus, which appears to be the focus of most of our emotions. If that area can be opened so that feelings flow between partners, sexuality is bound to follow.

Sometimes the question is one of draining off limitations, inhibitions, and loadings. Methods can be cultivated for "letting go" at the time and for working on the problem at other times. These methods fall into the realm of the therapeutic, and include techniques used by sensitivity groups, psychodrama, experiencing the now, acting "as if," and so on, as well as symbolic or fantasy-type methods.

An imaginative individual can visualize a spigot where the solar plexus lies (in that area from the lower part of the breastbone down to the navel). Once the spigot is "felt," he can turn it on and let all the negative feelings and difficulties flow out. As the area clears, he is amazed to feel the pressure and weight lessening, and finally the flow of feelings beginning between himself and his mate.

This flow is enhanced if the couple stand or lie facing each other, closely touching the length of their bodies, especially close in the solar plexus areas. Once one individual is open to the flow of feelings, the other is usually carried along into openness, and both develop feelings of affection, warmth, and love—with sexuality following closely behind.

Although frigid women have sexuality cut off from feeling, it is usually the man who doesn't really feel. It is as though, in our society, men are allowed two feelings: hostility and sexuality. Women are allowed the gentle emotions of warmth, tenderness and affection. This is a phenomenon which is not usually recognized, let alone understood. Since men use the same words women do about feeling, and since they *think* they feel and *speak* as though they feel (not knowing themselves that something is lacking), it is very difficult for them to know that they do not feel. It is much the same as with a color-blind person before he discovers his difficulty: he has names for the colors red and green and discriminates between the two in his perceptions. However, he is perceiving shades of gray and brown, not red as it exists distinct from green.

Actually, almost all men in our culture have a deficit of feeling to some extent: it is greater in professional men (accountants, lawyers and doctors, particularly surgeons) than in artists, and seems to be greatest of all in mechanical engineers. It is only as one observes the miracle of the birth of feeling that the picture begins to clarify, both for the man who feels, and for the observer.

The causes for this cutoff of feeling are probably twofold: first, the rigid cultural differentiation which allows little girls to feel and to cry freely but requires that boys suppress all forms of "sissy" feelings; and the cutting off of feeling very early in a sensitive child because of too much pain. In engineers one sees sensitive men who had so much emotional pain and confusion when they were young that they not only shut off feelings but carried the process even further by moving away from people and toward things in their vocation in order to make doubly sure they would not be further hurt.

The lack of feeling areas of emotion—the stronger emotions for a woman, the gentler for a man—puts a limitation on sexual experiencing. One of the important functions which modern men and women can perform for each other is to widen their partner's capacity to feel. The man helps the woman open to her feelings of sexuality and aggressiveness and to allow them fully. She is much more conditioned against sex than he: if for two decades one must say, "No, no, a thousand times no!" it is difficult to suddenly reverse the programming and say, "Yes!" The woman in turn teaches the man the value of tenderness and sensitivity and how the gentle emotions can act to embellish even strong passion.

There are other specific techniques which help bring feeling. A very simple one is the movement of hands over the body of the partner, not just the erogenous zones, but the whole body so that tactile feelings come into play. This might start with a massage or back rub of the one who feels cut off, moving at times into breast and genital areas and away again so that sexuality is subtly brought into play.

It is interesting to consider the semantic link between "to feel" as in tactile and "to feel" emotionally. Even the word emotion comes from *ex* (out of) and *movere* (to move): arising out of, or from motion, or moving out from. It is quite possible that adults who are too restricted in their feelings were prevented as children from moving and feeling freely in their environment and thus suffered from too early a constraint of exploratory and mastery urges. They were probably not allowed to "touch" bodies—their own or others—or probably even (valuable?) objects; they were certainly not allowed to feel whenever and whatever they wanted, and it is quite possible that when they reached out for new experiences and for learning about things by touching them and putting them into their mouths, their hands were slapped. The fear of having fingers or hands chopped off may very well be as serious a castration worry as the fear of loss of a penis and would be a source of restriction for girls as well as for boys.

While we are discussing aids to the feeling of sexuality, we should not overlook some of the obvious means available to any couple. In the first place, the constant orientation should be toward opening up sexually: both individuals should move toward sexual feelings at any and every (appropriate) opportunity. If listening to music together opens them to each other and to sex, they should plan for music, maybe even making love to special pieces; if dancing is of benefit, they should have a time of rocking and rolling together before maybe indulging in a double striptease as they go to bed. If reading poetry or erotic passages enhances feeling, that should be done; romantic movies often stimulate and awaken sexual desire, and so forth.

Each individual and every couple has different likes and dislikes; various stimuli make them more open to each other and to sexual feelings. These different aids should be assiduously sought out and cultivated so they can be used to help the couple toward greater openness and feelings.

Selective and careful drinking can be of great benefit for those who have no reservations about alcohol and whose barriers lower with a drink or two. Care must be taken against too much liquor (which varies among individuals and with conditions) because even a little bit too much blurs feelings, allows negative elements from the unconscious to be expressed, and depresses rather than relaxes.

Also, the man should not be afraid to use force judiciously in his lovemaking. Many women at heart want to be overwhelmed and carried away into passionate feelings. However, there is a very delicate line, as no woman wants to be forced against her "real" will; nor does a normal woman want to be hurt in lovemaking beyond the love bites or strawberry bruises which enhance passion and are not even felt as pain during strong sexual interaction. The distinction between rape and force is the discriminating line: it should be the force of strength which is applied in the lovemaking and not the force of imposition of action against the will of the other person.

There is also another technique which has been found to be very effective in arousing sexual feelings in both men and women and has served as a valuable tool against impotence: nursing. It may sound strange to consider having a man "nurse" at his wife's breast; however, it works relatively rapidly and in almost every case arouses both the husband and the wife. It is as though the man goes back to get some basic nourishment which he failed to receive in childhood (some men swear that they can taste milk coming from their wives and that when the technique is successful they feel wonderfully full of milk, deliciously satisfied, and sexually aroused); at the same time, the woman has great feelings of adequacy at providing "nourishment" for the man she loves.

Breasts are highly erogenous zones; any stimulation of them should be arousing, but nursing appears to be especially so. Also, sexual feelings while a mother is nursing her child are universal; if they are not felt the chances are that the mother is frightened of her sexuality toward her child and blocks the feelings from her awareness. The nursing technique taps into their process.

The progression of a man from sexual immaturity and impotence has been observed in patients merely by means of the addition of a nursing "schedule" of ten to fifteen minutes night and morning, with any resulting sexual feelings carried through to completion.

Psychological impotence (and "immature" penis and "immature sexuality" which all appear to be different forms of the same phenomenon) arises from fear or hostility or a combination of the two. Probably a large component of the "immaturity" contains unaccepted and unacceptable animal and so-called sadistic elements of the man's feelings, a combination of hostility and unresolved oral dependency (experienced as the desire to bite that which one loves) and fear of betraying himself in giving any indication of the presence of these feelings. Suppression of any element of strong feeling supresses sexuality itself. The man chooses to appear immature and undeveloped rather than to reveal such "dangerous" feelings.

Hostility (often unconscious) on the part of either the man *or the woman* can result in the inability to achieve and maintain an erection. Hostility on the part of the man can be from feeling that he is expected to do too much or that his body processes are under control of the woman, or at invalidly imposed guilt about sexuality. The fear can arise because of strict childhood repression of any show of sexuality, from fear of being caught masturbating, fear of having an erection (which haunts a pubescent boy's days, particularly in school situations), fear of inadequacy and nonperformance, and so on.

The technique of nursing takes the husband and wife back to the most basic situation of nourishment, and redoes it while both allowing and rewarding sexual feelings. The "child" has the experience of relearning that there *is* enough to nourish him and that he *will* get his share, and—almost more important in our situation—that he will not only be allowed body feelings by mother, but that she will feel these feelings with him, and will help him to fulfilment and nourishment in *both* of the two basic areas of food and sex.

At the same time a couple is using nursing as a technique to open sexuality and to overcome feelings of inadequacy and impotence, there should be some sort of regular daily hostility discharge for both of them. Hostility must be separated out from sexuality; as it begins to separate, the need for a discharge mechanism arises. There are a number of therapeutic techniques for this: punching bag for the man (not a speed bag, rather a canvas or duffel bag filled with torn newspapers), pounding a couch or bed for the woman; throwing "tantrums" on the bed when alone for both; smashing up cardboard cartons; and throwing clay (and then working it with the hands) among others.

Getting the hostility out by direct fighting of the couple is not recommended. When fights start (and they will inevitably arise during this period of working through old and uncreative neurotic patterns), the couple should immediately separate and write down, each of them, the events which led up to the difficulty. These "reports" should be gone over together simultaneously with either a professional counselor or a very competent "referee" so that the mechanics of each individual's difficulty become clear to them both. Half the battle—provided, of course, that the couple want to solve the problem—is in making unconscious neurotic mechanisms conscious and overt. If their true desire is to maintain the interlocking neurosis while they make verbal noises about wanting to solve the problem, this will very soon become apparent to an objective third party. The couple should then be helped to see what it is they really want, and how to go about relieving the situation of unrealistic pseudo-desires so that they can move directly toward achieving their goal, no matter how neurotic (so long as it is not harmful to either), in order that they may see how the achievement of the goal feels, and find out if that is really what they want.

If the avowed goal is sexuality but the real goal is control, this will become evident as overt mechanisms are initiated to move toward the sexuality, discharging hostility and unraveling conflict along the way. Then the real problem of wanting to control more than wanting to relate or to experience sexuality can be dealt with and hopefully brought to resolution. It is impossible, however, to solve any problem of sexuality when sexuality is not the problem but merely a reflection of it.

Desert Retreat

by William E. Hartman, Ph.D., and Marilyn A. Fithian

EDITORS' NOTE: *Dr. William Hartman is professor of physiology at California State College and Director of the Center for Marital and Sexual Studies in Long Beach, California. Marilyn Fithian is Associate Director of the Center for Marital and Sexual Studies. The two are coauthors of the book,* Nudist Society.

In the following article taken from Nudist Society, *they describe a physical therapy program used in the treatment of sexual dysfunction and report on what they have observed about this current widespread experiment.*

In the context of this article the word "marathon" refers to a weekend counseling situation for sexually malfunctioning couples. These married couples represent a spouse who is unable to achieve an orgasm through penilevaginal stimulation, or who ejaculates before his mate is able to be satisfied sexually or a combination of these phenomena. These couples are part of a program where approximately twenty hours of counseling time has been invested before the marathon takes place.

The first clue for the need of a weekend counseling situation away from home came from the research of Masters and Johnson. They reported being less effective in treating sexually dysfunctioning couples in the St. Louis area, in which their offices are located, than was true for out-of-town couples who came seeking treatment away from family, business, and social pressures.

The therapeutic program of the Center for Marital and Sexual Studies, taking into account these findings, attempted to establish a programmed situation where married couples would spend forty-eight hours with a male-female counseling team out of town. These couples traveled with the counselors to the setting without their children or any other than the therapeutic foursome being present.

The marathon idea or technique is based on the pioneering of the mid-1960s by Fred Stoller, George Bach and Jerry Nims. Essentially, it involves a 24-hour uninterrupted counseling session which we use in the present paper with some variation. We chose the Palm Springs area of Southern California as the setting.

The desert area was considered symbolic of the initial marital situation which we encountered in our beginning work with most of our couples. It was a dry, barren wasteland. At the same time one could see that with some water and tender loving care, an oasis could develop—a virtual paradise of pleasure. Also, connected with this, is the dying and rebirth process of mythology where death and love are closely related. Death like sex is obscene; it is pornographic and is not to be talked about. The ability of the couple to make the initial decision to seek help in a dying marriage represents, usually, the first attempt to come to grips with that which is not discussed. Death is the symbol of final inevitable impotence, but death and love are related also to creation; the rebirth, the fruition, the blooming of the paradise is that which we are attempting to attain. So, the symbolic element of locale is important in our work.

A trailer park located in the hot water area of the lower desert was selected. The major reasons were the location of a large house trailer belonging to the senior author, the relaxing atmosphere and the hot mineral water, and the importance of the water to birth and rebirth rites. In a sense they were being reborn into a new life as a sexually functioning individual through a rite of passage.

Our culture has no set rite of passage for our young from that of an adolescent to that of a sexually mature functioning adult. The closest we have is a marriage ceremony which really makes no preparation for that which is to come. We have made a preparation for what is to come by counseling with the couple for a period of time prior to our desert session. The desert counseling starts them on their journey, and our follow-ups allow us to see that the rite of passage was completed out of the wilderness of aloneness into a life of meaningfully relating.

En route to the desert a carefully arranged stop was made at Hadley's Fruit Ranch and Orchard in Cabazon. The store caters in freshly dried fruits and nuts, mostly from that area. One needs nourishment to sustain one through the journey on which we are to embark. Not just any type or kind of food but a food of nature, symbolic of the naturalness of man. Also, symbolically speaking, the wide variety of dates, nuts, and figs were reminiscent of early sexual symbols, and with a background of one of the counselors in mythology, sex can be openly and freely discussed in the context of the situation. At the store each individual is asked to choose a package of fresh nuts or fruits which they regarded as their favorite and from which they received the greatest enjoyment. We found that these favorites eaten at a later time brought back a recurring and positive feeling about the desert experience as well as enhancing the enjoyment of the marathon itself.

Couples were also given the opportunity to visit the wine tasting room where free samples were available. Although our discussions throughout the weekend are not geared as planned counseling sessions (there are only eight hours of specific sit-down-and-talk sessions over the weekend), almost all of our time with the couple is in a sense counseling. For instance, while visiting the wine room we can discuss the benefits of a glass of wine at dinner in relation to the relaxation it might provide for sexual functioning as opposed to the heavy drinking of the alcoholic who may be seeking an avoidance of sex.

The fruits and nuts were provided by the counselors as a gift and were usually comprised of fresh dates, dried apricots, dried figs, pears, peaches, or salted or unsalted cashew nuts. Other items were available but these were the usual choice. Couples who chose to purchase wines did so of their own volition—often drinking a glass with their dinners during the weekend session which helped to relax the situation. No one ever drank more than one glass and then only at the evening meal.

Upon arrival at the trailer park in the desert, typically scheduled for 6 P.M., couples were shown to their bedroom and given an opportunity to unpack their personal belongings. A tour was then taken of the facilities with the male counselor while the female counselor prepared the evening meal. The facilities included an Olympic size swimming pool, two hot water therapy pools, a Jacuzzi [whirl] pool and steam and sauna baths. Following a tour of the facilities, a counseling session, in the swimming pool, is usually suggested, all four to be involved. Water in the pool is typically at a temperature of 95 degrees. In this setting couples were instructed to float across the 25-foot width of the pool by pushing from the side, face down in the water repeating to themselves, "I am completely relaxed." After approximately 10 laps the suggestion was given that as they floated across the pool they would suggest to themselves, "I give myself completely." The theory behind the suggestion was that in the 20 hours work with the couples sexual problems frequently noted had to do with the inability of one or both spouses to relax, somewhat typifying the "uptight" culture of the day, and secondly, the inability or unwillingness of one or both spouses to completely let themselves go or give themselves completely in sexual embrace. We hypothesized that establishing a new habit pattern in thought and behavior might carry over to coital activity. Improved sexual functioning suggested that this might have been one of the important contributing factors.

Following dinner a session was scheduled where each member of the therapeutic couple had the opportunity to give the other a facial massage, under the direction of the counselors. They were instructed to attempt to convey in non-verbal language as many warm and positive feelings as possible to the spouse. Following the massage session some hypnotherapy of 30 to 45 minutes duration was usually scheduled including the use of post-hypnotic suggestion involving relaxation and improved sexual functioning. Since each program was designed for the individual couple there was some variation in sequential order of therapy work.

The setting then is in an atmosphere of complete relaxation or of one most conducive to relaxation including warm mineral water, non-verbal communication, and hypnotic suggestion before retiring for the night. No directions for actual sexual intercourse are given at that time. Some couples had intercourse that night, others did not.

The schedule for Saturday called for further swimming activities, hiking, and Honda riding across the desert. Although eight hours of scheduled work included a follow up of possible sexual activities of Friday evening and specific suggestions for improved sexual functioning during Saturday, much of the effectiveness of the approach seemed to be in the informal conversations with the therapists through most of the day. Most of the discussion concerned sexual behavior generally as well as reproductive biology and physiology.

The sexual symbolism of orgasm involves in the minds of many females the concept of "shooting the moon" or some increasing upward spiraling of sexual stimulation until complete satisfaction and release is achieved. The experience begins with the Jacuzzi pool at 100 degrees temperature and in a hotter therapy pool at 105 degrees. Some of the couples were taken up the world's longest tramway in aerial cars. The experience of up and over symbolically suggested to the non-orgasmic female that with increased warmth of body and emotional feeling in an environment of complete relaxation she would be closer to "shooting the moon" than had ever previously been true. This was reinforced through post hypnotic suggestion.

Following the return to the trailer after the tram ride the couples were directed in complete body massage which added another dimension of warm emotional response to their increasingly intimate non-sexual embrace which carried over to their sexual functioning that night. It was in this setting that non-orgasmic women and premature males were most effectively treated. The emphasis on the weekend session was on improving the relationship between spouses, emphasizing a warmer, more intimate relationship *per se* rather than achievement of orgasm on the part of the female or delayed ejaculation on the part of the male. In all instances these goals were achieved, namely that a warmer, more intimate relationship evolved, which was the primary objective and as well the secondary of more increasingly effective sexual functioning.

All couples involved in the weekend retreat were involved in sexual intercourse on at least three occasions of their own volition. They came into the program initially to improve sexual functioning, so without requirement or direction they voluntarily engaged in coital activities on frequent occasions in the desert setting.

One therapist always slept in the front part of the trailer with the couple in the back bedroom. On one occasion sleep was interrupted by the cry of a frustrated non-orgasmic woman so that this provided the basis of somewhat extended discussions the following day. In the case of one couple the woman was found to be orgasmic in a clinical situation later though she reported never having experienced orgasm previously. This involved her developing an awareness of what she was already experiencing. She was blocking the existing orgasm from consciousness. In another situation the wife on coming into the program would not permit her husband to touch her sexually. Within two weeks following the desert experience they reported intercourse involving eight different coital sessions in the previous week's time.

The follow-up aspect of the desert experience included hour long sessions in an attempt to determine the effectiveness of the weekend situation. By this time approximately 30 hours had been invested in the therapeutic setting with the couples routinely reporting the marathon experience the turning point in their sexual functioning and the most therapeutic aspect of our program. One woman reported in a follow up some months after the desert experience that the word "desert" evoked a warm feeling in her vagina whenever it was mentioned.

One contrast to the desert experience is a two-day intensive program with a couple residing in a local motel. While this has also proved to be effective the couple's response was not thought to be as positive by the counselors as in the desert setting where they could provide undivided personal and professional attention. The program in the motel involved accessibility to us at the Center any time they wished, with all aspects of the Counseling program conducted in the therapist's office. In the motel set-up no use of symbolic reference could be utilized and this was more of a straight counseling situation.

A summary of the desert counseling situation involving a modified marathon is to take sexually dysfunctioning couples away from home without their children into an environment of relaxation where with warm mineral water, hypnotherapy, and formal and informal interaction with counselors who encourage, approve and suggest sexual activities *verboten* in the socialization process, dramatic improvements in sexual function were uniformly reported by the couples involved in this program.

The modified marathon experience appears to have application beyond sexually inadequate couples. Ideally it involves a male-female team willing to invest two days of professional time in scheduled formal sessions with their clients. It further involves the challenge to be warm human beings in the unscheduled, informal interaction which inevitably takes place when a foursome take up residence together in a setting specifically designed to improve the interaction patterns for the marital unit who came to this situation with this goal in view.

The Doctor as Marriage Counselor

by Cornelius Lansing, M.D.

EDITORS' NOTE: *The following is reprinted from the textbook,* Marriage Counseling in Medical Practice, *a compendium for physicians edited by Nash, Jessner, and Abse. This chapter's author, Dr. Cornelius Lansing, is on the staff of the Department of Psychiatry of Dartmouth Medical School in Hanover, N. H. Dr. Lansing takes a dim view of popular books on sex. He says many are either blueprints for mechanical activity or gushy treatises on togetherness. He has an equally poor opinion of the competence of the average doctor to deal with sexual problems. He points out wryly that they are often too embarrassed to ask their patients about their sex lives but not at all embarrassed to inquire closely into the quality and frequency of bowel movements. Is sex a part of the health picture or isn't it? The author is one physician who believes that it is.*

The popular books on sex make it all sound so simple. One kind emphasizes a careful mechanical approach: a woman is a delicately balanced machine, trickier and more complicated than a man, but capable of control through mastery of anatomical, physiological, and psychological understanding and technique. All factors are taken into account: the calendar, the clock, the lights, the music, the menu, the words, the sighs. The evening is programed like a giant computer, all systems are "Go," the correct buttons are pushed, and the machine is marvelously in orbit. Still, it is also somewhat reminiscent of my uncle's account of the maneuvers used for winter starting of a capricious and headstrong Model T. When it comes to sex, is all this effort necessary? And if so, is it worth it? The books generally gloss over any functional problems that the *man* might have. Most of them are written by men, and there is an inescapable suspicion that the author is anonymously bragging about his own success with the ladies, implying: "Do as I do. Just be manly but patient, and you won't have a bit of trouble."

Another kind of book, giving much less space to How To Be a Great Lover, Even Though Married, emphasizes togetherness, communication, sympathy, understanding, and mutual consideration. If the husband is amorous, but the wife is tired, anxious, tense, and uninterested, the husband simply sets disappointment aside, summons up a modicum of sympathetic emotional maturity, and the problem is settled.

People who can profit from this sort of advice do not need it. Those who need it generally find the problems to be more stubborn and complicated than the books will admit, and some will seek medical or other professional aid. This is not easy for them: sex is quite a taboo subject for polite conversation, and if it is to be talked about at all, boasting is preferred to admission of difficulty, since the latter is often equated with failure or personal inadequacy. People who spend a fortune on their skin and hair, and are very kind to their stomachs, may let their libidos take an awful beating rather than run the risk of being mocked or scolded by revealing a "shameful" secret. Of course, many prefer self-medication to professional consultation anyway—note the widespread sale of anodynes, antacids, hypnotics, cold cures, and vitamins. Many people dislike having a doctor tell them what to do, unless they are seriously worried or hurting badly. But good health *is* socially approved, and there is no danger of loss of face if you get a regular physical examination, visit your dentist twice a year, eat a balanced diet, and get plenty of sleep, fresh air, and exercise. A man who gets a checkup from his doctor may publicly tell what a brave and conscientious fellow he is, how he took his medicine like a man, and so forth.

But no one can brag publicly about anything to do with sex, which in our culture is in a peculiar position. Its importance is openly acknowledged in print, but not in spoken words. If normal sex actually became taboo, advertising would be revolutionized, and products would have to be sold strictly on their intrinsic merits, instead of by association with the sensuous charms of professional models posing as consumers and displaying an almost perverse infatuation with the product. If abnormal sex likewise became taboo, much of the excitement would disappear from the local news, and the papers might be obliged to print more about world events. But the public importance of sex is always *officially* ignored or denied, playing down in words what is so heartily played up in pictures. Whatever its real importance, it cannot command an air of respectability; sober attention to the achievement of satisfactory sex life is not attended by the same high moral tone that accompanies correction of anemia or regulation of the bowels. Although sexuality is essential for the survival of the race, it is well known that lack of it poses no immediate threat to the life of the individual; sex is commonly regarded as a mildly nefarious self-indulgence, somewhere between coffee and tobacco, or between tobacco and dope, depending on social and religious affiliations.

In other cultures and other times, sexual interest, performance and satisfaction have been matters of public concern, and the subject of long (and even dull) scientific and religious treatises. Difficulties found no lack of professional practitioners sincerely devoted to restoring the sufferer to a state of health. But in our culture, prudery lays its chilly hand even on the medical profession, whose members, despite being *allowed* to know all about sex, often do not. In a paper at the Toronto meeting of the American Psychiatric Association in 1962, Dr. Harold Lief pointed out that doctors are "woefully ignorant about sex," which makes it difficult for them to help patients with problems in this area. Possibly because they assist in the birth process, doctors are reputed to know all about sex. Children think they do, and their early sexual explorations are commonly called the "Doctor Game." This myth of sexual omniscience lives on in popular literature, where the wily medical student gives the cavalryman and sailor a run for their money as champion in the art of seduction. This myth may also be fostered by the fact that some female patients become emotionally and sometimes sexually involved with male physicians. Even though this kind of situation is comparatively rare, it is still a possibility in the public mind and adds force to the notion of the doctor as a sexual expert. Yet in medical schools very little is taught on the subject beyond anatomy and purely automatic functioning, and I do not quite see how the physician is supposed to learn the rest without study, as his personal sexual experiences are in fact not much different from anyone else's, and the possession of more detailed anatomical knowledge adds little to his capacity as performer or advisor. A century ago, when ignorance and prudery were rampant, perhaps the doctor's routine anatomical knowledge really did put him ahead of properly brought-up people; he actually *did* know where babies came from, and quite a few otherwise intelligent people were not quite sure about it.

I think this myth of sexual omniscience is a heavy burden on our profession, and cramps our style. Many doctors, as students, believe the stories and assume that *only they* are somewhat ignorant of the ramifications of sex, and to all their colleagues they ascribe the standard myth of sexual omniscience. Hence they do not like to ask questions about it, or even to be caught reading about it, since this would seem to be admitting an exaggerated or perverse interest, or worse yet, a childish ignorance and naïveté. Yet how else can one learn except by study and reading? Personal experience, however extensive and varied, is not enough to cover the whole field. We all eat, but we are neither dietitians nor nutritionists. We breathe, but we are not respiratory physiologists. We eat, digest, and defecate, but this does not qualify us as gastroenterologists. Hopefully, we provide sterling examples of reasonably normal and satisfying sex life, but that does not give us leave to pose as experts on the subject.

There is certainly no reason for physicians to think that they deserve a monopoly on advising people about sexual problems. They do not advise people on dancing, gymnastics, piano duets, or contract bridge, all activities requiring skill and cooperation for maximum enjoyment. But since physicians do concern themselves with the structure and function of the human mind and body, their scientific training provides an excellent background for expert counseling in the field, although they can hardly expect to become proficient without study. Physicians and medical students should be encouraged to study the subject of sex. There are a great many books written about it, some good, some bad, some unbelievably tedious. The last word has not been said, and the safest literary diet is a varied one. A briefly annotated bibliography is appended to this chapter. The comments represent no official position, merely the author's personal opinions.

I will now specify and describe a few varieties of sexual problems, interpret their possible significance, and outline some ideas about treatment. Since this volume deals with the problems of married people, I will similarly restrict myself to sexual symptoms arising in this group. The problems of the unmarried are interesting and important, especially to those concerned, but they do not ordinarily involve permanent interpersonal relationships. The problems of a married person, on the other hand, impinge continuously on the spouse, affect the total interpersonal relationship, and are affected by it. It is this interpersonal aspect on which I would like to lay particular emphasis.

Another restriction on the topic is that the symptom must be such that one or both members of the married pair consider it a problem for which they may be seeking some sort of help. People often settle sexual problems by compromises that would not appeal to you or me, but as long as they are satisfied with the solution, we as physicians are not going to hear about them. Let me give an example. Although it has been shown that a substantial number of elderly people retain sexual interest and potency into the seventies and some even into the eighties, nobody is concerned that a great many do give up most sexual activity in the sixties. Now, if a couple in their late twenties decided to give up sex, it would be most unusual, yet if both were *really* in agreement about it and remained otherwise harmonious and devoted, it would not constitute a medical problem, and one would only hear about it inadvertently. This couple obviously does have a personal problem, but they have dealt with it (I shall not say solved it) in their own way. As long as the method actually works and does not lead to some kind of disabling symptom, such as hysterical or psychosomatic manifestations, it is not our business to *insist* on change. In the same way, we do not interfere by brute force with phobic, hysterical, or compulsive symptoms, which may represent the best adjustment the patient is capable of at the time.

Another example of a "sick" solution to a marital sexual problem is one in which a man deals with frustration or anger at his wife by having affairs with other women. No man is going to seek medical help about this unless he feels guilty about it, or his wife finds out and is angry, or he becomes involved in some sort of publicly disreputable behavior. Presumably such behavior is based on some kind of a personality problem in husband or wife or both, but the unprofessional solution of taking a mistress may be highly effective, albeit sometimes risky. Many people cope with their sexual problems without seeking advice, or even thinking of it. Some go to lawyers seeking divorce, and I understand that many lawyers try to get the warring couple to settle their differences. And some people wind up talking to the district attorney, so to speak, as in the famous case of Frankie and Johnnie.

Let me summarize by saying that I am going to discuss problems involving the sexual aspect of relationships and activities of married couples which are *perceived* as problems by one or both partners, or where neurotic "solutions" to the problem create social difficulties in the family or community.

I would now like to specify the conditions or broad diagnostic categories under which sexual problems may come to the attention of the physician. I am considering the problems as *symptoms*. I cannot emphasize too strongly that although the patient may have nothing on his mind but his sexual problem, it should always be considered as one aspect of a potentially more complex situation requiring diagnosis, and not simply as an isolated problem requiring blind treatment. I have made four categories, which I think cover all situations, although a case might come under more than one category. These categories are convenient aids to thinking in the course of taking a history and, if kept in mind, will prevent one from missing the obvious. While the patient goes on giving a perhaps too meticulous description of the malfunctioning of his genitalia, the physician can be thinking, "Could this fellow be psychotic? Has he a neurosis? Does he beat his wife, or vice versa? Or does he really have gonorrhea?" The categories I have chosen are:

1. Symptoms associated with physical disease.
2. Symptoms associated with psychosis.
3. Symptoms associated with neurosis.
4. Symptoms arising predominantly in the framework of a neurotic marital relationship.

Physical Disease: Sexual incapacity may be associated with physical diseases such as local acute or chronic inflammation, trauma, infection, or tumor; neurological disturbances; toxic, systemic, and metabolic disorders. The preponderance of sexual disorders are psychological and functional in origin, and in my opinion it would be fatuous to indulge in a heroic hunt for organic disease in every case, but thorough history-taking, a careful routine physical and neurological examination, routine laboratory work including serology, and meticulous examination of the affected parts are certainly in order.

Psychosis: Sexual symptoms, or some alteration of sexual habits, may be early manifestations of a psychotic disorder. Along with fatigue, insomnia, loss of appetite, and general slowing of physical activity, loss of libido is a common symptom of depressive reactions. Not all depressive reactions are psychotic, but it would be important to keep the possibility of this diagnosis in mind, since early discovery and appropriate treatment may forestall more serious developments. A manic or schizophrenic process may be ushered in by an increase in sexual activity or orgastic capacity, or by peculiar or bizarre ideas about sex or the sex organs. In such cases, diagnosis of the mental disorder can be made on the basis of the mental examination and many other aspects of the history. It should be remembered that bizarre ideas about sex do not necessarily imply psychosis. Such a condition is normal in children, even when they are adequately educated, and some individuals shy away from getting better information in later life. A colleague recently told me of seeing a college student who was disappointed by his discovery that Comparative Anatomy is not the study of the difference between the sexes!

Neurosis: In this category I would like to include sexual problems of psychogenic origin which are symptomatic of intrapsychic conflict, but where psychosis is not present or imminent. Obviously people whose problems arise within the marital relationship also fall within the neurotic category, but I would like to make a somewhat arbitrary distinction here, between cases where the inciting cause lies *within* the marital relationship, and those where it lies *outside* it. The latter category would include people with neuroses and personality disorders that might give rise to symptoms in the sexual area. It would for instance include all sexual deviations, such as exhibitionism, fetishism, sadism, masochism, homosexuality, etc. People with personality disorders generally do not suffer from much anxiety and so do not often seek help spontaneously, but they may come in at the behest of their spouses, or if their actions are detected and defined as criminal by public authority. If their "abnormal" actions are successfully concealed and if the "normal" sexual role is adequately performed, there is no complaint, and they do not seek help.

Neurotic disturbances such as hysteria, phobia, and anxiety reaction may be manifested by sexual difficulties, usually associated with such unpleasant emotions as fear, anxiety, guilt, and shame, and are manifested less by action than the lack of it. In the case of women, frigidity and dyspareunia come readily to mind, while impotence and premature ejaculation are chief among such problems in men. These are basically related to emotional immaturity, and the persistence of fearful or negative childhood attitudes into adult life. In our culture sex is officially an adult game, like automobile driving, and children are forbidden in no uncertain terms to play it. If they are "sat on" often enough and hard enough, and scared enough into the bargain, they may not realize that they have grown up even when they reach physical and legal maturity, and the fears and taboos may persist despite all logical efforts to dislodge them. Sometimes, of course, this leads to avoidance of marriage, but commonly such people do marry and some sooner or later discover that they are missing something that others enjoy or that the spouse is disappointed that they *do not* enjoy. In addition to the persistence of childhood fears, orgastic impotence or lack of enjoyment may be associated with envy and hostility toward the opposite sex, poor sexual-role identification, or excessive self-love that precludes actually loving another person.

Let me give some examples of cases in which neurotic intrapsychic conflicts gave rise to sexual problems:

1. A young man has had difficulty in breaking away from his domineering but neurotically helpless mother, who uses physical symptoms and "hysterics" to control her children. He marries a more stable woman, but whenever she becomes ill or at all emotional, he suffers anxiety and premature ejaculation. Her actions are not neurotic, but they remind him unconsciously of the complex and disagreeably close relationship with his mother, and although he loves his wife, under such conditions he wants to get out of there fast.

2. A woman marries a man somewhat like her father. She becomes frigid whenever her relationship with her husband evokes certain feelings which remind her of an erotically tinged situation with her father, repressed since she was a little girl. Guilt over forbidden childhood sexual wishes prevents her from enjoying her perfectly lawful marital relationship at times.

3. A normally aggressive man encounters unexpected success in his professional work. As a child he had a strong wish to compete with and surpass his father, but he never really expected to do so. Since his field of work is entirely different from his father's, he now feels as though he had won a victory by stealth and anticipates some horrid but unspecified doom, like a teen-ager who has been caught smoking his father's cigars and drinking his brandy, but whose fate has not yet been decided. After a time, his anxiety culminates in impotence, which irritates his wife.

4. A young woman marries an older man, a widower, and although she is apparently devoted to him she finds sexual intercourse painful and disgusting. Her "devotion" is rather like that of a little girl for a parent, and she actually wants to be treated not as a real wife but like a princess or a favorite child. She is too immature and self-centered to be capable of adult love and sexuality.

5. A man loses his father, with whom he had never gotten along well. He feels as though his failure to answer a letter had somehow hastened his father's death. He feels depressed and has loss of libido out of proportion to the depression. Much of his hostility had been engendered by his father's virtual abdication of family responsibility and

his many extramarital affairs. While disapproving of this, the patient had unconsciously envied his father's seductive skill and happy-go-lucky attitude, especially during adolescence.

In most of these cases, the sexual symptoms have not been the only complaints, and I have tried to present them as strictly *neurotic* problems, in which interference with sexual function or enjoyment is simply one aspect and may or may not be the presenting complaint. Much depends on the attitude of the spouse. In Victorian days it was not ladylike to enjoy sex, and many men who liked a lusty wench would nonetheless have been shocked if their *wives* became "involved" sexually; *they* hardly complained of a wife's frigidity, but nowadays it is often quite a different story. In the third example, above, where the man first had anxiety symptoms, the later impotence was an hysterical symptom, and for *him* giving up sexual activity "solved" his internal dilemma nicely. His wife did not like it a bit, however, and nagged him into getting help. If she had been frigid, or strongly inhibited sexually, or afraid of pregnancy, his symptom might have suited her fine, and he might not have sought help until he himself got tired of being impotent. We must also keep in mind that his impotence might have subsided spontaneously in time.

Neurotic Marital Relationship: The last category of marital sexual difficulties are those which are related to the neurotic elements in the relationship of a married couple. In addition to specific strengths, virtues, and other admirable qualities that stir up enough mutual admiration to lead to the altar, each spouse brings to the marriage his own conflicts, sensitivities, and special needs. Significant incompatibilities may be present, which do not manifest themselves until some time after the marriage has begun, which may appear so insidiously that they are hard to recognize as such until both partners are suffering from profound irritation, and which make adjustment and compromise all the more difficult. Perhaps the state of "being in love" is responsible for much of this, the marvelous self-deception that persuades the young man that he has found the girl of his dreams, and the same for the young lady. Dream girls and boys do not exist this side of the Pearly

Gates, yet young people in love insist on attributing the most angelic qualities to each other and expecting the same of themselves, a happy delusion that must somehow be worn away if they are ever to create a workable adult human relationship. Where mutual expectations are unrealistic, the letdown is cruel, and disillusion is painful when couples are confronted too abruptly with each other's frailties.

Some couples attempt to avoid acknowledgment of childish feelings and utilize deficiencies of character to escape the pain of facing these. Instead of living, they try a kind of play-acting. The man may assume the role of the tyrannical husband if his partner will play the hysterical wife. Or vice versa. From his side of the stage, the husband is being the sick little boy, casting his wife in the role formerly occupied by his controlling, aggressive mother. On her side, the wife is engaged in portraying to herself the long-suffering neglected girl, while assigning to her husband the role of her coarse, lazy, incompetent father. Neither is aware that the other is writing a different play, and neither has access to the real list of characters, which shows both of them as overgrown children trying to be adults, unable to escape from their past family relationships and busily and tragically recreating them in the present. The saddest part of all is that each resists maturing tendencies in the other and tries to coerce the partner into truly living the assigned role. If the husband achieves more stature, the wife uses her knowledge of his sensitivities to cut him down to size; if the wife becomes less bitchy, the husband does all he can to provoke her to return to the neurotic status quo.

The actual manifestations of this problem are the same as those mentioned under the heading of neurosis; the difference is that *both* partners are neurotically involved, and the difficulty lies more between them than within either one. It is somewhat like a *folie à deux*, in which two people participate in the same psychosis and share the same delusions about people in the outside world. The neurotic couple usually see the outside world clearly enough but have strongly distorted perceptions of each other, which they tend to perpetuate rather than amend.

Let me give an example of a typical complicated interaction involving sex in a relatively normal couple. It begins with a common source of confusion, the normal difference between the sexual urges of men, which are fairly steady, and those of women, which tend to vary with the menstrual cycle. The husband has been away on a trip, feeling a bit sexy, looking forward to fun in bed on his return, and recalls what a delightful time he had with his wife the night before he left, just a week ago. She is very glad to see him back, and they are quite romantic at dinner. They have some wine and are both relaxed, in fact he is quite tired after his long day's journey. She is feeling cuddly but not sexy, but he does not know this, and when he makes a lazy pass at her, she is suddenly revolted. It reminds her of mashers and the lecherous uncle who used to feel her up slyly at family reunions when she was a teen-ager. She reacts with disgust, and he is quite taken aback, so sudden and unexpected is this turn of events, which was definitely not on his program for the evening. He feels like a child arbitrarily and unjustly cut off in the midst of innocent fun, and he reacts in one of his characteristic ways, by turning away, hurt and pouting. This in turn makes his wife feel anxious and guilty. Her father used to act like this when angry, and she always felt it was somehow her fault. Although she is actually quite angry, she assumes an air of remorse and artificial friendliness and tries in a babyish way to be "nice." This unconsciously reminds the husband of certain contradictory attitudes of his mother, which always used to confuse and bother him, and he now becomes angrier still. At this point either of two things might happen: the husband becomes totally uninterested in sex and retreats nursing a grudge surprisingly reminiscent of an adolescent's feeling of not being understood, thwarting his wife's guilty and highly ambivalent attempts to act loving or sexy; or, alternatively, his anger takes an active form, in which he aggressively shows the little bitch that she is not going to treat *him* like a kid, and she responds spontaneously to his now ruthless ardor, and they have a fine time, and later recall that they have gotten into this bind on previous occasions. Where honest communication of feeling is possible, unpleasant situations like this can often be resolved in a way that leads to more realistic mutual perception. Where such communication is lacking, a stalemate ensues, often followed by endless repetition of the same dreary sequence.

It sometimes happens that in couples whose attitude toward sex is healthy, difficulty may nevertheless arise as a by-product of conflict in other areas. Sexual passion is frequently aggressive, and the emotion of love lies very close to that of hate. Where one or both partners have strong conflicts about hostility and aggression, sexual activity may have to be kept rather tame in order to prevent the adjacent feelings from getting out of control. A husband who needs such control may be a frustration to a wife who would like him sometimes to be a caveman. If she can communicate her wishes convincingly, they may find common ground; if not, he may merely think that her messages constitute a trap of some kind and remain all the more vigilantly calm.

Treatment: As in all other areas of scientific medicine, accurate diagnosis is the cornerstone of therapeutics. Once the underlying disturbance is recognized, therapy can proceed rationally. In the *physical* category, appropriate physical treatment is of course indicated; however, one must keep in mind that physical disease does not confer immunity against emotional problems, which may either be coincidental or secondary to the disease itself.

With patients in whom *psychosis* is suspected, psychiatric consultation should be considered, to verify the diagnosis and find what form of treatment is indicated. However, if the situation is chronic and stable, and the amount of social disturbance is slight, it may not be necessary to refer the patient elsewhere. Sympathetic support, or modest drug therapy, may provide all the stabilization that is needed. It must be kept in mind that even though the patient complains of something—in this case presumably a sexual problem—he *may* not really want to get rid of the symptom. If the symptom departs, well and good; if it does not, this is no reason to send the patient elsewhere or smother him with medicine, unless he is becoming otherwise more disturbed and hard to manage. If he maintains his job and family life and keeps coming to see you, let him complain as much as he wants. The symptom may represent the "ticket of admission" that permits him to maintain therapeutic contact with the physician.

There are many different ways in which *neurotic* patients can be treated, depending on the particular case. Simple reassurance as to the benign nature of the symptom may help a great deal. People are always worrying that they might be abnormal in some way, especially in regard to sexual feelings and fantasies. Reassurance and sex education, both by discussion and having the patient read a book, may bring great relief from guilt and anxiety. Of course the physician should be well acquainted with the wide range of what is "normal," which may not coincide with his personal view of what is optimal. The "Kinsey Reports" are good sources of information for physicians, but are not recommended for patients.

A "talking-out" type of psychotherapy may be very helpful, and this is well within the capacity of the average practitioner in many cases, if he can arrange the time. Patients with bothersome symptoms and relatively healthy personalities are the best motivated for formal intensive psychotherapy and can profit the most from it. Such patients also have the best chance of spontaneous recovery and can be greatly assisted by the tolerant understanding and non-interfering sympathy of a family doctor, especially if the problem is a fairly acute one. This is particularly true of male patients, who are aided not only by having a patient listener but by identification with a mature and healthy male, such as most doctors are. Neurotic female patients with sexual problems are trickier, since some will be prone to develop complex emotional attachments to a male physician and may indulge in highly seductive maneuvers, all of which are difficult to deal with unless you have had special training or happen to be personally skilled in avoiding entanglement without rejecting the patient. The most trying developments can be minimized by referring such patients to a female physician, but since these patients are often very immature, they tend to develop strong, sticky, dependent attachments that may be equally tedious to deal with, if less alarming. I do not recommend the use of drugs for patients with isolated sexual complaints. If the symptom is merely one aspect of a more complex neurotic problem, or if the measures already suggested are of no avail, psychiatric consultation is in order.

Patients with neurotic personality disturbances, who translate their conflicts into action (such as "running around") instead of perceiving them as feelings or symptoms, are very difficult patients to treat. Although some may seek psychiatric help, often they are poorly motivated and are merely complying with somebody's pushing. As in the case of alcoholism, family pushing may be 50 percent pulling. A masochistic wife may foster philandering at the same time that she is complaining of it, to maintain her status as a woman wronged. If you can see the interaction of such people and tell them about it quite bluntly, it may be of some help. Psychiatric treatment will be of little avail unless the patient sees himself as actually sick and wants to change. It will be a waste of time to insist that a truly reluctant person visit a psychiatrist. Those whose actions have gotten them in trouble with the law are still harder to treat, but the unambiguous quality of the threat of legal prosecution may be helpful.

In the case of *neurotically interacting couples,* the family physician may have as good a chance as anyone else in ferreting out the distortions and irrational elements in the relationship. The simple presence of an impartial referee sometimes enables couples to get things off their collective chest and resume normal communication. After talking to both alone and hearing some of the complaints, the doctor might get them together, and say, "I have the impression that you're both rather angry at each other, and afraid to admit it. Now why don't we talk about this?" This is really a way of saying, "Why don't you stop pouting and try to settle your problems like grown-ups?" while at the same time providing physical presence and moral prestige as a reassurance that nobody is going to get maimed in the discussion. Psychiatrists, social agencies, and marriage counselors often handle problems of this sort, and the physician should feel free to call on them. No doctor should try to do work of this sort unless he really wants to, but it can be highly interesting and rewarding.

In closing, let me reiterate my "permission" and exhortation to all physicians to read up on the subject of sex, if they wish to be able to help patients who come with such problems. Many patients have sexual problems that they would like help with, except that they wait to be asked about them. Many physicians feel embarrassed asking patients about sex, probably because they do not feel themselves well-grounded in the subject. If the patient brings it up, well and good, he has taken the responsibility himself. If the physician brings it up, the patient *might* become angry or offended. However, the possibility of such a reaction never seems to stop doctors from asking patients about their excretory functions in the course of history-taking. If the patient is alarmed, the doctor can usually reassure him that such questions are scientific, necessary, and routine. There is really no reason why sex should not be given an equally important place on the list of pertinent questions.

Bibliography

Eisenstein, Victor W. 1956. "Sexual Problems in Marriage," in Victor W. Eisenstein (ed.), *Neurotic Interaction in Marriage*. New York: Basic Books, Inc.

Ellis, A. 1951. *The Folklore of Sex*. New York: Boni.
Interesting survey of "public" attitudes toward sex as displayed in contemporary mass media.

Ford, C. S., and F. A. Beach. 1951. *Patterns of Sexual Behavior*. New York: Harper & Brothers and Paul B. Hoeber.

An important treatise on various kinds of sexual activities in primates and lower animals, including the natural occurrence of what human beings often call "perverse." A relatively short book, well-written and readable.

Gebhard, P. H., W. B. Pomeroy, C. E. Martin, and C. V. Christenson. 1958. *Pregnancy, Birth, and Abortion*. New York: Harper & Brothers and Paul B. Hoeber.

This is the third of the celebrated "Kinsey Reports," sober statistical studies of sexual attitudes and practices, based on extensive surveys. They have been criticized on technical grounds by statisticians, some of whom feel the sampling procedure to be biased; nevertheless, these will remain definitive studies until something better comes along. Being crammed with facts, charts, tables and "statistics," they make heavy reading, and will not be especially helpful for laymen, unless there is a need to convince a patient that something is "normal" to the extent of being prevalent. A good antidote for pious moralizing. Enormous bibliographies.

Herndon, C. N., and E. M. Nash. May, 1962. "Premarriage and Marriage Counseling: A Study of Practices of North Carolina Physicians," *J.A.M.A.*, 180: 395–401.

Survey of attitudes and practices of 514 physicians in a variety of specialties, regarding premarital examinations, contraceptive advice, counseling about marital problems. Statistics in easily assimilable form.

Kinsey, A. C., W. B. Pomeroy, and C. E. Martin. 1948. *Sexual Behavior in the Human Male*. Philadelphia: W. B. Saunders Co.

Kinsey, A. C., W. B. Pomeroy, C. E. Martin, and P. H. Gebhard. 1953. *Sexual Behavior in the Human Female*. Philadelphia: W. B. Saunders Co.

Lewinsohn, R. 1958. *A History of Sexual Customs*. New York: Harper & Brothers.

A thorough and interesting survey of sexual attitudes and customs in various parts of the world. The historical approach permits valuable insight into some of our ancestors' aberrations and some contemporary "tribal customs." Suitable for intelligent patients seeking explanations.

Prange, A. J., Jr., M. G. Sandifer, C. R. Vernon, and D. R. Hawkins. June, 1959. "A Brief Appraisal of Pain and Normal Sexual Behavior as Subjects of Medical Instruction," *N. Carolina Med. J.*, 20:222–25.

Brief survey of small sample of students from many medical schools, regarding presence or absence of instruction in sexual behavior; 90% had instruction on sexual behavior in children, but only 45% were instructed regarding adults.

Robinson, M. N. 1959. *The Power of Sexual Surrender*. New York: Doubleday & Co. Also published as a paperback (P 2100) by Signet Books.

An important book, written by a woman analyst, explaining the psychology of frigidity and offering sensible "self-help." It can be recommended equally for physicians, patients, and husbands. Very well-written, easy to read, and free of jargon.

Van de Velde, T. H. 1930. *Ideal Marriage: Its Physiology and Technique*. New York: Covici, Friede.

Excellent book for married people, leisurely and respectful; an "old standby" for many years, but by no means outdated. Emphasis on love and sentiment may not appeal to some, but will be welcomed by those who find mere mechanics rather sterile.

PART IV

Young People and Sex

Sexual Freedom and Culture Change

by Margaret Mead, Ph.D.

EDITORS' NOTE: *Dr. Margaret Mead is presently Curator Emeritus of Ethnology at The American Museum of Natural History where she maintains her office. She is Adjunct Professor of Anthropology at Columbia University and Chairman and Professor in the Social Sciences Division of the Liberal Arts College, Lincoln Center Campus, Fordham University, both in New York City. Dr. Mead is currently involved in creating a new exhibition hall on the Peoples of the Pacific in The American Museum of Natural History. Her professional specialty is the study of contemporary cultures in the light of perspective gained by the study of small, homogeneous, stable societies and the further development of cultural theories of human behavior.*

In this warm and compassionate address, delivered at San Francisco State College in 1967, when it sounded even more radical than it does now, Dr. Mead makes a dramatic appeal for more, not less, sexual freedom for young, unmarried adults. She's against casual, beach-party sex but is not against mutually responsible monogamous relationships even though such relationships do not necessarily lead to lifelong commitments. She says the birth-control pill has made this possible. However, she suggests the ideal pill would be sawed in half with each partner prescribed to swallow. She feels we need to develop a new form of sex relations in this country based on regard of one individual for another.

When we talk about young people today, we are not

talking about age-old conflicts between youth and age, or how youth is perennially idealistic, or progressive, or rebellious, or radical or conservative. We are talking about the position of younger people in a society that is changing so rapidly that the only people that have a clue as to what it's about tend to be the very young.

We are living in a situation that in time is analogous to the founding of the United States. It was founded by adults who came with their characters already formed and lived here as immigrants as best they could. Their children were born here and lived here. All of us who are pre-Sputnik, pre-atom bomb, and pre-computer are learning about what is going on today as the immigrants did who first came to the shores of this country. But the post-Sputnik, post-atom bomb, post-computer young people are the ones who live here, who were born here and belong to this period.

Our problem in talking with younger people, and in trying to work out new forms of culture appropriate to the world we live in today, is much more complicated than it has ever been before. We need to work out some way of combining the wisdom of older people with the native approach of those young people who were born in this age and are responding to it as natives and not as immigrants and strangers.

As I understand it, we are not going to discuss the virtues of the Pill versus other forms of contraception. We are primarily concerned with the Pill as a symbol of the fact that today we have reliable forms of contraception available—reliable, bearable, durable, and not inevitably too expensive. We are considering what the relationship is between reliable contraception and the sex behavior of young people, and, to some extent, of somewhat older people. I am stressing the word "reliable" because contraception, of course, is very old. Through the ages peoples have found a variety of methods of contraception or of dealing with unwanted children, including abortion and infanticide.

The thing that is important today is that we actually can have reliable contraception. We can move from the exceedingly ambiguous position we have been in for about the last fifty years in which, unless the parents belonged to a religious group that forbade contraception and observed the rules, children had to suspect that maybe they were accidents—which I think is a horrible thing to do to a child. One of the things we will be able to do with reliable contraception is to see that children are not accidents—to be able to say so, so that no child will ever have to wonder if he or she was wanted.

With reliable contraception, we are moving into a world in which we can ask quite different questions about what young people are to do and how they are to live. One of the principal reasons why society has to regulate sex relations between adults is for the safety of the children. Every society in the world has to set up rules which will make certain that the child has an identity, a place in society and people to care for it.

Through history, with few exceptions—the people who lived on various small islands and knew it, like Japan—every human society has felt that its members must have as many children as they could. This is partly due to the fact that so many children and mothers died. The only way a people could insure that the society would ever maintain itself was to encourage many children being born. So societies could never afford to emphasize very many individuals' contribution, as individuals, as against their contribution as parents.

This is particularly true of women. We could let men be statesmen, generals, painters, poets and builders as long as their wives were willing to spend the bulk of their lives producing and rearing the next generation. Today we face a new situation. Except for a few dying little societies here and there that might be worried, we know that nowhere in the world do we need more people. In general, every society in the world needs fewer people, better brought up and better cared for.

That gives us a totally new context for looking at sex behavior and the way in which we regulate it. We can, for the first time, separate the contribution of the individual, as an individual, from the contribution of an individual merely as one who carries on the existence of the group. This means also that in the world of the next 50 years, ideally, we will have fewer families with children, and many, many more people who will decide that they want to contribute to life as individuals. We have to look at the sex relationships that we build up among adolescents, late adolescents, and young adults and ask what kind of preparation these relationships are going to be for two possible kinds of marriage which will exist—whether or not we make them legal and formal—the marriage that is parental, devoted to bringing up several children in which the parents give a tremendous amount of their time and energy to caring for the children, and the marriage in which the principal point is not children, in which both husband and wife go out of the home as individuals doing things that are needed in society.

We can ask what kind of preparation for these future roles is the adolescent behavior today going to be. This may seem to you as if, in a sense, I am disallowing the importance of what young people themselves have to say. But what I am trying to present is a framework within which they can speak and discuss what they want to discuss and what they feel.

There's been a good deal of discussion on campuses about sexual freedom. There are several things that sexual freedom *might* mean. They have not been very well defined. It may merely mean a freedom to have sex relations with anybody, anywhere, at any time, without any responsibility whatsoever. This is sometimes the way the term is construed. It is very doubtful that this kind of freedom is likely to lead toward the kinds of marriages in which we, as Americans, have always believed.

When we talk about revising the Puritan Ethic, this does not mean we are actually going to get over it. We will simply say people *ought* to have some kind of sexual freedom. The *ought* is going to be there just as firmly as it was when we said people *ought not* to have sexual freedom, and it is much more inappropriate to insist on pleasure than it is to insist on pain. This is one of the problems we are facing in the California version of American culture. Everybody in California thinks they *ought* to be happy; they *ought* to enjoy the climate. This has been called, "suppressing your superego." It is extraordinarily puritanical. When we ask how much sexual freedom young people ought to have, we are still asking an essentially puritan question.

And we do indeed have to ask: What kind of marriages are we likely to have in the next 25 years? What will be the relationships between the kinds of adolescent life that we set up as styles and the kinds of people that today's youth want to be later? What will the repercussions be and will the sequences we establish be appropriate?

We know from the study of many peoples that there is no one form of marriage that necessarily fits the human race. We know that there are many forms of premarital behavior followed by different kinds of married relationships. There are societies which have great premarital freedom and marital stability; there are societies which have no premarital freedom and great marital instability. We can look over the world and find societies where what happens in adolescence and young adulthood fits what happens in maturity, and societies where there is no such fit.

One of the ways in which we can try to build a new set of standards is to think about what kind of adults we are going to need in the next 25 years. We are going to need desperately the full contribution of every gifted, every intelligent, every talented, every sensitive person in this country. We need to ask what kinds of adults are we going to need, and how will the styles set up in adolescence prepare them to be the kind of adults we need—not just for their own state or our own nation, but as Americans in a community and in a world in which we are only one part.

What the world needs, and what *we* need, are one today. Americans are members of the whole human race living on this planet in intercommunication with each other. So we can ask what the people of this planet need from Americans, who happen to be living in the richest country on this planet, and who are, in many ways, the most materially fortunate people in the world today.

We have, at present, a kind of marriage which has been described as the all-purpose marriage. When you marry, you expect your marriage partner to be totally satisfying —in bed, out of bed, early in the morning, late at night, in the car, on the mountain, as a parent, as a partner . . . skiing. We have done something no people have ever tried to do before—to take another human being and make him into an absolutely all-purpose utility. This is an exceedingly brittle form of marriage, very, very trying, and very hard to live in. When anything goes wrong—in bed, or out of bed, or skiing—people immediately think, "I've made a mistake. I must get a divorce. He isn't what I *thought* he was." No human being could be what an American spouse is expected to be. This brittleness, whenever the spouse fails in any respect, is one of the weaknesses of American marriages. It is not only in sexual fidelity, but in many other respects. He or she does not have quite the ethical sensitivity, or the same views on politics, or take the toothpaste cap off the same way.

We can ask what kind of relations in adolescence will fit into this very demanding kind of marriage. I think we can say that very rapid change of partners, and breaking up immediately if there is any kind of disappointment, is very poor preparation for standing the kinds of disappointment that are bound to occur in marriages where we ask so much. The kind of adolescent freedom which means a month with one boy, and two months with another, and a third month with two others, and then they don't suit, going on from one piece of inexperienced experimentation to another, throwing one relationship after another aside as unsatisfactory, is an extraordinarily poor preparation. It is seldom a way of acquiring tolerance. It is very often a way of acquiring the habit of disappointment.

We also have to face the fact that Americans are violently opposed to much association between the experienced and the inexperienced. We do not really like marriages where there is more than a five-year age difference. When a man of 40 marries a girl of 20, we shake our heads. Of course, if a woman of 40 marries a man of 20, we don't even bother to shake our heads. We *know*. People are certain such a marriage is undesirable and doomed. So, in the United States, we have very effectively interfered with any teaching from a person who knows anything about sex to those who don't know anything about it. This is partly due to our standards of monogamy, but even more to our standards of peer relationships—that good relationships must be between peers. Whether it's premarital experimentation of adolescents, or marriage itself, the ignorant and inexperienced teach the ignorant and the inexperienced, and clumsiness and lack of skill are perpetuated.

This does not apply only to sex; it also applies to cooking. Mothers do not teach their daughters how to cook today. They throw them out of the kitchen—one of the reasons for early marriage. The girls then, getting a kitchen of their own, are expected to teach themselves to cook. They get a cookbook, and they do astonishingly well. But you can't learn lovemaking from books.

Yet we do not believe that you learn by being taught by a master; you do it yourself. The whole country is a mass of do-it-yourself activities, and one of the things we have is do-it-yourself sex. I think our feeling for the peer group, for ties among members of narrow generations who share the same ideas, is going to be so strong that this emphasis on peer group sex is probably going to survive. This means that if we are going to try to treat sex as a serious form of communication between human beings—a serious form of commitment of one person to another, as a way in which one person takes responsibility for another person's delight and another person's sense of himself (none of which we do today)—if we are going to do this, we also have to allow for a period of learning in which young people somehow learn from other young people, because we disapprove of any other form of learning.

It would seem all the more important, therefore, that we do not plunge our young people into parenthood, unready and inexperienced in the art of living with another person, but that we give them an opportunity to form what might be called individual marriages without the commitment of parenthood, to learn to live with and to love one other person first.

One of the principal questions students ask when a period of marriage without children is proposed is, "Why get married?" They often mean they can sleep with someone in the back of the car, in a motel for an hour—that it is fairly easy to get sex anywhere. They are saying, in effect, "Why get married at all until you want children?" This shows we have no recognition of sex relations as part of a relationship between human beings, as individuals, who are taking each other's happiness in their hands. If we propose and protect the position of young people who want to live together, if we legalize it and bless it so they can live quite happily and publicly together as companions who are trying to make something of their relationship to each other but without the commitment to parenthood yet, we will be giving young people a chance to make something of the human relationship between a man and a woman which is not the same as being parents.

With the need to control population increase, and as each child needs more and more from both parents, we seem to be moving toward a society where there will be fewer children, and where it is even more important for people to learn to make something of a sex relationship for its own sake. It includes learning to live with another person *24 hours* out of 24. I suppose many of the people who ask, "Why get married?" have very little idea how tough 24-hour relationships are. It includes the way people look in the morning; it includes their half-remembered dreams; it includes their bad tempers and their good. It includes remembering to telephone if you are late. It includes saying to all the other people around you, "I am taking responsibility for this person as a human being."

The fact that it seems so hard to discuss this point suggests the crux of our difficulty at present is that we are talking about sex freedom as if a sexual act were simply a disassociated event in which another person was used, and not as a part of an important human relationship between two people. Here, again, we are still puritans. We still tend to disallow sex, and only justify it if it leads to parenthood. It reflects the belief that it is better to marry than to burn—and it is better to have children; this puts one in a more respectable position. Sex becomes a sort of virtue instead of a vice, according to the historic definition of the difference between vice and virtue. If the pleasure comes before the pain, it's vice; if the pain comes before the pleasure, it's virtue. Worrying about virtue and vice in this sense is an intrinsic part of our puritan inheritance.

It is not at all sure whether we are going to be able to do something more than simply reverse the position. We have said sex is bad, except when children are the outcome, or at least the desired outcome. Today we are inclined to say sex is good; you *ought* to have some. In fact, you ought to have quite a lot. In fact, it's quite abnormal not to have some sex. Today nobody wants to employ unmarried men. Employers are very suspicious of them, and they are getting suspicious of unmarried women who used to be protected by the fact that they could not find anybody they thought was "fit to marry." Americans today are increasingly demanding a sex life from everyone.

At the same time, we are postponing a sex life, in the sense of permitted parenthood, later and later because of the need for people to be students much longer. A great deal of what has been going on, a great deal of the discussion and argument, has focused around this question of whether students who are not yet economically self-sufficient and are not full members of society should, nevertheless, marry and have children.

In the last 20 years, the whole question of sexual freedom has gotten muddled by the fact that all over this country, especially for high school students, pregnancy is seen, and has become, one route to marriage. When we consider the possibility that certain sure contraceptive methods may change our whole attitude toward many of these things, we have to realize that a large number of young people who get pregnant do so to get married. This has nothing to do with sexual freedom. It is simply the best way to get mother and father to agree to give them a car, and to continue to finance their children after marriage as well as before.

Adults have given up completely as far as chaperonage is concerned. They gave up when the use of the automobile became general. Adults also tend today to push young people toward greater heterosexual maturity. We have almost eliminated one-sex friendships in this country, and have substituted dating between junior high school boys and girls at a stage when they have almost nothing to say to each other. As a result, we push them further into heterosexual activity, often before they are ready for it. We have popularized and publicized sex activity, without giving any background or basis for treating sex activity seriously as a responsible relationship to other human beings. We are facing the need for a new style that will permit young people to pair off and to have a full, committed experience as individuals before they become parents. This will, in turn, protect our children. Any system that we set up must protect our children—children who are going to be more vulnerable than they have been in the past.

I think we are missing the point of the argument most of the time. The Pill itself dramatizes one very important point about this era we are moving into. It is based on trust. A young man who does not wish to marry yet, or does not yet wish to have a child if he is married, is entirely dependent on what his wife tells him. He has no way of finding out whether she is telling the truth or not unless he stands over her day by day. This is a case where men have to trust women. It is a one-sided trust, which is not ideal. There is possibility of fear of cheating, and of a great deal of cheating. It might perhaps be ideal if we are going to continue with something like the Pill to have a pill that has two halves, that would *only work if both people took their half*.

This sounds like a pleasant biochemical joke. Specialists understand its impossibilities probably, but it symbolizes the position to which we have got to come. We have got to come to a relationship between the existence of reliable forms of contraception which gives us the ability not to have children except under appropriate and responsible circumstances, and the development of mutual trust—a kind of trust in which individuals are not exploiting each other merely as temporary sexual objects and passing forms of experimentation. We need forms that will differentiate relationships between individuals based on companionship, and respect, and publicly avowed sexual relations on the one hand, and parental marriages on the other, where those who wish to have children take on a different order of responsibility.

If we can fit these things together—the long, long period young people need to prepare for their vocations, the problems of delayed responsibility inherent in our present system, the breakdown of the old sanctions against premarital sex without the development of new and responsible sanctions as to how we are to engage in sex relations —if we can face all these things, we ought then to be able to develop a new style of sex relations in this country based on the regard of one individual for another, on a recognition that sex is part of a full human relationship. We need to feel that sex does not need to be justified by parenthood, but also that today it very often should not be immediately or necessarily followed by parenthood.

It is because we have reached a stage in the history of the world where population control is essential for the survival of the human race that we have the research that has given us better forms of contraception. We now have social permission to discuss openly the possibility of a world in which much of the time we dissociate, for many people, sex activity from parenthood. But keep in mind that it is always going to be important to see that such forms of sex activity also protect parenthood. The children will be fewer. They will be more fragile because we keep almost every child that is born today, instead of letting 50 percent die and only saving the stronger 50 percent.

The education the children of tomorrow will need will be infinitely more complicated than any education a child has ever had. We will need good parents. We will need the type of society that can protect the children that are growing up at the same time that we also develop the kind of society in which individuals can be related to each other as people, using their sex relationships as part of their recognition and responsibility for one another as individuals.

The Sexual Hang-ups of Young Adults

EDITORS' NOTE: *Is the Masters and Johnson Reproductive Biology Research Foundation a passing phenomenon? As indicated in the final pages of Part I of this book, Masters and Johnson hope so. It all depends, of course, on whether the current generation of young people are sexually healthier and better informed than their parents. It's said that there is a sexual revolution going on and that problems in sexual expression are about to disappear.*

To help find out, we asked five young middle-class Americans to talk about the here-and-now sex attitudes of their age group. Participating in the session were three men and two women between the ages of 20 and 24. Two were college students. Two were college dropouts and working at self-supporting jobs. One had no college. One is married. (His wife did not take part in the discussion.) A young man and woman in the discussion group were living together. Two—one man and one woman—were single.

It seems that today's young adults have as many sexual problems as their parents even though they "rap" about them more freely and in language that would have made grandma reel. Some of their problems are old absurdities like comparative size of penises. Others are new, brought by the hallucinogenic drug scene. Here's how the session went.

The group is gathered in the kind of small city apartment young adults can afford. The room has prints and an art student's original paintings thumbtacked to the walls. There are two straight chairs and a sofa. Young people scarcely ever breathe without the beat of music. 'Cellist Aldo Parisot's performance of Vivaldi's "Cello Concerto" is coming through on the New York FM station

WBAI. On a small table in the middle of the group there is one bottle of wine and five jelly glasses. The session starts as the wine bottle clinks against the glasses.

JIM: Well, what we are here to talk about is: Can we screw better than our parents? Forty or 50 percent of the people in our parents' generation are supposed to have been knocked out of bed by various physiological or psychological sexual difficulties. What about us? I think our parents are envious of us—they think we can screw better than they can. Are we going to perpetuate that mystique or bust it?

KEN: Oh, I think it should definitely be busted. Even though we get better odds.

JIM: Because we get more practice?

STEVE: Why do you think we have better odds?

KEN: Maybe through taking LSD.

STEVE: I don't think LSD is all that good for sex.

KEN: I don't mean that you ball when you're tripping. But the ultimate effect of tripping is to straighten you out—counteract all the things that make you sexually inadequate. I think what LSD does is make you have sex more intensely. I'm not talking about the ability to do it, I mean the ability to *feel* it.

SHIRLEY: You mean like breaking out of parochial school or something?

KEN: I mean the ability to be close enough to someone so that you can really get into it. You shouldn't ball to fulfill a preconceived idea but to go with it where it takes you. LSD can help with that. Acid gets a lot of things out of your gut—like the idea that sex is dirty. You get back to when you were four or five years of age and what it was like then. When I first tried to ball on an acid trip I got this real, loud "No! No!" from my psyche. My parents must have been yelling "No! No!" when I was a kid.

STEVE: When I'm on acid my cock feels very, very different.

JIM: In what way?

STEVE: It starts off by feeling it's not there at all.

JIM: But you're still aware of sex, right?

STEVE: Not really. Or, it's like I'm aware of it in a new way. Like being reborn.

JIM: Where do our ideas about sex first get born? From our parents?

KEN: I don't think many of our parents were sexually happy. It has to do with whether you were toilet trained too early or if you weren't breast fed or if you *were* breast fed and were weaned too soon.

JIM: How about us?

KEN: We're all afflicted with the attitudes that were built into us. Because the sex function—actually I think it was a rather poor job of engineering—is built into the human disposal system, the no-no and the do-it-now commands get all mixed up. You should urinate when mom holds you over the pot and says "wee-wee." But no matter what the agony you shouldn't poop in your pants. "Wait 'til we get to the next gas station." The same thing gets transferred to the sex function. You should be able to do it on command. Like when the Army medic says, "Milk it." But if you want to be a great lover you should be able to hold out for two hours until your girl has had about forty responses— why the hell should you do that, by the way? It's tiring.

JIM: Maybe the women's liberation movement is sneaking in here. . . .

BETTY: My parents like never balled, never. . . . My mother was furious when she caught me kissing my date goodnight. I was 15. She said never to do that again until I was engaged. She really said that. I remember my grandmother complaining to my mother how I wasn't toilet trained until I was two and how messy I was. . . .

JIM: Is the girl's messy bedroom and a guy's messy clothes a sexual spinoff? Because you resent the intrusion on your sexual privacy?

STEVE: Well, maybe. When I came home from a date the question was, "How'd you make out?" My father was trying to be a pal. But that was an intrusion.

SHIRLEY: My parents didn't want to know.

JIM: But they were worried?

SHIRLEY: Yeah. Finally, a couple of years ago, my mother said to me something like, "I hope you aren't. I wish you wouldn't. But if you're going to . . ." And she offered me a pill prescription. It wasn't exactly a jolly go-ahead. No "God bless" or any sign that it was going to lead to joy. It was more like cooperating with a series of dentist's appointments. As for real information about sex, I had a lot of ridiculous ideas. Like about the way the penis works. I thought it was something like a telescope. That it was sort of coldly expanded or shortened at will. (*Laughter.*) And of course I had no idea of dimension—I mean, the long and short of it.

JIM: Are we hung up on genital size?

STEVE: When I was about 13 at camp we used to compare cock sizes.

JIM: Do we pretty much accept the idea it's not the size but what you do with it that counts?

SHIRLEY: I think girls do.

BETTY: The only girls I ever knew who said "Wow, was he ever big" were pretty insecure types.

STEVE: The way I feel is that if you have a big cock it might hurt the girl . . .

SHIRLEY: You think so?

STEVE: But I think it would be good to have a really big cock just for display you know. Like big tits.

BETTY: Oh, that's such a drag!

KEN: Well, the legend about John Dillinger, that he had an enormous prick . . . It's one of the most persistent rumors I ever heard. I heard it in second grade.

JIM: And is it true?

KEN: About Dillinger's cock being on display at the Smithsonian? That it was six feet . . .

STEVE: No, no, two feet!

BETTY: I hear all these experts say it doesn't make any difference—the length—but a married friend of mine who prostitutes on the side said, "Don't try to tell me that!"

STEVE: It's true that blacks have bigger cocks.

KEN: No, that's been scientifically debunked. Absolutely! A team of physiologists went along the west coast of Africa and on up the west coast of Europe measuring cocks and they discovered absolutely no. . . . (*Everyone breaks into laughter and a voice says,* "What an assignment!") Magazines like *Playboy* perpetuate all these myths. *Playboy* views sex as acrobatics. Maybe that's why people read it. When I was at Yale in every dorm there would be one dude who subscribed to *Playboy* and passed it around to everyone.

SHIRLEY: My father reads *Playboy*.
JIM: Don't knock it. There was a great crusade they went all out on. Some cat was arrested on charges of sodomy and they went to bat for him and it took three years but they got him released.
KEN: If we could have a real sexual revolution, *Playboy* would be the first to go broke. *Playboy* exists by titillating us about what most of us can't hope to do. Or don't dare to do.
JIM: That brings us to what you might call big screen sex. You know, you're just an ordinary guy. You've got normal sex connections but you're afraid you might be missing something. So do you go in for pornography, sexy movies, nude parties, maybe an orgy if you get invited?
KEN: I went to a nude party once. It was a bore. It was mostly older married couples. They stripped and started painting each other's bodies.
JIM: Were they actually having sex or just taking off their clothes?
KEN: No, just painting and then taking showers together.
STEVE: I think nude parties are shitty; if people walked around naked there would be much less to it. . . .
KEN: Aw, come on, man, there would be more to it.
STEVE: You think so. I don't.
JIM: Well, nude parties and wife swapping and whatnot are defended by some as a legitimate quest for variety. Some experts say a little infidelity is good for a marriage. I don't dig that myself. If I got bored with my wife I might be unfaithful but I wouldn't think it was good for my marriage. Supposedly, the way to keep from getting bored is to come up with new techniques, new positions for balling. Okay, so we read the *Kama Sutra* and learn how to have intercourse practically standing on our heads. . . .
STEVE: But you can't will a big experience just by trying a new, exotic position.
JIM: Yeah, that's what Masters and Johnson say . . . you can't will ecstasy.
SHIRLEY: Not one-sided, you can't. But two people together can expand their horizons.
STEVE: It's all in how you were brought up. If your par-

ents are balling, you know it even if you're a little kid. By the way your parents act, you know it's good.

JIM: But all of us have seen middle-aged couples—our parents and their friends—and you can sort of look at them and figure out which ones are still balling and which ones have agreed to quit.

KEN: Well, these marriages degenerate into placid agreements. You can tell. They get sort of round-shouldered. Nothing sticks out in front, everything sags. It has nothing to do with age, really. You can see young chicks sagging and trying to hide. You can tell they're nonorgasmic, even though they're 18. Know what I mean?

SHIRLEY: Yeah. And you feel sorry. Want to help?

KEN: Not really.

JIM: Well, we are supposed to be talking about sexual adequacy or inadequacy so let's get down to the basic orgasmic experience. Is our generation doing it better?

KEN: Well, it's a spectrum, you know. You have sexual adequacy ranging from feeling kind of let-down to feeling very good.

SHIRLEY: When I think of sexual inadequacy I think of some guy looking at himself in the mirror and asking himself if Joe next door does it better. . . .

BETTY: I wonder if sex is inadequate the way we're doing it?

KEN: You mean in the act of balling if you feel inadequate? Look, if you feel bad afterwards, let-down rather than exhilarated that's the main complaint of inadequacy. You can feel physiologically satisfied—that you've had an outlet—and still feel depressed afterwards. With masturbation you can relieve sexual tension, maybe more expertly than another person could relieve you because you can time yourself and call all the shots and fantasy what you want—that you're laying some very fabulous woman like Jeanne Moreau or Melina Mercouri and she's telling you how great you are . . . but it's not the same as a reciprocal experience.

JIM: Well, what is a good lay and how do we—in our supposedly uninhibited era—get there?

STEVE: Well, I think the hang-up is egotism. The girl is worrying about whether she is giving the guy a good time. He's worrying whether she thinks he's a competent lover. That's a price our generation has paid, you know. In our parents' generation they played the game of let's pretend—you're my first. My ideal as I grew up was to be able to tell myself, "I really gave her a good lay." Or, "That chick's not gonna forget me for a while." You perform for the projection of your image, not for your pleasure or your relationship to the girl or even really for yourself. You say, "Wow, I balled for 69 innings" but who's going to pin a medal on you?"

JIM: How about prostitutes—can they do it better?

BETTY: It's a big mystique, that whores know how better than other women. The most important thing about sex is not what your body does but what you feel. Any girl can learn how to tighten her vagina, just by buying a book.

KEN: You're right, it's like an acrobatic trip. There are plenty of chicks who are into that, too. Yeah, I guess the traditional red light district is going, gone. The new non-pro's have run them out of business.

SHIRLEY (*angrily*): Go jump in the lake!

BETTY (*coldly*): Look, brother, women are assuming the sexual privileges men have had for centuries but that doesn't make them amateur whores. It means women are putting out for the guys they like and for their own fun. In our generation premarital sex for women is dignified.

KEN: Okay, okay.

JIM: How about homosexuality—dudes, gay power, faggots, dykes?

SHIRLEY: I think we're living with that better than our parents did. We don't shoot homosexuals. And we accept the fact that a lot of people go through homosexual experiences.

KEN: Well, maybe it's all come home to roost. Y'know, western civilization was founded by faggots. Socrates, Plato. That's where all those ancient Greeks were at. And Sappho, who was a dyke.

BETTY: Well, what do you expect? How else could a woman combat all that obnoxious male intellectualism?

JIM: The ancient Greeks indulged in a lot of sex fantasies and of course they did all the ground work in Freudian analysis. Like getting sexually involved with your mother or father, or being tied to a mast so you couldn't get involved with a dangerously sensual dame. Or dispersing your sexual output by knitting or weaving. How about today? Does sexual fantasy play a big role in our lives? Obviously, fantasy leads to masturbation. Do we feel more free to fantasy and masturbate than our parents? You know, Masters and Johnson say that a person who can't masturbate successfully is sexually inadequate, even if she or he is a perfectly functioning heterosexual.

STEVE: You mean you should be able to do it yourself? Or you're no good?

SHIRLEY: Kee-rist!

KEN: Well, I think we're probably fantasying less because we're doing it more. Face it, we're living in a more open society. The chicks are more honest. That's the big thing. A girl that you're balling isn't going to jump up crying, "But I thought you were going to marry me."

SHIRLEY: No, she's more likely to stand up and say "drop dead."

KEN: Sister!

SHIRLEY: I mean it.

STEVE: There's a new double standard, you're right. The biggest problem in sex I'm aware of is the demands chicks are making on men. They're not taking what they can get and saying, "Thank you, sir," like our mothers undoubtedly did. They're demanding their own innings. And if they don't get it from one guy they feel free to say, "Forget it!" and go elsewhere. And since I'm just a male reluctant to give up his self-image as a good swordsman—every male needs this—I want to be able to fuck the shit out of whoever I'm fucking. . . .

BETTY (*pityingly*): You mean you care more about scoring than enjoying?

STEVE: Oh, God!

BETTY (*in earnest*): But don't you realize that if you stayed with one girl for maybe three months you'd find the longer you stayed together the better—there'd be less to bridge and it would be a growing relationship?

KEN: But then you'd have to start all over with each chick. Monogamy is the best answer, it seems.

JIM: Amen.

STEVE: Yeah, if you can get it.

BETTY (*mockingly*): Try harder!

JIM: Well, Masters and Johnson think our early sex experiences occur under such lousy, hurried, guilty circumstances that a sort of imprint is made on our brains and our nervous systems and it's a wonder any of us ever learn to do it right.

KEN: Yeah, that's the great untold secret we're unwilling to tell our parents. Or even ourselves. The fact is, our early experiences at balling were disappointing and humiliating and like any other activity it takes practice. . . .

JIM: And information?

BETTY: Yeah, it helps if one of them knows how. Two green kids, they just blunder around. Like granny and grandpa.

JIM: Or maybe worse. Granny and grandpa might have lived on the farm and helped with the animals. If so, they saw how it worked from an early age. You know, even animals have to be taught, too? A green mare has to be hobbled and tied before she'll receive a stallion. And a green dog who's put on to a bitch in heat—well, the professional breeders stand by and actually hand-manipulate that dog until he gets the idea.

STEVE: No kidding? It sounds perverse.

KEN: Well, we should give it some thought. The sexes shouldn't be so polarized.

BETTY: Maybe sexuality shouldn't be so polarized. Women who are young rarely kiss or touch each other. Unless of course they're lesbians. When they get older they peck cheeks. Men either pump hands or pound each other on the back. It's all an embarrassed renunciation of sensuality.

SHIRLEY: Too bad. Maybe if we spent more time touching each other, breathing on each other, and sort of leaning against each other all these painful sexual hangups would fade away.

JIM: We'd have to change society first. We're all so afraid of committing ourselves. If you pat or kiss or pinch somebody it's not just a pleasant sensual experience. You fly into a panic and think, "What have I done?" And you feel guilty. Then you have to explain it. We still haven't broken the back of Puritanism in this country. We're a nation of people with dirty minds. If you point a finger to the sky, no one will think you're saying that it's going to rain.

KEN: Yeah, there's a whole catalogue of hand gestures that relate to sexy, sensual acts that will get you a punch in the nose almost anywhere. All these acts have got transferred into insults. Too bad.

SHIRLEY: Yeah, sad. The whole picture is still rough. To answer your original question, our generation is bolder and more open but I don't know that we're better off. Maybe we can raise a generation of sexually healthy kids?

KEN: But the point is, man. . . .

SHIRLEY: Woman.

KEN: The point is, woman, what I'm convinced of, there's no end to sex fulfillment. It doesn't have a limit except mortality.

JIM: Maybe not even then. More Paisano, everybody?

(The tape ends.)

PART V

The Cultural Reflex

Impersonal Sex in Public Places

by Laud Humphreys, Ph.D.

EDITORS' NOTE: *Dr. Humphreys, who began his career in the ministry of the Episcopal Church, received his Ph.D. in sociology from Washington University in St. Louis in 1968. He is now assistant professor in sociology at Southern Illinois University in Edwardsville.*

The following article, reprinted from Dr. Humphreys' recent study of homosexuals entitled Tearoom Trade, *is a valuable introduction to the next Masters and Johnson work, scheduled for publication in 1975, which will be a report on their research on homosexuality.*

At shortly after five o'clock on a weekday evening, four men enter a public restroom in the city park. One wears a well-tailored business suit; another wears tennis shoes, shorts and teeshirt; the third man is still clad in the khaki uniform of his filling station; the last, a salesman, has loosened his tie and left his sports coat in the car. What has caused these men to leave the company of other homeward-bound commuters on the freeway? What common interest brings these men, with their divergent backgrounds, to this public facility?

They have come here not for the obvious reason, but in a search for "instant sex." Many men—married and unmarried, those with heterosexual identities and those whose self-image is a homosexual one—seek such impersonal sex, shunning involvement, desiring kicks without commitment. Whatever reasons—social, physiological or psychological—might be postulated for this search, the phenomenon of impersonal sex persists as a widespread but rarely studied form of human interaction.

There are several settings for this type of deviant activity—the balconies of movie theaters, automobiles, behind bushes—but few offer the advantages for these men that public restrooms provide. "Tearooms," as these facilities are called in the language of the homosexual subculture, have several characteristics that make them attractive as locales for sexual encounters without involvement.

The methods employed in this study of men who engage in restroom sex are the outgrowth of three ethical assumptions: First, I do not believe the social scientist should ever ignore or avoid an area of research simply because it is difficult or socially sensitive. Second, he should approach any aspect of human behavior with those means that least distort the observed phenomena. Third, he must protect respondents from harm—regardless of what such protection may cost the researcher.

Because the majority of arrests on homosexual charges in the United States result from encounters in public restrooms, I felt this form of sexual behavior to provide a legitimate, even essential, topic for sociological investigation. In our society the social control forces, not the criminologist, determine what the latter shall study.

Following this decision, the question is one of choosing research methods which permit the investigator to achieve maximum fidelity to the world he is studying. I believe ethnographic methods are the only truly empirical ones for the social scientist. When human behavior is being examined, systematic observation is essential; so I had to become a participant-observer of furtive, felonious acts.

Fortunately, the very fear and suspicion of tearoom participants produces a mechanism that makes such observation possible: a third man (generally one who obtains voyeuristic pleasure from his duties) serves as a lookout, moving back and forth from door to windows. Such a "watchqueen," as he is labeled in the homosexual argot, coughs when a police car stops nearby or when a stranger approaches. He nods affirmatively when he recognizes a man entering as being a "regular." Having been taught the watchqueen role by a cooperating respondent, I played that part faithfully while observing hundreds of acts of fellatio. After developing a systematic observation sheet, I recorded fifty of these encounters (involving 53 sexual acts) in great detail. These records were compared with another 30 made by a cooperating respondent who was himself a sexual participant. The bulk of information presented in *Tearoom Trade* results from these observations.

Although primarily interested in the stigmatized behavior, I also wanted to know about the men who take such risks for a few moments of impersonal sex. I was able to engage a number of participants in conversation outside the restrooms; and, eventually, by revealing the purpose of my study to them, I gained a dozen respondents who contributed hundreds of hours of interview time. This sample I knew to be biased in favor of the more outgoing and better educated of the tearoom population.

To overcome this bias, I cut short a number of my observations of encounters and hurried to my automobile. There, with the help of a tape recorder, I noted a brief description of each participant, his sexual role in the encounter just observed, his license number and a brief description of his car. I varied such records from park to park and to correspond with previously observed changes in volume at various times of the day. This provided me with a time-and-place-representative sample of 134 participants. With attrition, chiefly of those who had changed address or who drove rented cars, and the addition of two persons who walked to the tearooms, I ended up with a sample of 100 men, each of whom I had actually observed engaging in fellatio.

At this stage, my third ethical concern impinged. I already knew that many of my respondents were married and that all were in a highly discreditable position and fearful of discovery. How could I approach these covert deviants for interviews? By passing as deviant, I had observed their sexual behavior without disturbing it. Now, I was faced with interviewing these men (often in the presence of their wives) without destroying them. Fortunately, I held another research job which placed me in the position of preparing the interview schedule for a social health survey of a random selection of male subjects throughout the community. With permission from the survey's directors, I could add my sample to the larger group (thus enhancing their anonymity) and interview them as part of the social health survey.

To overcome the danger of having a subject recognize me as a watchqueen, I changed my hair style, attire and automobile. At the risk of losing more transient respondents, I waited a year between the sample gathering and the interviews, during which time I took notes on their homes and neighborhoods and acquired data on them from the city and county directories.

Having randomized the sample, I completed 50 interviews with tearoom participants and added another 50 interviews from the social health survey sample. The latter control group was matched with the participants on the bases of marital status, race, job classification and area of residence.

This study, then, results from a confluence of strategies: systematic, first-hand observation, in-depth interviews with available respondents, the use of archival data, and structured interviews of a representative sample and a matched control group. At each level of research, I applied those measures which provided maximum protection for research subjects and the truest measurement of persons and behavior observed.

Like most other words in the homosexual vocabulary, the origin of *tearoom* is unknown. British slang has used "tea" to denote "urine." Another British usage is as a verb, meaning "to engage with, encounter, go in against." According to its most precise meaning in the argot, the only "true" tearoom is one that gains a reputation as a place where homosexual encounters occur. Presumably, any restroom could qualify for this distinction, but comparatively few are singled out at any one time. For instance, I have researched a metropolitan area with more than 90 public toilets in its parks, only 20 of which are in regular use as locales for sexual games. Restrooms thus designated join the company of automobiles and bathhouses as places for deviant sexual activity second only to private bedrooms in popularity. During certain seasons of the year—roughly, that period from April through October that midwestern homosexuals call "the hunting season"—tearooms may surpass any other locale of homoerotic enterprise in volume of activity.

Public restrooms are chosen by those who want homoerotic activity without commitment for a number of reasons. They are accessible, easily recognized by the initiate, and provide little public visibility. Tearooms thus offer the advantages of both public and private settings. They are available and recognizable enough to attract a large volume of potential sexual partners, providing an opportunity for rapid action with a variety of men. When added to the relative privacy of these settings, such features enhance the impersonality of the sheltered interaction.

In the first place, tearooms are readily accessible to the male population. They may be located in any sort of public gathering place: department stores, bus stations, libraries, hotels, YMCAs or courthouses. In keeping with the drive-in craze of American society, however, the more popular facilities are those readily accessible to the roadways. The restrooms of public parks and beaches—and more recently the rest stops set at programmed intervals along superhighways—are now attracting the clientele that, in a more pedestrian age, frequented great buildings of the inner cities. My research is focused on the activity that takes place in the restrooms of public parks, not only because (with some seasonal variation) they provide the most action but also because of other factors that make them suitable for sociological study.

There is a great deal of difference in the volumes of homosexual activity that these accommodations shelter. In some, one might wait for months before observing a deviant act (unless solitary masturbation is considered deviant). In others, the volume approaches orgiastic dimensions. One summer afternoon, for instance, I witnessed 20 acts of fellatio in the course of an hour while waiting out a thunderstorm in a tearoom. For one who wishes to participate in (or study) such activity, the primary consideration is finding where the action is.

Occasionally, tips about the more active places may be gained from unexpected sources. Early in my research, I was approached by a man (whom I later surmised to be a park patrolman in plain clothes) while waiting at the window of a tearoom for some patrons to arrive. After finishing his business at the urinal and exchanging some remarks about the weather (it had been raining), the man came abruptly to the point: "Look, fellow, if you're looking for sex, this isn't the place. We're clamping down on this park because of trouble with the niggers. Try the john at the northeast corner of [Reagan] Park. You'll find plenty of action there." He was right. Some of my best observations were made at the spot he recommended. In most cases, however, I could only enter, wait and watch—a method that was costly in both time and gasoline. After surveying a couple of dozen such rooms in this way, however, I became able to identify the more popular tearooms by observing certain physical evidence, the most obvious of which is the location of the facility. During the warm seasons, those restrooms that are isolated from other park facilities, such as administration buildings, shops, tennis courts, playgrounds and picnic areas, are the more popular for deviant activity. The most active tearooms studied were all isolated from recreational areas, cut off by drives or lakes from baseball diamonds and picnic tables.

I have chosen the term "purlieu" (with its ancient meaning of land severed from a royal forest by perambulation) to describe the immediate environs best suited to the tearoom trade. Drives and walks that separate a public toilet from the rest of the park are almost certain guides to deviant sex. The ideal setting for homosexual activity is a tearoom situated on an island of grass, with roads close by on every side. The getaway car is just a few steps away; children are not apt to wander over from the playground; no one can surprise the participants by walking in from the woods or from over a hill; it is not likely that straight people will stop there. According to my observations, the women's side of these buildings is seldom used at all.

What They Want, When They Want It

The availability of facilities they can recognize attracts a great number of men who wish, for whatever reason, to engage in impersonal homoerotic activity. Simple observation is enough to guide these participants, the researcher and, perhaps, the police to active tearooms. It is much more difficult to make an accurate appraisal of the proportion of the male population who engage in such activity over a representative length of time. Even with good sampling procedures, a large staff of assistants would be needed to make the observations necessary for an adequate census of this mobile population. All that may be said with some degree of certainty is that the percentage of the male population who participate in tearoom sex in the United States is somewhat less than the 16 percent of the adult white male population Kinsey found to have "at least as much of the homosexual as the heterosexual in their histories."

Participants assure me that it is not uncommon in tearooms for one man to fellate as many as 10 others in a day. I have personally watched a fellator take on three men in succession in a half hour of observation. One respondent, who has cooperated with the researcher in a number of taped interviews, claims to average three men each day during the busy season.

I have seen some waiting turn for this type of service. Leaving one such scene on a warm September Saturday, I remarked to a man who left close behind me: "Kind of crowded in there, isn't it?" "Hell, yes," he answered, "It's getting so you have to take a number and wait in line in these places!"

There are many who frequent the same facility repeatedly. Men will come to be known as regular, even daily, participants, stopping off at the same tearoom on the way to or from work. One physician in his late fifties was so punctual in his appearance at a particular restroom that I began to look forward to our daily chats. This robust, affable respondent said he had stopped at this tearoom every evening of the week (except Wednesday, his day off) for years "for a blow-job." Another respondent, a salesman whose schedule is flexible, may "make the scene" more than once a day—usually at his favorite men's room. At the time of our formal interview, this man claimed to have had four orgasms in the past twenty-four hours.

According to participants I have interviewed, those who are looking for impersonal sex in tearooms are relatively certain of finding the sort of partner they want. . . .

> You go into the tearoom. You can pick up some really nice things in there. Again, it is a matter of sex real quick; and, if you like this kind, fine—you've got it. You get one and he is done; and, before long, you've got another one.

. . . and when they want it:

Well, I go there; and you can always find someone to suck your cock, morning, noon or night. I know lots of guys who stop by there on their way to work—and all during the day.

It is this sort of volume and variety that keeps the tearooms viable as market places of the one-night-stand variety.

Of the bar crowd in gay (homosexual) society, only a small percentage would be found in park restrooms. But this more overt, gay bar clientele constitutes a minor part of those in any American city who follow a predominantly homosexual pattern. The so-called closet queens and other types of covert deviants make up the vast majority of those who engage in homosexual acts—and these are the persons most attracted to tearoom encounters.

Tearooms are popular, not because they serve as gathering places for homosexuals but because they attract a variety of men, a *minority* of whom are active in the homosexual subculture and a large group of whom have no homosexual self-identity. For various reasons, they do not want to be seen with those who might be identified as such or to become involved with them on a "social" basis.

Sheltering Silence

There is another aspect of the tearoom encounters that is crucial. I refer to the silence of the interaction.

Throughout most homosexual encounters in public restrooms, nothing is spoken. One may spend many hours in these buildings and witness dozens of sexual acts without hearing a word. Of 50 encounters on which I made extensive notes, only in 15 was any word spoken. Two were encounters in which I sought to ease the strain of legitimizing myself as lookout by saying, "You go ahead —I'll watch." Four were whispered remarks between sexual partners, such as, "Not so hard!" or "Thanks." One was an exchange of greetings between friends.

The other eight verbal exchanges were in full voice and more extensive, but they reflected an attendant circumstance that was exceptional. When a group of us were locked in a restroom and attacked by several youths, we spoke for defense and out of fear. This event ruptured the reserve among us and resulted in a series of conversations among those who shared this adventure for several days afterward. Gradually, this sudden unity subsided, and the encounters drifted back into silence.

Barring such unusual events, an occasionally whispered "thanks" at the conclusion of the act constitutes the bulk of even whispered communication. At first, I presumed that speech was avoided for fear of incrimination. The excuse that intentions have been misunderstood is much weaker when those proposals are expressed in words rather than signalled by body movements. As research progressed, however, it became evident that the privacy of silent interaction accomplishes much more than mere defense against exposure to a hostile world. Even when a careful lookout is maintaining the boundaries of an encounter against intrusion, the sexual participants tend to be silent. The mechanism of silence goes beyond satisfying the demand for privacy. Like all other characteristics of the tearoom setting, it serves to guarantee anonymity, to assure the impersonality of the sexual liaison.

Tearoom sex is distinctly less personal than any other form of sexual activity, with the single exception of solitary masturbation. What I mean by "less personal" is simply that there is less emotional and physical involvement in restroom fellatio—less, even, than in the furtive action that takes place in autos and behind bushes. In those instances, at least, there is generally some verbal involvement. Often, in tearoom stalls, the only portions of the players' bodies that touch are the mouth of the insertee and the penis of the insertor; and the mouths of these partners seldom open for speech.

Only a public place, such as a park restroom, could provide the lack of personal involvement in sex that certain men desire. The setting fosters the necessary turnover in participants by its accessibility and visibility to the "right" men. In these public settings, too, there exists a sort of democracy that is endemic to impersonal sex. Men of all racial, social, educational and physical characteristics meet in these places for sexual union. With the lack of involvement, personal preferences tend to be minimized.

If a person is going to entangle his body with another's in bed—or allow his mind to become involved with another mind—he will have certain standards of appearance, cleanliness, personality or age that the prospective partner must meet. Age, looks and other external variables are germane to the sexual action. As the amount of anticipated contact of body and mind in the sex act decreases, so do the standards expected of the partner. As one respondent told me:

> I go to bed with gay people, too. But if I am going to bed with a gay person, I have certain standards that I prefer them to meet. And in the tearooms you don't have to worry about these things—because it is just a purely one-sided affair.

Participants may develop strong attachments to the settings of their adventures in impersonal sex. I have noted more than once that these men seem to acquire stronger sentimental attachments to the buildings in which they meet for sex than to the persons with whom they engage in it. One respondent tells the following story: We had been discussing the relative merits of various facilities, when I asked him: "Do you remember that old tearoom across from the park garage—the one they tore down last winter?"

> Do I ever! That was the greatest place in the park. Do you know what my roommate did last Christmas, after they tore the place down? He took a wreath, sprayed it with black paint, and laid it on top of the snow—right where the corner stall had stood. . . . He was really broken up!

The walls and fixtures of these public facilities are provided by society at large, but much remains for the participants to provide for themselves. Silence in these settings is the product of years of interaction. It is a normative response to the demand for privacy without involvement, a rule that has been developed and taught. Except for solitary masturbation, sex necessitates joint action; but impersonal sex requires that this interaction be as unrevealing as possible.

People Next Door

Tearoom activity attracts a large number of participants—enough to produce the majority of arrests for homosexual offenses in the United States. Now, employing data gained from both formal and informal interviews, we shall consider what these men are like away from the scenes of impersonal sex. "For some people," says Evelyn Hooker, an authority on male homosexuality, "the seeking of sexual contacts with other males is an activity isolated from all other aspects of their lives." Such segregation is apparent with most men who engage in the homosexual activity of public restrooms; but the degree and manner in which "deviant" is isolated from "normal" behavior in their lives will be seen to vary along social dimensions.

For the man who lives next door, the tearoom participant is just another neighbor—and probably a very good one at that. He may make a little more money than the next man and work a little harder for it. It is likely that he will drive a nicer car and maintain a neater yard than do other neighbors in the block. Maybe, like some tearoom regulars, he will work with Boy Scouts in the evenings and spend much of his weekend at the church. It may be more surprising for the outsider to discover that most of these men are married.

Indeed, 54 percent of my research subjects are married and living with their wives. From the data at hand, there is no evidence that these unions are particularly unstable; nor does it appear that any of the wives are aware of their husbands' secret sexual activity. Indeed, the husbands choose public restrooms as sexual settings partly to avoid just such exposure. I see no reason to dispute the claim of a number of tearoom respondents that their preference for a form of concerted action that is fast and impersonal is largely predicated on a desire to protect their family relationships.

Superficial analysis of the data indicates that the maintenance of exemplary marriages—at least in appearance—is very important to the subjects of this study. In answering questions such as "When it comes to making decisions in your household, who generally makes them?" the participants indicate they are more apt to defer to their mates than are those in the control sample. They also indicate that they find it more important to "get along well" with their wives. In the open-ended questions regarding marital relationships, they tend to speak of them in more glowing terms.

Tom and Myra

This handsome couple live in ranch-style suburbia with their two young children. Tom is in his early thirties—an aggressive, muscular and virile-looking male. He works "about 75 hours a week" at his new job as a chemist. "I am *wild* about my job," he says. "I really love it!" Both of Tom's "really close" friends he met at work.

He is a Methodist and Myra a Roman Catholic, but each goes to his or her own church. Although he claims to have broad interests in life, they boil down to "games—sports like touch football or baseball."

When I asked him to tell me something about his family, Tom replied only in terms of their "good fortune" that things are not worse:

> We've been fortunate that a religious problem has not occurred. We're fortunate in having two healthy children. We're fortunate that we decided to leave my last job. Being married has made me more stable.

They have been married for eleven years, and Myra is the older of the two. When asked who makes what kinds of decisions in his family, he said: "She makes most decisions about the family. She keeps the books. But I make the *major* decisions."

Myra does the household work and takes care of the children. Perceiving his main duties as those of "keeping the yard up" and "bringing home the bacon," Tom sees as his wife's only shortcoming "her lack of discipline in organization." He remarked: "She's very attractive . . . has a fair amount of poise. The best thing is that she gets along well and is able to establish close relationships with other women."

Finally, when asked how he thinks his wife feels about him and his behavior in the family, Tom replied: "She'd like to have me around more—would like for me to have a closer relationship with her and the kids." He believes it is "very important" to have the kind of sex life he needs. Reporting that he and Myra have intercourse about twice a month, he feels that his sexual needs are "adequately met" in his relationships with his wife. I also know that, from time to time, Tom has sex in the restrooms of a public park.

As an upwardly mobile man, Tom was added to the sample at a point of transition in his career as a tearoom participant. If Tom is like others who share working class origins, he may have learned of the tearoom as an economical means of achieving orgasm during his navy years. Of late, he has returned to the restrooms for occasional sexual "relief," since his wife, objecting to the use of birth control devices, has limited his conjugal outlets.

Tom still perceives his sexual needs in the symbolic terms of the class in which he was socialized: "about twice a month" is the frequency of intercourse generally reported by working class men; and, although they are reticent in reporting it, they do not perceive this frequency as adequate to meet their sexual needs, which they estimate are about the same as those felt by others of their age. My interviews indicate that such perceptions of sexual drive and satisfaction prevail among respondents of the lower-middle to upper-lower classes, whereas they are uncommon for those of the upper-middle and upper classes. Among the latter, the reported perception is of a much higher frequency of intercourse and they estimate their needs to be greater than those of "most other men."

Aging Crisis

Not only is Tom moving into a social position that may cause him to reinterpret his sexual drive, he is also approaching a point of major crisis in his career as a tearoom participant. At the time when I observed him in an act of fellatio, he played the insertor role. Still relatively young and handsome, Tom finds himself sought out as "trade," i.e., those men who make themselves available for acts of fellatio but who, regarding themselves as "straight," refuse to reciprocate in the sexual act. Not only is that the role he expects to play in the tearoom encounters, it is the role others expect of him.

"I'm not toned up anymore," Tom complains. He is

gaining weight around the middle and losing hair. As he moves past 35, Tom will face the aging crisis of the tearooms. Less and less frequently will he find himself the one sought out in these meetings. Presuming that he has been sufficiently reinforced to continue this form of sexual operation, he will be forced to seek other men. As trade he was not expected to reciprocate, but he will soon be increasingly expected to serve as insertee for those who have first taken that role for him.

In most cases, fellatio is a service performed by an older man upon a younger. In one encounter, for example, a man appearing to be around 40 was observed as insertee with a man in his twenties as insertor. A few minutes later, the man of 40 was being sucked by one in his fifties. Analyzing the estimated ages of the principal partners in 53 observed acts of fellatio, I arrived at these conclusions: the insertee was judged to be older than the insertor in 40 cases; they were approximately the same age in three; and the insertor was the older in 10 instances. The age differences ranged from an insertee estimated to be 25 years older than his partner to an insertee thought to be ten years younger than his insertor.

Strong references to this crisis of aging are found in my interviews with cooperating respondents, one of whom had this to say:

> Well, I started off as the straight young thing. Everyone wanted to suck my cock. I wouldn't have been caught dead with one of the things in my mouth! . . . So, here I am at 40—with grown kids—and the biggest cock-sucker in [the city]!

Similar experiences were expressed, in more reserved language, by another man, some 15 years his senior:

> I suppose I was around 35—or 36—when I started giving out blow jobs. It just got so I couldn't operate any other way in the park johns. I'd still rather have a good blow job any day, but I've gotten so I like it the way it is now.

Perhaps by now there is enough real knowledge abroad to have dispelled the idea that men who engage in homosexual acts may be typed by any consistency of performance in one or another sexual role. Undoubtedly, there are preferences: few persons are so adaptable, their conditioning so undifferentiated, that they fail to exercise choice between various sexual roles and positions. Such preferences, however, are learned, and sexual repertories tend to expand with time and experience. This study of restroom sex indicates that sexual roles within these encounters are far from stable. They are apt to change within an encounter, from one encounter to another, with age, and with the amount of exposure to influences from a sexually deviant subculture.

It is to this last factor that I should like to direct the reader's attention. The degree of contact with a network of friends who share the actor's sexual interests takes a central position in mediating not only his preferences for sex role, but his style of adaptation to—and rationalization of—the deviant activity in which he participates. There are, however, two reasons why I have not classified research subjects in terms of their participation in the homosexual subculture. It is difficult to measure accurately the degree of such involvement; and such subcultural interaction depends upon other social variables, two of which are easily measured.

Family status has a definitive effect on the deviant careers of those whose concern is with controlling information about their sexual behavior. The married man who engages in homosexual activity must be much more cautious about his involvement in the subculture than his single counterpart. As a determinant of life style and sexual activity, marital status is also a determinant of the patterns of deviant adaptation and rationalization. Only those in my sample who were divorced or separated from their wives were difficult to categorize as either married or single. Those who had been married, however, showed a tendency to remain in friendship networks with married men. Three of the four were still limited in freedom by responsibilities for their children. For these reasons, I have included all men who were once married in the "married" categories.

The second determining variable is the relative autonomy of the respondent's occupation. A man is "independently" employed when his job allows him freedom of movement and security from being fired; the most obvious example is self-employment. Occupational "dependence" leaves a man little freedom for engaging in disreputable activity. The sales manager or other executive of a business firm has greater freedom than the salesman or attorney who is employed in the lower echelons of a large industry or by the federal government. The sales representative whose territory is far removed from the home office has greater independence, in terms of information control, than the minister of a local congregation. The majority of those placed in both the married and unmarried categories with *dependent* occupations were employed by large industries or the government.

Median education levels and annual family incomes indicate that those with dependent occupations rank lower on the socio-economic scale. Only in the case of married men, however, is this correlation between social class and occupational autonomy strongly supported by the ratings of these respondents on Warner's Index of Status Characteristics. Nearly all the married men with dependent occupations are of the upper-lower or lower-middle classes, whereas those with independent occupations are of the upper-middle or upper classes. For single men, the social class variable is neither so easily identifiable nor so clearly divided. Nearly all single men in the sample can be classified only as "vaguely middle class."

As occupational autonomy and marital status remain the most important dimensions along which participants may be ranked, we shall consider four general types of tearoom customers: (1) married men with dependent occupations, (2) married men with independent occupations, (3) unmarried men with independent occupations, and (4) unmarried men with dependent occupations. As will become evident with the discussion of each type, I have employed labels from the homosexual argot, along with pseudonyms, to designate each class of participants. This is done not only to facilitate reading but to emphasize that we are describing persons rather than merely "typical" constructs.

Type I: Trade

The first classification, which includes 19 of the participants (38 percent), may be called "Trade," since most would earn that appellation from the gay subculture. All of these men are, or have been, married—one was separated from his wife at the time of interviewing and another was divorced.

Most work as truck drivers, machine operators or clerical workers. There is a member of the armed forces, a carpenter, and the minister of a pentecostal church. Most of their wives work, at least part time, to help raise their median annual family income to $8,000. One in six of these men is black. All are normally masculine in appearance and mannerism. Although 14 have completed high school, there are only three college graduates among them, and five have had less than 12 years of schooling.

George is representative of this largest group of respondents. Born of second-generation German parentage in an ethnic enclave of the midwestern city where he still resides, he was raised as a Lutheran. He feels that his father (like George a truck driver) was quite warm in his relationship with him as a child. His mother he describes as a very nervous, asthmatic woman and thinks that an older sister suffered a nervous breakdown some years ago, although she was never treated for it. Another sister and a brother have evidenced no emotional problems.

At the age of 20 he married a Roman Catholic girl and has since joined her church, although he classifies himself as "lapsed." In the 14 years of their marriage, they have had seven children, one of whom is less than a year old. George doesn't think they should have more children, but his wife objects to using any type of birth control other than the rhythm method. With his wife working part time as a waitress, they have an income of about $5,000.

"How often do you have intercourse with your wife?" I asked. "Not very much the last few years," he replied. "It's up to when she feels like giving it to me—which ain't very often. I never suggest it."

George was cooking hamburgers on an outdoor grill and enjoying a beer as I interviewed him. "Me, I like to come home," he asserted. "I love to take care of the outside of the house. . . . Like to go places with the children—my wife, she doesn't."

With their mother at work, the children were running in and out of the door, revealing a household interior in gross disarray. George stopped to call one of the smaller youngsters out of the street in front of his modest, suburban home. When he resumed his remarks about his wife, there was more feeling in his description:

> My wife doesn't have much outside interest. She doesn't like to go out or take the kids places. But she's an A-1 mother, I'll say that! I guess you'd say she's very nice to get along with—but don't cross her! She gets aggravated with me—I don't know why. . . . Well, you'd have to know my wife. We fight all the time. Anymore, it seems we just don't get along—except when we're apart. Mostly, we argue about the kids. She's afraid of having more. . . . She's afraid to have sex but doesn't believe in birth control. I'd just rather not be around her! I won't suggest having sex anyway—and she just doesn't want it anymore.

While more open than most in his acknowledgement of marital tension, George's appraisal of sexual relations in the marriage is typical of those respondents classified as Trade. In 63 percent of these marriages, the wife, husband or both are Roman Catholic. When answering questions about their sexual lives, a story much like George's emerged: at least since the birth of the last child, conjugal relations have been very rare.

These data suggest that, along with providing an excuse for diminishing intercourse with their wives, the religious teachings to which most of these families adhere may cause the husbands to search for sex in the tearooms. Whatever the causes that turn them unsatisfied from the marriage bed, however, the alternate outlet must be quick, inexpensive and impersonal. Any personal, ongoing affair —any outlet requiring money or hours away from home— would threaten a marriage that is already shaky and jeopardize the most important thing these men possess, their standing as father of their children.

Around the turn of the century, before the vice squads moved in (in their never-ending process of narrowing the behavioral options of those in the lower classes), the Georges of this study would probably have made regular visits to the two-bit bordellos. With a madam watching a clock to limit the time, these cheap whorehouses provided the same sort of fast, impersonal service as today's public restrooms. I find no indication that these men seek homosexual contact as such; rather, they want a form of orgasm-producing action that is less lonely than masturbation and less involving than a love relationship. As the forces of social control deprive them of one outlet, they provide another. The newer form, it should be noted, is more stigmatizing than the previous one—thus giving "proof" to the adage that "the sinful are drawn ever deeper into perversity."

George was quite affable when interviewed on his home territory. A year before, when I first observed him in the tearoom of a park about three miles from his home, he was a far more cautious man. Situated at the window of the restroom, I saw him leave his old station wagon and, looking up and down the street, walk to the facility at a very fast pace. Once inside, he paced nervously from door to window until satisfied that I would serve as an adequate lookout. After playing the insertor role with a man who had waited in the stall farthest from the door, he left quickly, without wiping or washing his hands, and drove away toward the nearest exit from the park. In the tearoom he was a frightened man, engaging in furtive sex. In his own back yard, talking with an observer whom he failed to recognize, he was warm, open and apparently at ease.

Weighing 200 pounds or more, George has a protruding gut and tattoos on both forearms. Although muscular and in his mid-thirties, he would not be described as a handsome person. For him, no doubt, the aging crisis is also an identity crisis. Only with reluctance—and perhaps never—will he turn to the insertee role. The threat of such a role to his masculine self-image is too great. Like others of his class with whom I have had more extensive interviews, George may have learned that sexual game as a teen-age hustler, or else when serving in the army during the Korean war. In either case, his socialization into homosexual experience took place in a masculine world where it is permissible to accept money from a "queer" in return for carefully limited sexual favors. But to use one's own mouth as a substitute for the female organ, or even to express enjoyment of the action, is taboo in the Trade code.

Moreover, for men of George's occupational and marital status, there is no network of friends engaged in tearoom activity to help them adapt to the changes aging will bring.

I found no evidence of friendship networks among respondents of this type, who enter and leave the restrooms alone, avoiding conversation while within. Marginal to both the heterosexual and homosexual worlds, these men shun involvement in any form of gay subculture. Type I participants report fewer friends of any sort than do those of other classes. When asked how many close friends he has, George answered: "None, I haven't got time for that."

It is difficult to interview the Trade without becoming depressed over the hopelessness of their situation. They are almost uniformly lonely and isolated: lacking success in either marriage bed or work, unable to discuss their three best friends (because they don't have three); en route from the din of factories to the clamor of children, they slip off the freeways for a few moments of impersonal sex in a toilet stall.

Such unrewarded existence is reflected in the portrait of another marginal man. A jobless Negro, he earns only contempt and sexual rejection from his working wife in return for baby-sitting duties. The paperback books and magazines scattered about his living room supported his comment that he reads a great deal to relieve boredom. (George seldom reads even the newspaper and has no hobbies to report.) No wonder that he urged me to stay for supper when my interview schedule was finished. "I really wish you'd stay awhile," he said. "I haven't talked to anyone about myself in a hell of a long time!"

Type II: Ambisexuals

A very different picture emerges in the case of Dwight. As sales manager for a small manufacturing concern, he is in a position to hire men who share his sexual and other interests. Not only does he have a business associate or two who share his predilection for tearoom sex, he has been able to stretch chance meetings in the tearoom purlieu into long-lasting friendships. Once, after I had gained his confidence through repeated interviews, I asked him to name all the participants he knew. The names of five other Type II men in my sample were found in the list of nearly two dozen names he gave me.

Dwight, then, has social advantages in the public restrooms as well as in society at large. His annual income of

$16,000 helps in the achievement of these benefits, as does his marriage into a large and distinguished family and his education at a prestigious local college. From his restroom friends Dwight learns which tearooms in the city are popular and where the police are clamping down. He even knows which officers are looking for payoffs and how much they expect to be paid. It is of even greater importance that his attitudes toward—and perceptions of—the tearoom encounters are shaped and reinforced by the friendship network in which he participates.

It has thus been easier for Dwight to meet the changing demands of the aging crisis. He knows others who lost no self-respect when they began "going down" on their sexual partners, and they have helped him learn to enjoy the involvement of oral membranes in impersonal sex. As Tom, too, moves into this class of participants, he can be expected to learn how to rationalize the switch in sexual roles necessitated by the loss of youthful good looks. He will cease thinking of the insertee role as threatening to his masculinity. His socialization into the Ambisexuals will make the orgasm but one of a number of kicks.

Three-fourths of the married participants with independent occupations were observed, at one time or another, participating as insertees in fellatio, compared to only one-third of the Trade. Not only do the Type II participants tend to switch roles with greater facility, they seem inclined to search beyond the tearooms for more exotic forms of sexual experience. Dwight, along with others in his class, expresses a liking for anal intercourse (both as insertee and insertor), for group activity, and even for mild forms of sadomasochistic sex. A friend of his once invited me to an "orgy" he had planned in an apartment he maintains for sexual purposes. Another friend, a social and commercial leader of the community, told me that he enjoys having men urinate in his mouth between acts of fellatio.

Dwight is in his early forties and has two sons in high school. The school-bound offspring provide him with an excuse to leave his wife at home during frequent business trips across the country. Maintaining a list of gay contacts, Dwight is able to engage wholeheartedly in the life of the homosexual subculture in other cities—the sort of involvement he is careful to avoid at home. In the parks or over cocktails, he amuses his friends with lengthy accounts of these adventures.

Dwight recounts his first sexual relationship with another boy at the age of "nine or ten":

> My parents always sent me off to camp in the summer, and it was there that I had my sexual initiation. This sort of thing usually took the form of rolling around in a bunk together and ended in our jacking each other off.... I suppose I started pretty early. God, I was almost in college before I had my first woman! I always had some other guy on the string in prep school —some real romances there! But I made up for lost time with the girls during my college years.... During that time, I only slipped back into my old habits a couple of times—and then it was a once-only occurrence with a roommate after we had been drinking.

Culminating an active heterosexual life at the university, Dwight married the girl he had impregnated. He reports having intercourse three or four times a week with her throughout their 18 married years but also admits to supplementing that activity on occasion: "I had the seven-year-itch and stepped out on her quite a bit then." Dwight also visits the tearooms almost daily:

> I guess you might say I'm pretty highly sexed [he chuckled a little], but I really don't think that's why I go to tearooms. That's really not sex. Sex is something I have with my wife in bed. It's not as if I were committing adultery by getting my rocks off—or going down on some guy—in a tearoom. I get a kick out of it. Some of my friends go out for handball. I'd rather cruise the park. Does that sound perverse to you?

Dwight's openness in dealing with the more sensitive areas of his biography was typical of upper-middle and upper-class respondents of both the participant and control samples. Actual refusals of interviews came almost entirely from lower-class participants; more of the cooperating respondents were of the upper socioeconomic ranks. In the same vein, working-class respondents were most cautious about answering questions pertaining to their income and their social and political views.

Other researchers have encountered a similar response differential along class lines, and I realize that my educational and social characteristics encourage rapport with Dwight more than with George. It may also be assumed that sympathy with survey research increases with education. Two-thirds of the married participants with occupational independence are college graduates.

It has been suggested, however, that another factor may be operative in this instance: although the upper-class deviants may have more to lose from exposure (in the sense that the mighty have farther to fall), they also have more means at their disposal with which to protect their moral histories. Some need only tap their spending money to pay off a member of the vice squad. In other instances, social contacts with police commissioners or newspaper publishers make it possible to squelch either record or publicity of an arrest. One respondent has made substantial contributions to a police charity fund, while another hired private detectives to track down a blackmailer. Not least in their capacity to cover for errors in judgment is the fact that their word has the backing of economic and social influence. Evidence must be strong to prosecute a man who can hire the best attorneys. Lower-class men are rightfully more suspicious, for they have fewer resources with which to defend themselves if exposed.

This does not mean that Type II participants are immune to the risks of the game but simply that they are bidding from strength. To them, the risks of arrest, exposure, blackmail, or physical assault contribute to the excitement quotient. It is not unusual for them to speak of cruising as an adventure, in contrast with the Trade, who engage in a furtive search for sexual relief. On the whole, then, the action of Type II respondents is apt to be somewhat bolder and their search for "kicks" less inhibited than that of most other types of participants.

Dwight is not fleeing from an unhappy home life or sexless marriage to the encounters in the parks. He expresses great devotion to his wife and children: "They're my whole life," he exclaims. All evidence indicates that, as father, citizen, businessman and church member,

Dwight's behavior patterns—as viewed by his peers—are exemplary.

Five of the 12 participants in Dwight's class are members of the Episcopal church. Dwight is one of two who were raised in that church, although he is not as active a churchman as some who became Episcopalians later in life. In spite of his infrequent attendance to worship, he feels his church is "just right" for him and needs no changing. Its tradition and ceremony are intellectually and esthetically pleasing to him. Its liberal outlook on questions of morality round out a religious orientation that he finds generally supportive.

In an interview witnessed by a friend he had brought to meet me, Dwight discussed his relationship with his parents: "Father ignored me. He just never said anything to me. I don't think he ever knew I existed." [His father was an attorney, esteemed beyond the city of Dwight's birth, who died while his only son was yet in his teens.] "I hope I'm a better father to my boys than he was to me," Dwight added.

"But his mother is a remarkable woman," the friend interjected, "really one of the most fabulous women I've met! Dwight took me back to meet her—years ago, when we were lovers of a sort. I still look forward to her visits."

"She's remarkable just to have put up with me." Dwight added:

> Just to give you an idea, one vacation I brought another boy home from school with me. She walked into the bedroom one morning and caught us bareassed in a 69 position. She just excused herself and backed out of the room. Later, when we were alone, she just looked at me—over the edge of her glasses—and said: "I'm not going to lecture you, dear, but I do hope you don't swallow that stuff!"

Although he has never had a nervous breakdown, Dwight takes "an occasional antidepressant" because of his "moodiness." "I'm really quite moody, and I go to the tearooms more often when my spirits are low." While his periods of depression may result in increased tearoom activity, his deviant behavior does not seem to produce much tension in his life:

I don't feel guilty about my little sexual games in the park. I'm not some sort of sick queer. . . . You might think I live two lives; but, if I do, I don't feel split in two by them.

Unlike the Trade, Type II participants recognize their homosexual activity as indicative of their own psychosexual orientations. They think of themselves as bisexual or ambisexual and have intellectualized their deviant tendencies in terms of the pseudopsychology of the popular press. They speak often of the great men of history, as well as of certain movie stars and others of contemporary fame, who are also "AC/DC." Irving Goffman has remarked that stigmatized American "tend to live in a literarily defined world." This is nowhere truer than of the subculturally oriented participants of this study. Not only do they read a great deal about homosexuality, they discuss it within their network of friends. For the Dwights there is subcultural support that enables them to integrate their deviance with the remainder of their lives, while maintaining control over the information that could discredit their whole being. For these reasons they look upon the gaming encounters in the parks as enjoyable experiences.

Type III: Gay Guys

Like the Ambisexuals, unmarried respondents with independent occupations are locked into a strong subculture, a community that provides them with knowledge about the tearooms and reinforcement in their particular brand of deviant activity. This open participation in the gay community distinguishes these single men from the larger group of unmarrieds with dependent occupations. These men take the homosexual role of our society, and are thus the most truly "gay" of all participant types. Except for Tim, who was recruited as a decoy in the tearooms by the vice squad of a police department, Type III participants learned the strategies of the tearooms through friends already experienced in this branch of the sexual market.

Typical of this group is Ricky, a twenty-four-year-old university student whose older male lover supports him. Ricky stands at the median age of his type, who range from nineteen to fifty years. Half of them are college graduates and all but one other are at least part-time students, a characteristic that explains their low median income of $3,000. Because Ricky's lover is a good provider, he is comfortably situated in a midtown apartment, a more pleasant residence than most of his friends enjoy.

Ricky is a thin, good-looking young man with certain movements and manners of speech that might be termed effeminate. He is careful of his appearance, dresses well, and keeps an immaculate apartment, furnished with an expensive stereo and some tasteful antique pieces. Seated on a sofa in the midst of the things his lover has provided for their mutual comfort, Ricky is impressively self-assured. He is proud to say that he has found, at least for the time being, what all those participants in his category claim to seek: a "permanent" love relationship.

Having met his lover in a park, Ricky returns there only when his mate is on a business trip or their relationship is strained. Then Ricky becomes, as he puts it, "horny," and he goes to the park to study, cruise and engage in tearoom sex:

> The bars are o.k.—but a little too public for a "married" man like me. . . . Tearooms are just another kind of action, and they do quite well when nothing better is available.

Like other Type III respondents, he shows little preference in sexual roles. "It depends on the other guy," Ricky says, "and whether I like his looks or not. Some men I'd crawl across the street on my knees for—others I wouldn't piss on!" His aging crisis will be shared with all others in the gay world. It will take the nightmarish form of waning attractiveness and the search for a permanent lover to fill his later years, but it will have no direct relationship with the tearoom roles. Because of his socialization in the homosexual society, taking the insertee role is neither traumatic for him nor related to aging.

Ricky's life revolves around his sexual deviance in a way that is not true of George or even of Dwight. Most of his friends and social contacts are connected with the homosexual subculture. His attitudes toward and rationalization of his sexual behavior are largely gained from this wide circle of friends. The gay men claim to have more close friends than do any other type of control or participant respondents. As frequency of orgasm is reported, this class also has more sex than any other group sampled, averaging 2.5 acts per week. They seem relatively satisfied with this aspect of their lives and regard their sexual drive as normal —although Ricky perceives his sexual needs as less than most.

One of his tearoom friends has recently married a woman, but Ricky has no intention of following his example. Another of his type, asked about marriage, said: "I prefer men, but I would make a good *wife* for the right *man*."

The vocabulary of heterosexual marriage is commonly used by those of Ricky's type. They speak of "marrying" the men they love and want to "settle down in a nice home." In a surprising number of cases, they take their lovers "home to meet mother." This act, like the exchange of "pinky rings," is intended to provide social strength to the lovers' union.

Three of the seven persons of this type were adopted— Ricky at the age of six months. Ricky told me that his adoptive father, who died three years before our interview, was "very warm and loving. He worked hard for a living, and we moved a lot." He is still close to his adoptive mother, who knows of his sexual deviance and treats his lover "like an older son."

Ricky hopes to be a writer, an occupation that would "allow me the freedom to be myself. I have a religion [Unitarian] which allows me freedom, and I want a career which will do the same." This, again, is typical: all three of the Unitarians in the sample are Type III men, although none was raised in that faith; and their jobs are uniformly of the sort to which their sexual activity, if exposed, would present little threat.

Although these men correspond most closely to society's homosexual stereotype, they are least representative of the tearoom population, constituting only 14 percent of the participant sample. More than any other type, the Rickys seem at ease with their behavior in the sexual market, and their scarcity in the tearooms is indicative of this. They want personal sex—more permanent relationships—and the public restrooms are not where this is to be found.

That any of them patronize the tearooms at all is the result of incidental factors: they fear that open cruising in the more common homosexual market places of the baths and bars might disrupt a current love affair; or they drop in at a tearoom while waiting for a friend at one of the "watering places" where homosexuals congregate in the parks. They find the anonymity of the tearooms suitable for their purposes, but not inviting enough to provide the primary setting for sexual activity.

Type IV: Closet Queens

Another dozen of the fifty participants interviewed may be classified as single deviants with dependent occupations, "closet queens" in homosexual slang. Again, the label may be applied to others who keep their deviance hidden, whether married or single, but the covert, unmarried men are most apt to earn this appellation. With them, we have moved full circle in our classifications, for they parallel the Trade in a number of ways:

1. They have few friends, only a minority of whom are involved in tearoom activity.
2. They tend to play the insertor role, at least until they confront the crisis of aging.
3. Half of them are Roman Catholic in religion.
4. Their median annual income is $6,000; and they work as teachers, postmen, salesmen, clerks—usually for large corporations or agencies.
5. Most of them have completed only high school, although there are a few exceptionally well-educated men in this group.
6. One in six is black.
7. Not only are they afraid of becoming involved in other forms of the sexual market, they share with the Trade a relatively furtive involvement in the tearoom encounters.

Arnold will be used as the typical case. Only 22, Arnold is well below the median age of this group; but in most other respects he is quite representative, particularly in regard to the psychological problems common to Type IV.

A routine interview with Arnold stretched to nearly three hours in the suburban apartment he shares with another single man. Currently employed as a hospital attendant, he has had trouble with job stability, usually because he finds the job unsatisfactory. He frequently is unoccupied.

ARNOLD:

I hang around the park a lot when I don't have anything else to do. I guess I've always known about the tearooms ... so I just started going in there to get my rocks off. But I haven't gone since I caught my lover there in September. You get in the habit of going; but I don't think I'll start in again—unless I get too desperate.

INTERVIEWER:

Do you make the bar scene?

ARNOLD:

Very seldom. My roommate and I go out together once in a while, but everybody there seems to think we're lovers. So I don't really operate in the bars. I really don't like gay people. They can be so damned bitchy! I really like women better than men —except for sex. There's a lot of the female in me, and I feel more comfortable with women than with men. I understand women and like to be with them. I'm really very close to my mother. The reason I don't live at home is because there are too many brothers and sisters living there. . . .

INTERVIEWER:

Is she still a devout Roman Catholic?

ARNOLD:

Well, yes and no. She still goes to Mass some, but she and I go to seances together with a friend. I am studying astrology and talk it over with her quite a bit. I also analyze handwriting and read a lot about numerology. Mother knows I am gay and doesn't seem to mind. I don't think she really believes it though.

Arnold has a health problem: "heart attacks," which the doctor says are psychological and which take the form of "palpitations, dizziness, chest pain, shortness of breath and extreme weakness." These attacks, which began soon after his father's death from a coronary two years ago, make him feel as if he were "dying and turning cold." Tranquilizers were prescribed for him, "but I threw them out, because I don't like to become dependent on such things." He quoted a book on mental control of health that drugs are "unnecessary, if you have proper control."

He also connects these health problems with his resentment of his father, who was mentally ill:

ARNOLD:
> I don't understand his mental illness and have always blamed him for it. You might say that I have a father complex and, along with that, a security complex. Guess that's why I always run around with older men.

INTERVIEWER:
> Were any of your brothers gay?

ARNOLD:
> Not that I know of. I used to have sex with the brother closest to my age when we were little kids. But he's married now, and I don't think he is gay at all. It's just that most of the kids I ran around with always jacked each other off or screwed each other in the ass. I just seemed to grow up with it. I can't remember a time when I didn't find men attractive. . . . I used to have terrible crushes on my gym teachers, but nothing sexual ever came of it. I just worshipped them, and wanted to be around them all the time. I had coitus with a woman when I was 16—she was 22. After it was over, she asked me what I thought of it. I told her I would rather masturbate. Boy, was she pissed off! I've always liked older men. If they are under 30, I just couldn't be less interested. . . . Nearly all my lovers have been between 30 and 50. The trouble is that *they* always want sex—and sex isn't really what I want. I just want to be with them—to have them for friends. I guess it's part of my father complex. I just want to be loved by an older man.

Few of the Type IV participants share Arnold's preference for older men, although they report poorer childhood relationships with their fathers than do those of any other group. As is the case with Arnold's roommate, many closet queens seem to prefer teen-age boys as sexual objects. This is one of the features that distinguishes them from all other participant types. Although scarce in tearooms, teenagers make themselves available for sexual activity in other places frequented by closet queens. A number of these men regularly cruise the streets where boys thumb rides each afternoon when school is over. One closet queen from my sample has been arrested for luring boys in their early teens to his home.

Interaction between these men and the youths they seek frequently results in the sort of scandal feared by the gay community. Newspaper reports of molestations usually contain clues of the closet queen style of adaptation on the part of such offenders. Those respondents whose lives had been threatened by teen-age toughs were generally of this type. One of the standard rules governing one-night-stand operations cautions against becoming involved with such "chicken." The frequent violation of this rule by closet queens may contribute to their general disrepute among the bar set of the homosexual subculture, where "closet queen" is a pejorative term.

Sexual Patterns in Three Ethnic Subcultures of an American Underclass

by Bernard Rosenberg, Ph.D. and Joseph Bensman, Ph.D.

EDITORS' NOTE: *Dr. Rosenberg is a professor of sociology at the City College of New York and guest professor at the New School for Social Research. He is coauthor of* Mass Culture: The Popular Arts in America. *Dr. Bensman is also a professor of sociology at the City College of New York and is coauthor of* Small Town in a Mass Society *and author of* Dollars and Sense.

Dr. Rosenberg and Dr. Bensman, in their intensive survey of how poverty-stricken young people in American ghettos encounter sex tell us among other things that dominant Western ideas about love and sex have little relevance for them. Sexual fulfillment is experienced merely as a physical release; sexual conquest is the dominating force in most male-female encounters and the female, as trophy, becomes a nonobject whose human or sexual needs do not matter. The poor's information about sex is minimal—whatever these people know comes from hygiene classes at school. Pregnancy out of wedlock is a common occurrence and early marriage ensues with resignation.

The groups studied consisted of white Appalachians living in Chicago, Blacks in Washington, D.C., and Puerto Ricans in New York. The article is reprinted from The Annals of the American Academy of Politics and Social Science.

No American who wishes to discuss love and sex can avoid the long Western tradition from within which we, knowingly or unknowingly, come by all our perspectives. Jerusalem, Athens, Rome, and their several sequelae constitute, or symbolize, that tradition. From it, that is to say, from the Hellenic and Judaeo-Christian past, Western man derives not only certain prescriptions and prohibitions; but a whole framework of ideas, concepts, and theories that are his heavy cultural burden. Diffusion and dilution notwithstanding, the sexual analyst and those he discusses share that burden. To be sure, neither need recognize or acknowledge the connection that binds them together in an inescapable matrix.

We have come to our present sexual pass through devious and tangled paths, still strewn with innumerable laws, parables, images, aftereffects, and reflections. In this brief statement, we can do no more than touch upon a few highlights which may illuminate part of our rich and varied background.

For example, the poems of Sappho and those of Ovid, like a score of other such sources—including philosophical schools, and religious cults—have in common that they celebrate erotic joy. All of them say to us that love (as in the story of Ruth) and sex (as in the mythopoeic figure of Priapus) should involve deep feeling or great pleasure. This notion is currently fashionable among many otherwise disenchanted, proudly "rational," and highly sophisticated people. At the same time, they are affected by those provisions of the Decalogue, as interpreted by Talmudic and Scholastic commentators, that set severe limits upon love and sexuality while emphasizing the responsibilities inherent in sacramental and indissoluble relationships whose purpose is solely reproductive.

With *eros* and *agapé*, Plato spiritualized sex. St. Augustine, and, later on, many of the Schoolmen who introduced Aristotelian modifications, took over these Platonic ideas. In various guises, they became essential to both the Catholic and Protestant world view. The Christian churches also fashioned sexual codes of their own which, even when they were systematically violated, produced discrete and historically specialized sexual behavior. In Europe and America, sexual renunciation, with deep intellectual and religious roots, always seems to have had an obverse side, or to have proceeded in dialectical sequence to eroticism. Thus, to condemn the pleasures of the flesh may itself entail, or simply lead to, precisely those pleasures. The medieval denial of sex was in no way incompatible with chivalry and romantic love as practiced at the courts of Aquitaine and Provence. Here, if anything, as Denis de Rougemont has shown, are the beginnings of a romantic conception made universally familiar in our time by way of Hollywood films. Dante and Beatrice, Tristan and Iseult, Romeo and Juliet are prototypic cases in which sexual desire feeds upon the loved one's permanent inaccessibility.

Seventeenth-century Puritanism and nineteenth-century Victorianism, each in its complex and contradictory manner, left us with a dualistic dogma whose force is not yet fully spent. Mind and body (therefore, love and sex) were pitted against each other. As the underside of Victorian life is subjected to increasing exposure, one beholds not only the sexually etherealized woman of virtue, but her fallen sister, whether given to prostitution or not, who is cynically and mercilessly exploited. As hitherto unpublishable memoirs reach the contemporary reader, he comes to know the moralistic upper-class gentleman who collects pornography, indulges in exotic, probably inverted and polymorphous, perverse sexual tastes while practicing hypocrisy, if not perfecting it to a high art.

Victorianism and the revolt against it are our immediate antecedents. And that revolt is largely ideological. The exaltation of eroticism tends to be academic. Proponents of "sexual freedom" contrast it favorably with artificial and hypocritical Victorian conventions. Beginning with feminism as a political movement, proceeding in the 1920s under banners like companionate or trial marriage, through a strident call for emancipation and liberation, to the present "sexual revolution," learned men have set forth their ideas. Hedonists and rationalists, champions of homosexuality, of a return to infantile gratification with "love's body" and no mere fixation on genital pleasure: here is a peculiar gamut from Bertrand Russell to Albert Ellis, Herbert Marcuse, and Norman O. Brown. None of them, the logician, the psychotherapist, the Hegelian, or the Classical scholar, is primarily interested in the restoration of "natural" sexuality. All of them are passionately interested in proving or disproving theories.

Even Sigmund Freud, who did more than anyone else to free Western thought from the straightjacket of Victorianism, was himself a puritan—in perhaps the best Biblican sense of the term. Furthermore, Freud, in his sexual speculations and investigations, drew heavily upon Greek philosophy, specifically the ideas of *agapé, eros,* and *caritas.* Freud's "scientific" attitude toward sex is actually permeated with several of the oldest concepts of antiquity—with which they are perfectly continuous. Insofar as Freudian psychology fuels the sexual revolution, it is directed not at the demolition of Western norms, but only at one narrow version of a complicated social heritage.

Like speech, dress, manners, and a score of other visible stigmata, conduct in the sexual sphere has always been class-bound. To speak of the mores dominant in any period is necessarily to be elliptical. For example, the Victorian double standard was, in its own time, mainly an upper-middle-class phenomenon, rarely affecting higher and lower social strata. Similarly, the revolt against it seems to have liberated segments of the middle class at least from the idea of sexual repression. For some time now, as Theodore Dreiser noted over and over in his early novels, the relatively stable blue-collar working class has best exemplified puritanical prudery and sexual hypocrisy.

All the while, romantic writers, artists, and social scientists have been searching for "genuine" or "natural" sexuality, embodied in an eroticized and newly ennobled savage, uncontaminated by that odious sophistication which reduces the physical expression of love to *le contact de deux épidermes.* Thus occurs the idealization of peasants, "earthmen," primitives, those sexually spontaneous and unalienated humans who—when viewed from a safe distance—look so free and easy in all their ways. Are there such groups of people within the underclass of our own society? Does their alleged culture of poverty so far remove them from Western civilization that research in their midst will reveal what love and sex are really like when they are emancipated from history and intellectuality?

The Three Ethnic Subcultures

These are some of the questions implicit in the material that follows.* Three miserably, and more or less equally, impoverished areas in New York, Chicago, and Washington, D.C., were selected for prolonged study. Lander and his associates held poverty constant and introduced ethnicity as the variable. They concentrated on all the inhabitants of one social block (with dwellings that face each other) in each of the three cities. In New York, most of the subjects were Puerto Ricans, in Chicago, Appalachian whites, and in Washington, Negroes. Intensive nondirected "tandem interviews" (with two interviewers and one respondent) yielded the qualitative data about adolescent youth that we cite and sift in our analysis.

All three of these ethnic groups are composed largely of recent migrants, who had come to the urban centers from other parts of the United States (including Puerto Rico), and who had brought with them many of their ways of life, perhaps even accentuated by contrast with their new environment and their new neighbors.

A common culture presupposes that those who belong to it speak the same language. There is such a language for all Americans as there is an overarching culture that unifies urban dwellers and farmers, the young and the old, the privileged and the underprivileged. Subcultural segmentation produces "special languages" within the larger linguistic community, and they are intelligible only to initiates, that is, members of ethnic, occupational, regional, and religious groups. That the broadly conceptualized culture (or subculture) of poverty is somewhat illusory can be demonstrated by the variegated speech patterns characteristic of poor Appalachian whites, Negroes, and Puerto Ricans. Indeed, for each of our populations, it would be possible to assemble a glossary of terms widely used by insiders but meaningless to most outsiders. How luxuriant local variation takes place (in meaning, accent, and value)

---

*This essay stems from a much larger study conceived and directed by Bernard Lander under multiple sponsorship, including the President's Committee on Juvenile Delinquency and Youth Crime, Notre Dame University, and the Lavanburg Corner House Foundation.

is the proper subject matter of a highly technical discipline called ethnolinguistics. It is not our intention to turn that discipline loose on data gathered for other purposes. Nevertheless, this much must be said: each group living in its own slum moves toward a certain linguistic homogeneity, bringing ancestral speech ways, borrowing symbols from the larger society, and synthesizing them into distinctive configurations. Peculiarities of speech are a rough index of differential association and cultural isolation. Unique idioms emerge from intense in-group living, and disappear at the opposite pole of full acculturation. In between, we find a complex mixture reflecting uneven exposure to the wider institutional order, which is itself in constant flux. A few illustrations from the heterosexual sphere may be in order.

Chicago

In our sample, the adolescent males among the New York Puerto Ricans and Washington Negroes are unresponsive to questions about dating. The word does not appear in their lexicon, and, as it turns out, this fact points to a substantive difference in behavior between these boys and those in Chicago. Every respondent among the Chicago Appalachian whites knows what a date is. One at first defines it as "goin' out with a fox," then adds, "You just go out driving, make some love, catch a crib—and that's all." Here, indeed, are the cadences, the inflections, and the semantics of a special language in which "fox" means girl and "crib" stands for house or apartment, which, in turn, signifies a trysting place that one "catches" along with the "fox." Such expressions may have their origin in the hill country of Kentucky and Alabama, whence they were transplanted to the Midwest and, merged with much else, produced a dynamic amalgam that cannot be duplicated elsewhere.

There are fuzzy edges around every word that is variously defined not only at different levels of the social hierarchy, but within any one level. For those who generalize in the grand manner, dating is understood to be "an American" phenomenon; the more sophisticated family sociologists (who prepare textbooks for college students) see it as a peculiar ritual, a courtship pattern, practiced by middle-class youth in the United States. In our samplings of the underclass, only the poor white teen-agers date, and they do so in ways similar to and dissimilar from those of their middle-class counterparts. The telephone, for instance, plays no great part in their activities, as it does among more privileged adolescents, but the automobile is central. Neither matters much with Puerto Ricans and Negroes.

The Chicago boys, who will sometimes commit crimes to get a car, and need it to commit other crimes, and whose vocabulary is rich with the knowledge they have of car parts, may be said to live in a car complex. This circumstance provides them with a degree of physical mobility far greater than that of any other economically deprived group we have studied. In a crisis, occasioned, say, by the impregnation of a girl friend (scarcely a rare occurrence), they can always take to the road, ranging widely over Illinois and adjacent states. The automobile liberates them, up to a point, not only from their constricted neighborhood, but from the metropolis itself. And, given the car, they are able to date girls in a more or less conventional manner. The "portable bedroom" can be used for preliminary sex play most conveniently at drive-in movies, where two or three couples commonly occupy one car. Asked what he usually does on a date, a 15-year-old Chicago boy replies, in part:

> If your friend's got a girl he's taking to the drive-in, you take her with him. And you take your girl to the show, go out to eat, dance, stuff like that.

On the average, what does a date cost?

> Well, if you go to a show, you won't have to spend but about, at the most, five, maybe six dollars. . . . If you go to the drive-in, you spend a dollar and a half for each one to get in. That's three dollars. Give the kid who's driving the car a buck, split the gas bill, you know, help to pay for some of the gas—and you eat. Oh, it costs you about six dollars.

Bowling and roller-skating are other diversions deemed to be suitable on dates in our Chicago sample. Neither is a popular boy-girl pastime in the other cities—where boys like sports that they play with other boys. Pick-ups are made on the street from a car, in neighborhood movie houses, and in teen-age bars which are frequented with great regularity only by the Appalachians.

All of this sounds a great deal like the textbook account, even to a general preference for double-dating. Yet, the reasons behind that preference gives us a clue to something different, and specific to the Chicago group, namely, that a heavy streak of violence is woven into the texture of their heterosexual behavior. Hence: "I like to go out with other couples because it's better when you travel together. When you're alone, there's always other guys trying to start trouble." You date, but you appear alone with a girl at your own peril, as this little vignette makes clear:

> I saw her walking down the hall with another boy, and I got pretty jealous. I started saying, "If you like that guy so much, go ahead and go out with him," and he walked up and started smartin' off to me. So I hit him, and then I beat him up. She turned around and slapped me. She called me a brute or something. . . . So that didn't hit me just right, and I said, "Forget it."

If a date culminates in sexual intercourse, it is also useful to have someone else along:

> I was going with a girl. She was 16. She squealed on me, and they tried to get me on statutory rape. And, oh, she gave 'em a big long story, trying to get me into a lot of trouble. But there was another kid along with me on that date. And she claimed that he held her down and that I held her down. But this boy's stories matched and hers didn't. Otherwise, I would have been sunk.

With dating, there go the lineaments of a rating-dating complex, which does not precisely parallel Willard Waller's famous description of a widespread campus phenomenon, but does imply a measure of respect for the girls one dates, by contrast with the disrespect accorded girls and older women who are nothing but sexual objects. The following example is somewhat extreme but highly indicative:

> I consider a girl you go out with and a girl you have intercourse with two different kinds of girls. There's a girl I date. I like to hold hands with her and make out with her, kiss her, but that's as far as I want to go with any girl I take out. If I like the girl, I don't want to mess her up. But then, there is the other girls I just don't care about because they give it to the other guys—which means they don't care too much for theirselves.

The type of boy who makes this provisionally puritanical division between good girls (with lovers who hold back from final consummation) and bad girls who "give it to the other guys," is yet capable of treating "good girls" with even greater harshness. This double standard means that there are separate norms; less is expected of the promiscuous girl, much more of the girl you date who may, after all, become your wife. If so, unquestioning submission to male authority is expected:

> What if you married a girl who talked back to you? What would you do?
> Shut her up.
> How?
> Well, I'd fix her where she wasn't able to talk too much.

The specter of violence is omnipresent. It may issue from association with either type of girl, and although there are always two types, criteria for establishing them vary. (Asked whether he still considers girls decent if they go to bed with him, a Chicago boy answers, "It's a matter of how hard I have to work. If I have to work real hard I think a lot of them. If they give it to me right off I think they're pigs.") Infidelity in a girl friend will ordinarily provoke a physical assault of some sort. What to do if the woman you marry is unfaithful? "Beat the shit out of her" is the semiautomatic response.

Acts of aggression connected with sex are, no doubt,

intensified by heavy consumption of alcohol. Sex, liquor, and violence form a *Gestalt* in Chicago not nearly so discernible in New York or Washington. In another context, whiskey and beer act as a catalyst for serious fighting, possibly with recourse to knives and firearms. In the sexual context, alcohol is also believed to be useful as a means of emboldening the boy and rendering the girl more compliant to his advances:

> Do the girls get pretty wild when they've had a few drinks?
> Yes.
> Do most of the guys try to get the girls loaded?
> Yes.
> How often are you successful?
> We're not very successful at getting them loaded. I mean that takes a little money.

Beer is cheaper than whiskey and favored for that reason; a low alcohol content notwithstanding, it is believed to serve the purpose. Girls plied with beer are considered "better," that is, more available, than those who remain unlubricated. They can more easily be "cut"—which is typical and revealing Chicago argot for the sex act.

New York City

In the New York sample, there is no "cutting." The first few interviews with Puerto Rican youth revealed little about sex, a topic concerning which we had not anticipated that there would be unusual reticence. The breakdown in communication turned out to be no more than terminological. Once in possession of key words and phrases, the interviewers encountered no serious resistance to the free discussion of plain and fancy sex. There are taboo topics, notably religion as it shades off into magic, but sex is not one of them. The linguistic breakthrough occurred in this matter when a resident observer advised us to ask about "scheming." We did so, causing faces to light up that had remained blank as long as we struggled vainly to find the right conventional or unconventional sexual expression. "Scheming" was that expression. Equivalent, in a way, to "cutting" which suggests sex-and-sadism, "scheming" has mildly conspiratorial overtones. It stands for kissing, necking, petting, and full sexual consummation, everything from prepubertal exploration to real coitus, which is secret, exploitative, and pleasurable, but seldom brutal. With appropriate language, much information can be elicited, and comic misunderstandings are left behind. (To the question, "Did you ever have a girl sexually?" the young Puerto Rican respondent answers by asking, "Did I ever have a girl *sectionally?*" And some minutes are consumed, to no avail, in disentangling the adverbs. We want to know from another boy whether he goes to bed with girls, whether he sleeps with them, and he takes us literally: "No. I sleep by myself, in my own bed.")

Scheming is initiated at parties, and parties are called sets. They function as substitutes for going out, picking up, and dating. Young people at or around twenty may have apartments of their own which, like any of many vacant apartments on the block, can be used for sets, as they can be and are used for private or collective sexual adventures. At sets, boys and girls meet, play records, dance, drink beer or whiskey more or less moderately, smoke cigarettes and take pot more or less immoderately, and, under dim colored lights, engage in uninhibited foreplay. With twenty or more in attendance, sets seem to be fairly large affairs, and while some are organized during the week by hedonistic truants, there are sure to be others around the clock on week-ends. Since the youngsters use stimulants and depressants that are costly, and Saturday is the traditional day for pilfering small objects whose sale produces money with which to buy supplies, the best sets are most likely to occur on Saturday nights. You drink a little, you smoke a lot, you are high, a girl offers to dance with you, and by and by, when the dim lights go out altogether, you fondle her. Presently, you step outside with your girl and scheme in the hallway, at her place if no one is at home, on a rooftop—this one, or another at the nearby housing project. And:

> If you got a really good friend, and the girl is willing if she's really bad off or somethin', you know what she will do? *She'll pull the train.*
>
> Pull the train?
>
> Yes, that's what we call it: pulling the train. You

take one chance. Then another guy takes a chance. You know.

Usually, how many guys are there?

Two.

Not like 10 guys with one girl?

Oh, depends like on what kind of a girl. . . . I been in a situation with about six guys.

"Pulling the train" is by no means an everyday occurrence. Sets are. They may be regarded as a spontaneous expression of youth culture, an informal device contrived by teen-agers for their own pleasure, a technique for circumventing official and established organizations, an escape from uplift sponsored by benevolent adults. Sets provide an arena—or constitute a preparation—for scheming, which, in most cases, means private and secret sexual activity. Boys do boast, with a probable admixture of phantasy and exaggeration, about sexual conquests, but they are loath to name names and thus cause "trouble" for themselves or their girl friends. The set in which they begin to participate at about age fifteen is understood to be somewhat illicit. It may become a pot party or a sex party (our respondents are ambivalent and divided among themselves about which they like best)—and either one, if publicized, can lead to unpleasant sanctions.

Washington, D. C.

Boy-girl relations in the Washington poor Negro community are neither as car- and show-centered as in the Chicago white group nor as party-centered as in the New York Puerto Rican group. In Washington, the school, despite all its deficiencies, is much more pivotal than we would have supposed. Young people attend school dances now and then, meet classmates formally and informally, and, while ungoverned by any particular protocol, they begin to "go out" with one another. Soon there is sex play, and, in many cases, real sexual involvement. Things tend to begin in school, and there, too, the "facts of life" are transmitted most frequently and most effectively. Only in our Washington Negro sample do high school children use technical (now and then garbled) scientific terms for the sex act and the sex organs. They describe human reproduction as it has been explained to them by their biology teachers:

> We had it in school. I know how the sperms come down, when a boy is having sex relations with a girl; they meet the egg, go up through the vagina, stay in the womb and grow month after month. And then after a period of time, the woman have a baby.
>
> We're supposed to do that next half, after we finish with music (find out where babies come from and things like that).
>
> Well, I know the process of starting—I mean, you have to have two unions, I mean a fusion of, uh, male and female, between the two organs. I mean the vulva and the, um, penis. The vulva and the penis. And, um, it takes a union of sperm and meeting with the egg. And after that, I know the situation of—what do you call it?—the embry—yeah, embry—and that's the first stage of the child. . . . And the food which the child receives comes from the navel of the mother. It's connected to the child, I believe mouth-to-navel, something like that. And after a nine month period, the child's supposed to be born.

A boy whose parents told him "all about it" at age 12, says:

> They explained it to me, that it was the entrance of the penis into the woman's vulva. I mean, they used other terms, but that's the terms I would use because, let's say, I'm more up on it now, on this education.

Again:

> Well, uh, let's see, when the sperm, I think goes into the vagina, something like that, then, it meets the other sperm I think, and it starts doing something.

However imperfectly they may have absorbed their biology lessons, these teen-agers show a degree of sophistication unavailable to their counterparts among the New

York Puerto Ricans and in Chicago, where sexual knowledge is more likely to be associated with the street—and its earthy language—than with the classroom. (With the Puerto Ricans, a self-taught, semi-demi-social worker has helpfully taken it upon himself to provide some sex instruction in yet another linguistic style—largely Spanish, partly English argot.) For children to seek or parents to offer information, even when it is urgently needed, seems to be a rare occurrence. (We suspect that parent-youth embarrassment on this score is a class phenomenon. There is reason to believe that the middle-class parent now speaks freely to his children about the facts of life while evading questions about the facts of death.) The young mother of two illegitimate children in Washington tells us that she developed early: "At the age of 12 I was as developed as any girl of 14 or 15. Being young, I never paid too much attention to it, but older people in the community noticed." As she recounts it, men got fresh; some began to follow her home, and she took to making "smart" remarks. Then, after a while, "I had one man run me home from school." She ran and found sanctuary on a neighbor's porch, and "the man started to come after me till he looked up and spotted a lady and another man on the porch. After that my mother came over, and we told her about it, and the three of them walked around, but they didn't see him." This incident was but the first of several, including one "proposition" from a preacher, about which the mother was informed. She still divulged nothing to her daughter, and the daughter observes, "I just could not bring myself to look up at my mother and ask her what was happening."

The whole story, "the nitty gritty," came from experience with "fellows," who, however, were judged to be stupid, as well as girls on the street and an older sister. From her own account, but never officially, she was a sexual delinquent by age 13.

On the other hand, in Washington, a Negro boy may experience sexual initiation under his father's auspices. If there is an older woman who wishes to "come some," that is, who wishes to have a sex partner, the father sometimes encourages his son to cooperate. We have one such case on record:

She (the older woman) came down to see my sister, and she started liking me. She started paying my way to the movies and all that. So my father told me to go on and do it. So I did. . . . He say, "I know you going to do it when I ain't around." So he gave me a protector, and I go on and do it. . . . He say we were going to do it behind his back anyhow, and that he just wanted to help me along. I ain't never used the protection, though.

Attitude Comparisons

Although he tends to confuse protection against venereal disease with protection against pregnancy, the Negro teenager is generally more knowledgeable about this, too, than his Puerto Rican or poor white age mate. He more often recognizes and applies terms like contraceptive, diaphragm, coil, prophylactic, or rubber—for one reason, because he more often knows what they mean. Not that he or his girl friend is much inclined to use any of these objects, for their interposition threatens the individual with loss of his "cool"—an important but amorphous quality which must be maintained at all times. Although among all three ethnic samples, only a minority favor contraception, the Negro youth understand best, and Puerto Rican youth least, just what it is that they habitually decline to use. And, while amorality or *anomie* tends to prevail in sexual matters, it assumes a degree of egocentricity among the poor white boys unequalled elsewhere. In this exchange, we have an extreme but not atypical expression of the Chicago attitude:

Do you ever use contraceptives?
Nope.
How about women? Do they ever use anything?
Nope.
Do you ever think about it?
Nope.
Are you afraid of what might happen?
Nope. *They can't touch me. I'm under age.*

Seeing it exclusively from his own standpoint, and then only insofar as his conduct may lead to legal jeopardy, he is not afraid of making girls pregnant. Later on, when he does come of age, in order to avoid possible charges of statutory rape, such a boy will prefer sexual relations with older women. Even then, this respondent insists, he "ain't gonna use anything." Told by the interviewer about diaphragms and how they work, he vehemently protests against their use. They would interfere with his pleasure: "Might get in my way." To be sure, without contraception, it is possible to spawn an illegitimate child, something he at first claims to have done at least once—before second thoughts cause him to cast doubt on the "mother's" veracity. This is his complete verbatim statement on the matter:

> She told me were gonna have a kid. I said, "Tough." She said, "Ain't it though?" I said, "What you gonna do about it?" She said, "I ain't gonna do nothin' about it. How about you?" I said "Nothin'." She said, "That's good." I said goodbye and she said goodbye. And that's the last I saw of her. I mean I *saw* her in school. She's still goin' to school. I don't believe that we had a kid, though. She just said we did.

Risk or no risk, boys are generally hostile to the idea of prophylaxis. One objection is phrased purely in terms of the pleasure principle, most colorfully by a Chicago boy who explains why he never uses anything like a rubber, "I tried it once. It's like riding a horse with a saddle instead of bareback." Is he afraid of "knocking a girl up?" Answer: "Sure. *I worry about it afterwards. I guess I'm lucky so far. That's all.*" The cost factor appears again in Chicago where the poor-white boys are markedly more reluctant than the Negroes and Puerto Ricans in Washington and New York, respectively, to spend money on contraceptive frills. At the climactic moment, their impecuniosity can be frustrating. As a rule, in the white population, girls are no more eager than boys to insure against pregnancy, but once in awhile they are:

> Oh, I've used them a couple of times. Like one time, a broad got all worried, and she told us to lay off. . . . We had her pants off and everything. She ask me if I didn't have some rubbers. Uh-uh. "Get

off." I had to wait a little longer. I didn't have any money either.

In the Chicago underclass, there is, then, a minimum of anxiety about the consequences of sexual intercourse, a strong disinclination to take any responsibility for what happens. Most boys are poorly informed and unconcerned about measures taken or not taken by their sex partners. "I wouldn't know if they did or not [use anything to prevent pregnancy]. I don't care if they do or not." Does he know what girls might do to protect themselves? "Well, there's with the hot water, like that. Then, there's, they press on their stomachs someplace . . . on some cords, usually when you get done, the girl has to go to the bathroom. She goes in, she presses here and there, and it all comes out. They claim that's one of the best ways." Ignorance of the facts should not be discounted, but knowledge may or may not be correlative with action. Even if a girl asks for restraint, so that she will not have to cope with unwed motherhood, the boy is likely to refuse:

> Do many girls ask you to stop before you come?
> Most don't. Some do.
> They don't want to get pregnant?
> That's right.
> Do you usually oblige them?
> Well, not usually, no.

Biologists like Ashley-Montagu have established the existence of adolescent sterility, a period after the onset of puberty during which reproduction presumably cannot take place. Widespread premarital sexual experimentation, not always related to courtship, among "primitive peoples" to whom puritanism is unknown, has been noted for over a century. Adolescent sterility helps anthropologists to account for the smoothness with which such relations occur. In ever larger sectors of our own society, birth control has "sterilized" teen-agers, thereby insuring them against the many complications of illegitimacy. Neither of these mechanisms seems to be significantly operative in any of our cities. Adolescent *fertility* is high, and respondents (males only slightly more so than females) express a very nearly uniform distaste for every kind of contraceptive device. Significant differences are, in the first instance, more attitudinal than behavioral. How much responsibility does a boy who has got his girl with child feel? Some in the Puerto Ricans and Negroes of New York and Washington; virtually none in the whites of Chicago. That unimpeded sexual contact can and does lead to babies is something a transplanted Appalachian white boy is likely to know only too well. For the most part, he "couldn't care less"; the interviewer asks such a boy: "What's stopping you from knocking up girls?" Answer: "Nothin'. I've got four kids, maybe five. Two here in Chicago, two in Wisconsin, and when I left Wisconsin, I heard there was one more." Does he support any of them? "Shit no." After getting a girl pregnant, "I just take off."

Less able to "take off," as careless but more likely to be "trapped," hemmed in on every side, the New York Puerto Rican boy generally finds insemination of his girl friends a worrisome matter. It is seldom a question of direct responsibility to the "victim"—which would presuppose a kind of socialization or internalization of standards evident neither among "good boys" nor among "bad boys." What if the girl has a baby? "Maybe the parents might make him marry her." Coercion under these circumstances into unwanted matrimony is a nightmare in the New York group to the like of which no one in Chicago ever alludes. We pursue the issue one step farther: "Suppose they didn't make you. Would you marry her anyhow?" The response is a derisive, "Nah!" But then we want to know whether he would support the baby, and to this the answer is a subculturally typical *yes*. Even if, in order to do so, he would have to quit school (and this respondent values school)? Yes, even so, although, "that would be pretty bad."

The qualitative difference we wish to point up is more than a matter of nuance. Lloyd Warner and his associates were able to rank people, whom they interviewed in Yankee City, by class-typed responses to interview questions. We, in turn, can situate boys and girls (and could do so "blind," that is, without any accompanying data) in one of three impoverished subcultures, by their responses to a variety of straightforward, nondirective, and projective questions. Thus, a Puerto Rican boy who presents a tougher "front" than the one just quoted above is still unmistakably a Puerto Rican, and not an Appalachian or Negro boy:

> Do you try to avoid getting a girl pregnant or don't you care?
> I try to avoid it.
> Suppose you did, and she found out where you lived?
> I'd have to marry the broad.
> Would you like that?
> No, that's a hell of a mess.

The less insouciant type, a boy, for instance, whose presentation of self is somewhat gentler, simply says of the hypothetical girl he has impregnated: "You've got to marry her," leaving implicit why you have got to.

Since precautions to avert childbirth are unpopular, and pregnancy takes place willy-nilly, abortions should be common. If so, boys in Chicago tend to feel that it is no business of theirs. How different is the attitude that emerges in New York where, to select one of many examples, an advanced adolescent remarks apropos a girl friend who might get pregnant, "If I liked the girl enough I would marry her, or something." Suppose he didn't like her all that much, would he still feel obligated? "Yeah." In what way, we wonder. Would he arrange for an abortion? "No. That would mess her up too much. ... Cause some ladies, they just do it to get money out of it; they don't really do it to help a person at all." Nonmedical abortionists, charging about 80 dollars a job, are said to abound on the street. Nevertheless, the white boys recoil from availing themselves of these services, obviously not for financial reasons, which are important in Chicago, since the stated alternative, assuming marital or nonmarital responsibility for support, would be so much costlier than disposition of an undesired fetus.

The differential warmth, involvement, and concern for "the other" in sexual affairs, while significant, should not be exaggerated. It is nonetheless present whatever tack we take. The myth of *machismo*, incorporating an alleged need for constant dramatic assertions of masculinity, notwithstanding, our Puerto Rican teen-age boys do not preen themselves on their virility. Most of them accept the code which prohibits tattling "to other guys about girls they have schemed with." Some do engage in invidious talk about "street girls" whose well-known promiscuity makes it impossible to take pride in having "scored" with them. Similarly, the reaction to betrayal is a mild one. Violent assault on a girl may occur if she is suspected of having squealed to the police about stealing or fighting—not so about sexual defections. When they occur, New York boys say, "I walk away," "I tell her not to do that again," "I call it quits." The gorge does not rise very high, one's manhood is not called into question, and violence flares up but rarely. Likewise, the readiness to spare a girl friend undue embarrassment—or to share it with her by prematurely shouldering the parental responsibility—is quite exceptional. Commenting on the large number of unmarried girls with babies that boys refuse to support, a respondent explains, "Maybe one guy has her, then another, and then another. She doesn't know who the father is." Then what? "The last guy gets the blame." And getting the blame, more often than not, seems to mean accepting the blame, which, in turn (age permitting), means marriage. In this realm, as elsewhere, *fatalismo* apparently counts for more than *machismo*.

Sexual experience, which begins early and mounts in frequency, if not intensity, should not be equated with sexual sophistication. Indeed, the manifest naïveté is sometimes monumental. So:

> How do you avoid getting girls pregnant? (Long pause) I don't really know.
> Nobody ever told you about that?
> Nobody ever told me.
> Well, how do you keep the girl from having a baby?
> I guess you kill the baby.
> Do you know about killing babies?
> I don't know, but . . .
> Is that what they do around the block?
> If they gonna kill the babies, they gonna kill theirself.
> So you never heard about protection? Like a rubber?
> What did you say? Girdle? Maybe that's the only way. I know a girl lives in my neighborhood. She had

a baby, but you couldn't tell, and after a while they
found out she had a girdle on. But she still had a baby.
I don't really know how you could stop it. The only
way, I suppose, is wearing a girdle.

Another boy reports making a girl pregnant, but there
was no baby, "because she took it out." How he does not
know or will not say. Yet another, asked what he would
do if he got his girl friend pregnant, replies, "There's
nothing I could do," and, for lack of options, lets it go
at that.

Early marriage ensues, in a spirit best described as
resignation. This "solution" becomes all the more irrational whenever the boys protest, as they do with great
vehemence, that it is the one thing that they wish, above
all, to avoid. They speak of no marriage or late marriage,
drawing the lesson of delay and circumvention from their
own experience in unsatisfactory family relations. And,
pointing to others all around them, they declaim against
too many people marrying too soon, having too many
children. It is on this basis that they diagnose most of
their own trouble and most of the ills that others encounter
in a slum environment. It all starts, they say, when a
young man fathers a child he does not want—whose conception he will do nothing to prevent. Here, indeed, for
one part of the underclass is the way of all flesh: fully
aware of the danger, our young man tumbles headlong
into it, doing exactly what he had sworn not to do, classically entering a scene he had resolved to sidestep, with
some, no doubt, unconscious propulsion into a trap he
professes to abhor.

A finer distinction must be made among Appalachians
in Chicago. There, group-affiliated males show a consistent
unwillingness to marry, holding out for very long, while,
among the unaffiliated, there is a noticeably higher incidence of early marriage. When it takes place, males tend
to be several years older than females, even if both are
still in their teens. In the majority of cases, delay is secured through reinforcement of a powerful male peer
group that seemingly functions much like the one analyzed
by William Foote Whyte in *Street Corner Society*. It is
the opinion of two long-time resident observers in Chicago
that "most of the males find it impossible to maintain

regular and satisfying experiences with a girl and quickly withdraw their attention and return to the male peer group." They also indicate that despite a well-nigh-universal claim to early sexual experience, many of the male youths admit to prolonged periods of disengagement both from heterosexual activity and coed sociability. Much of the sexual play that does take place involves a group of boys who exploit one or two females, many of them "young runaways" or disillusioned young wives, viewed as "easy scores" for all. After a week or so of intensified sexuality with one such female, she usually disappears. Then the males resume their involuntary celibacy. Later, they embark once again on the same cycle. All of this is absolutely affectless.

Appalachian girls in Chicago stress early marriage as a female adjustment. They hope for husbands who "won't be unfaithful," "won't drink," "will be nice," and "will work hard." Demographic findings and intimate observation make it clear that, personal preference apart, a girl often marries the first young male adult with whom she has a steady relationship. Our resident observers also tell us that their "noncodified observations yield another interesting pattern of marital relationship in the next older group," which they feel may have a bearing on "the essentially brittle relations of the teen-agers." During our study, a number of marriages have been observed to dissolve into a peculiar pattern of realignment, such that: Male A, aged 35, establishes a liaison with Female X, his own age or older; wife of A establishes a liaison with unmarried Male B, aged 25 or 30 or with a formerly married male, aged 25 to 30 who, in turn, has separated from his younger wife. Consequently, for the second marriage, or for sexual adventures after a first marriage, the male is ordinarily younger than the female. We find, in short, that parallel to the traditional form (older husband, younger wife), there is a deviant form that leaves separated, divorced, and unfaithful women with younger husbands and lovers. There is a certain distinctiveness in this duality.

Cultural Values Compared

We suspected at the outset of our inquiry that the rhetoric and the activity of impoverished American subcultures would be far removed from traditional Western ideas of love and sex. They are. Middle-class standards, in all their present disarray, carry those ideas (or reactions against them) in a confusing mélange that can only bewilder young people who are their residuary legatees. Not so in the underclass, where, with all its diversity, these ideas appear—if at all—only in mutilated form.

With a mixture of envy and indignation, middle-class people often impute pure sensual pleasure to their social inferiors, who are thought to pursue this objective heedlessly, if not monomaniacally. There is no warrant for this judgment. Puerto Rican youth in New York seem, somewhat more than the other groups, to stress sensual pleasure, but even they are manifestly more interested in *collective* fun, in "the set" itself, than in pure hedonism. All the same, insofar as "scheming" is an act of rebellion against authority, it does not much differ from taking pot or ingesting alcohol. In any class, youthful manifestations of defiance are a tacit acknowledgement of that coercive culture which some choose to resist. On the face of it, a Puerto Rican boy willing to "accept the responsibility" of marriage to, or help for, the girl he has impregnated, responds in accordance with one element of the Western Catholic tradition. For him, heterosexual dalliance imposes an obligation, but only if "the worst should happen," and then only when he is actuated by a sense of fatality rather than by love or duty. Chance has dealt him a heavy blow, rendered him powerless to fight back, left him a plaything of mysterious forces, destroyed his capacity to act as a free agent.

That culturally induced responsibility for one's sex acts cannot be taken for granted is clear enough in the other two groups, whose members refuse to do what the New York Puerto Rican boy feels that he must do. In this milieu, a residue of the declining tradition may still be observed. Not so in the Washington and Chicago samples of Negroes and Appalachian whites.

Given time, any group encapsulated in a constricted

ghetto can be severed, not just from the mainstream of a larger culture but from its ancestral subculture as well. The unique circumstances of isolation and contact, impoverishment and opportunity, continuity and rupture with the past, will produce new codes, new standards, new articulations, and new behavior patterns. The Appalachian whites and the Washington Negroes are in most ways slightly less "Westernized" (that is, made into middle-class people) than Puerto Rican youth in New York. All, however, have rural, but by no means identical, origins. And all have moved into hideous urban ghettos where, to varying degrees, they are shut off from the major values of Western society. For people from the Southern hill country or the Southern plantation, lack of contact with outsiders is an old story. Urbanization, even in ghettos, reduces their isolation. The Appalachian white may have been culturally on his own since the pre-Revolutionary settlement of this country. For lower-class Negroes, isolation may have begun with the capture of their ancestors in Africa, and continued through Southern slavery to Northern segregation. The Negro subclass has had practically no exposure to Western sexual ideals, and the Appalachian white's exposure occurred so long ago that its effects are virtually inoperative.

For these submerged peoples, our dominant sexual ideologies have little relevance. Neither emotional and material responsibilities, nor their opposite, pure joy in unrestrained sexuality, is much in evidence. Sexual fulfillment is experienced merely as a physical release—the "friction of two membranes"—in which the female is the necessary but unequal partner. Otherwise, sexual conquest provides a trophy calculated to enhance one's prestige in peer-group competition. Masculinity is affirmed as part of a game whose competitors must incessantly prove themselves before an audience of others engaged in the same pastime. Since it is a competitive game, the boy who plays cannot expect to earn points for scoring over an easy mark, a "pig." Victory consists in overcoming the largest possible number of inaccessible girls. The conversion of females into trophies reduces them to nonpersons. Their personal, sexual, or simply human, needs do not matter. They exist to be tricked, deceived, manipulated—and abandoned. Skill in all these techniques is a sign of stylistic virtuosity. For a boy to abuse his sexual partner in many ingenious ways makes him a big winner. To all this, the lush rhetoric and varied responses elicited from our interviews are ample testimony. Customary allusions to Western concepts of love and sex are "foreign" to people who cannot express them verbally or in terms of their actual conduct. They are historically and personally alienated from the amorous and sexual context that Western idealism, with all its twists and turns, has to offer. That condition, for which no single urban ghetto is a carbon copy, can only deepen as subcultural segregation runs its course.

Investigation of ethnic underclass sexual mores in our own society, while it points to important differences, certainly does not provide us with examples of "natural," spontaneous, unrepressed, and nonneurotic sensual pleasure. Sexual practices are indissolubly linked to nonsexual aspects of life-style. For this reason, it would in any case be impossible to transfer the really illusory freedom of slum sex codes to an academic and bureaucratic world. If in that world, "intellectualized," "artificial," and "abstract" standards prevail, they cannot be banished by sexual personalism. No more than primitive or peasant society do subcultures of poverty offer us solutions to our sexual dilemma.

On Sexual Apathy in the Male

by Ralph R. Greenson, M.D.

EDITORS' NOTE: *Dr. Greenson is clinical professor of psychiatry at the University of California, Los Angeles School of Medicine and Scientific Director of the Foundation for Research in Beverly Hills, California. The following article, reprinted from the professional publication,* California Medicine, *details Dr. Greenson's observations about growing male indifference to sexual intercourse. He believes it is caused by newly aggressive women, by over-concern with health, by eating too much rich food, by making too much money, by a preference for alcohol to sex.*

This presentation was prompted by clinical findings in the private practice of psychiatry and psychoanalysis that indicate men and women have changed in their sexual behavior and responses in the last 25 years. It is my definite impression that, in general, women are becoming sexually more assertive and demanding, and men are more indifferent and lethargic. Before World War II, the term "frigidity" was used exclusively in regard to women. Today I find far more men who display sexual coldness or disinterest. This is not only true for the chronologically mature and the middle-aged but it appears to be equally valid for the youth of this "cool" generation. There are other changes in sexual behavior, but I shall limit this communication to a description of some typical forms of sexual apathy and will attempt to explain some of the underlying causes.

I do not claim that my findings are statistically valid, but I have confirmed my own observations with many colleagues who practice psychoanalysis or psychiatry or who have made pertinent observations as gynecologists, urologists and general practitioners.

I propose to use the term *sexual apathy* to refer to behavior which indicates a conscious indifference, disinterest, unconcern and coldness toward sexual intercourse. I underline the fact that this is a conscious phenomenon because it is a well known fact that people may react and behave as if they had no sexual appetite but on closer scrutiny will be found to have hidden and distorted manifestations of libido. I prefer the term *apathy* to *frigidity* because it is broader in scope and avoids the feminine connotation associated with frigidity in the past.

The different categories I have selected for discussion are neither precise nor systematic. I chose to emphasize certain easily recognizable large groups.

Sexual boredom in middle age. Men and women of 45 to 55 years of age and married some 20 to 25 years tend to find sex boring and uninteresting, a chore and an obligation. It is not rare to find men who use sexual intercourse with their wives primarily as a means of getting rid of unpleasant sexual tension, a guilt-free form of masturbation. In the past, women who had given up any hope of sexual pleasure would submit to this procedure passively in order to "relieve" the husband.

Today I find the situation changed, at least in the middle and upper economic and educational classes. The middle-aged woman of today, who has experienced sexual satisfaction in the early years of marriage, expects—in fact, it would be more precise to say, *demands*—sexual gratification. Even in the past, the middle-aged woman was far less apathetic about sex than the middle-aged man, a point which has been confirmed by the works of Kinsey,[4,5] Masters and Johnson.[6]

It would seem that the freedom from the fear of pregnancy, which the menopause brings, adds to the middle-aged woman's sexual assertiveness. There are other factors involved in this change, some of which I shall discuss later. At this point, I wish to focus on the sexual apathy of the middle-aged man.

There are many factors which contribute to the male's disinclination toward sex in middle age. After 25 years of marriage, his sexual practices (in marriage) tend to become stereotyped and routinized. There are no more surprises or improvisations. Actually, he has stopped allowing himself to fantasy or to act upon his imaginings in the sexual situation. At age 45, the male has more or less achieved his full professional and economic status. If he is successful he is concerned about maintaining his masculine "image." If he is a failure, he is loath to reveal any further defects in his virility. As a consequence of his insecurity about his masculinity, the middle-aged American male is inhibited in giving full rein to his sexual fantasies, because libidinal fantasies in general tend to have an infantile cast. A rich sexual life depends on one's freedom to enact with another person the different sensual longings which arise spontaneously in the sexual situation. The sexually healthy male and female enjoy one another's sexual infantilisms in the foreplay of the sexual act. Frightened people become inhibited and try to play it safe by following a set pattern. The resultant rigidities and routines make for sex without passion, which is boring.

Another complicating circumstance is the typical middle-aged man's notion that at this time of life his body has to be preserved from any undue stress and strain. He may play 36 holes of golf at his country club and cards afterwards, but at night, in bed with his wife, he is apt to feel sex is too strenuous and depleting. It is not rare to find men who act in bed as though the sexual act is a dangerous obligation they contracted for when they were young and foolhardy. They are more interested in preserving their body than their marriage. Sexual relations have become for them merely a biological need, a gonadal exercise, and no longer an intimate emotional experience. They want sex to be performed as a service, with little active participation on their part.

One of the typical clinical manifestations of sexual frustration in middle age is the prevalence of somatic dysfunctions on a psychological basis.

Ever since Freud,[2] we have become increasingly aware of the human propensity to become fixated to, or to regress to, earlier forerunners of the drive for sexual intercourse. I am sure all physicians are familiar with the man who is a passionate collector of various possessions and who is correspondingly disinterested in sex. The obese patient has obviously sexualized eating and de-sexualized love-making.

The drinker has substituted the quest for the drunken stupor in place of orgasm. The swallowers of tranquilizers have replaced the dull haze and partial oblivion of the drug for the fantasy life required by a good sex life. In all these patients there is a regression in the direction of anality, orality and narcissism and a turning away from human relations, love and sex.

In this group one should include those patients who have displaced their conflicts about sex into somatic channels and who develop physical problems on a psychological basis. The specific organ system afflicted often reveals the psychological fixation point. Thus, disorders of the stomach and small intestine point in the direction of oral fixations, while illnesses of the lower bowel may indicate anal regression. All these patients are more or less apathetic about sex and use their somatic symptoms as a rationalization for avoiding sexual relations as well as a hidden substitute satisfaction. It is important for the physician to recognize that "prescribing" sexual intercourse will not correct these disorders. Also, careful medical evaluation is important in each case. The finding of pathological psychodynamics does not rule out other etiological factors.

The sexuality of the "cool" generation. I believe it is important to interpolate at this point that the designation "cool" generation does not apply with equal validity to all the youth. I find it helpful to distinguish the cool "cools" from the warm "cools." The cool "cools" are best exemplified by the "beatniks," the removed, isolated and withdrawn individuals who refuse to become involved and committed to anything or anyone which has its roots in the past. Home, family, country, tradition, convention and ideals are all abhorred. They do relate to their fellow "cools," but even then it is limited to the group as a whole and individual relations are marginal and tangential.

The warm "cools" also have a rebellious attitude toward most values of the past but they do become passionately involved in causes. They have been called "Vietniks" to distinguish them from the beatniks. They protest vociferously against the war in Viet Nam, they are intensely involved in the civil rights movement, they march in Selma, riot against the police on the Berkeley campus. The warm "cools" do become emotionally involved with individuals as well as groups, and although they do bear some similarity to the cool "cools," they also resemble the youth of the time before World War II.

It is a striking fact that most of the youth today are much more open about their sexual practices than they used to be. Teen-agers in the middle and upper classes think nothing of displaying quite intimate forms of necking and petting in the presence of their parents, something which was unheard of 30 years ago. It is worth noting that the young parents of this generation are willing, if not eager, to watch. In both boys and girls, sexual intimacy often precedes romantic love.[9] They get to know each other sexually before they become close emotionally or intellectually. This development is more pronounced in girls because in the past it was the female who required the feeling of being loved before she was able to respond sexually. In the past, it was the unpopular girl who used her sexuality for bait as a means of competing with the more attractive rivals. Today, even the most attractive and popular girls indulge in a variety of sexual practices with little emotional involvement.

This public sexuality does not lead to real sexual satisfaction, but on the contrary, indicates some degree of orgastic impotence. Quick and easy bodily intimacy and familiarity make for promiscuity and "organ pleasures," but not for a rich sensual experience. A confirmation of this hypothesis, I believe, is to be found in the frequent use of LSD and marijuana by the youth. They use drugs in a vain attempt to bring color to their relatively colorless lives. The drabness stems from the emotional thinness of their interpersonal relations.

There seem to be several etiological factors responsible for these developments. On the one hand, the parents of the cool generation want their children to be popular, to be "in"; and the parents, too, want to be popular with the younger generation. Modern parents dread to say no to their offspring. They feel every deprivation might be a trauma—a word they use without real understanding. They also cannot bear to arouse the youngsters' anger. They want peace of mind, even if it causes peace-of-mindlessness. Clinical experience has demonstrated that people who cannot cope with the different varieties of hate, anger and resentment, will also have trouble with the different forms of love.

Insecure parents often need to alleviate their own anxiety by using the social success of their children. Young parents of today often push their children to "date" prematurely and, as a consequence, the youngster is emotionally unprepared for this experience. I believe one of the reasons the young males and females of today wear their hair alike and dress alike stems from their fear of the opposite sex. The boy and girl of today seek a twin, not a sweetheart or a lover. They are only secure with someone who resembles themselves. It is natural for the young to fear the opposite sex, but it becomes more pronounced when they are pushed into dating prematurely by their parents. The twinship in our present day youth is an attempt to compensate for lack of a close friendship with someone of the same sex, an occurrence which their parents mistrust and oppose. (There is an increased dread of homosexuality in young parents.) The twinship means sameness, familiarity and security. Once some degree of safety is established, sex becomes possible but it is low key and relatively unsatisfying.

The opposite sex is unfamiliar and strange, and therefore frightening. However, sexual differences also make for excitement and fascination. This is most clearly to be seen in the attitudes toward the genitals of the opposite sex, where the differences are most pronounced. If fear predominates, the sexual organs are felt to be repulsive and threatening. If the anxiety is overcome, the genitals of the opposite sex are perceived as tantalizing and attractive. One can observe a broad spectrum of reactions, from disgust and horror to captivation and rapture. This varies from person to person, and also within the same person, depending on his emotional state at a given time.

Another contributory factor to this clinical syndrome of impoverished sexuality is a past history of a life with a relative absence of frustration and the prevalence of quick and easy satisfactions. The height of sensual pleasure is achieved when sex is interwoven with romantic love. The full flowering of romantic love and passion requires a background of dealing with obstacles, suffering and frustration. The anthropologists, especially Margaret Mead,[7] have demonstrated this convincingly. The great lovers in real life and in literature were willing to endure great misery and pain for their loved ones. They were willing to wait, to struggle and to endure, all of which went to make the loved person more precious. The "cool" set is accustomed to quick and easy gratifications. Instant warmth and instant sex make for puny love, cool sex, and a turning to LSD and "pot."

If we turn to adults between 25 and 45 years of age, we now seem to find an increase of sexual apathy in the male and sexual demandingness in the female. In both sexes there is a mounting tendency to divorce sexual relations from emotional involvement. This is particularly pronounced in the male. There are many men who can be libidinously very ardent and vigorous as long as it does not imply emotional commitment. A young woman patient of mine reported to me that she has been dating a 35-year-old man for several months. Each time he sees her he takes her out to dinner to an expensive restaurant, then to a fashionable nightclub or theatre and then wants to go to bed. During the course of the evening, however, the young man only speaks pleasant trivia or broad clichés. When my patient pointed out his evasiveness, he did not deny it. He replied that he liked her, he was quite eager to dine with her, dance with her and go to bed with her, but he didn't want to get "involved." It was not only his fear of marriage with the ensuing responsibilities; his behavior, I later learned, was based on the alienation of sex from love.

There are many patients who do not display a generalized sexual apathy but who are apathetic toward one type of love object. I refer here to people who are only able to feel passionate about someone strange or forbidden, and feel lethargic toward someone familiar and permissible. This is a very widespread phenomenon in our society, as our high divorce rate and flagrant marital promiscuity indicate. Every physician has seen patients who are sexually apathetic to their marital partner yet are carrying on a torrid love affair outside the marriage. If you explore this matter you will find that the person involved is unable to feel passion to the person he is married to. It is quite typical to get a history that before marriage, and even in the early years, there was a great deal of sexual desire which slowly petered out. I should note at this point that, in the past, this situation was predominant in the male. Now it is equally true of the female.

The underlying psychopathology in such cases seems to be based on several crucial elements. In the first place, people in this category were never able to overcome that taboo of childhood, when it was forbidden to have sexual impulses toward members of the family. Unconsciously, the people one lives with becomes familiar—that is, family—and therefore desexualized.

Another important factor is the increase in hostility and fear between the sexes, above all in men, which seems to have mounted with the increasing ascendency of women.[1] As women in our society have become more assertive and daring, men seem to have become more passive and timid, in life in general, and particularly in sexual matters. As women have gained greater freedom economically and politically, and are less afraid of pregnancy, due to the "pill" and other modern contraceptive devices, they are able to achieve orgasm far more readily than they did in the past. Today, women tend to feel entitled to equal orgasms along with their other equal rights. In the past, a woman needed the feeling of being loved as a prerequisite for sexual gratification. Now she seems just as able as men to enjoy fornication without romantic love. The separation and estrangement of love from sex is an extremely important source of today's sexual problems, and although it is a complicated topic, I want to sketch briefly some of the underlying psychological causes.

As I observe some of the most obvious clinical signs, I conclude that women are far more certain of their femininity than men of their masculinity. For example, a woman is at her most feminine in the company of men. Many men in our society feel most manly at a "stag" party or poker game—that is, in the company of men. In the past, we would have explained this on the basis of the male's fear of the castrating, penis-envying woman. Although there is some validity to this concept, I believe today we would be more inclined to recognize the fact that one's gender identity, one's sense of belonging to a given sex and not another, stems from very early childhood experiences that long pre-date the phallic phase.[3,8] In early childhood the child tends to identify as he perceives and learns. Since children are reared by mothers, both boys and girls will identify with the mother. Girls learn to become feminine by their contact with mother. The boy has to switch his identification and has to have meaningful contact with a masculine father to become manly. This is harder to obtain in our society because fathers spend far less time with the young child and have increasing difficulty in asserting their maleness.

Furthermore, the mother is by far the source of the greatest pleasure and security in early childhood of both boys and girls. It is an all too human tendency to envy, to want to possess for oneself, that which is so valuable. We have long recognized the female's envy of the male in our society. But we have neglected the much deeper and older envy of mother, particularly in men. On the surface, men have contempt for women. But below the surface is a repressed envy. This is true for all inappropriate contempt—it covers hidden envy. I believe the deep seated *unconscious* hatred and fear of women is the underlying basis for the sexual apathy in the male. The original source of this hatred is the male child's dependency on the omnipotent-appearing mother. As long as women were timid and demure about sex, men were able to assume a dominating and aggressive role. Now that women have become sexually more aggressive and outspoken, it seems that the latent fear became mobilized and manifests itself in the male's avoidance of sex.

There are many other factors which should be mentioned, even if I cannot discuss them. The welfare state tends to act like a mother, taking care of the sick, the poor, the unemployed and the aged. This tends to feminize men and to blur the distinction between males and females. This is particularly true in all collectivist states and in people living on the dole. I believe this is observable in the Soviet Union, in the Kibbutz in Israel, and in armies which use women. Finally, the emphasis on security as the goal of life makes for the quest of peace-of-mindlessness, early retirement and a general emotional uninvolvement. Loving is risk-taking. It implies daring to be vulnerable and hurt. In this sense, the search for security is the enemy of loving and in our society the emphasis is on security. One of the results of this attitude is the splitting off of love from sex, and consequently we so frequently find love without passion and sex without emotional involvement.

References

1. Borgese, E.: Ascent of Woman, George Braziller, New York, 1963.
2. Freud, S.: Three Essays on the Theory of Sexuality, Standard Edition, 7:125, London, 1962.
3. Greenson, R.: On homosexuality and gender identity, Int. J. Psychoanal., 45:217–219, 1964.
4. Kinsey, A., Pomeroy, W., and Martin, C.: Sexual Behavior in the Human Male, W. B. Saunders Co., Philadelphia. 1948.
5. Kinsey, A., Pomeroy, W., Martin, C., and Gebhard, P.: Sexual Behavior in the Human Female, W. B. Saunders Co., Philadelphia, 1953.
6. Masters, W., and Johnson, V.: Human Sexual Response, Little, Brown & Company, Boston, 1966.
7. Mead, M.: Male and Female, William Morrow & Co., New York, 1949.
8. Stoller, R.: A contribution to the study of gender identity. Int. J. Psychoanal., 45:220, 1964.
9. Wolfenstein, M.: Changing Patterns of Adolescence, Ciba-Symp., pp. 195–208, J & A Churchill, Ltd., London, 1965.

PART VI

A Psychoanalytic View

Paradoxes of Sex and Love

by Rollo May, Ph.D.

EDITORS' NOTE: *The following is excerpted from the second chapter in Dr. May's book* Love and Will. *Dr. May is a practicing psychotherapist and teaches at the William Alanson White Institute of Psychiatry, Psychoanalysis and Psychotherapy in New York.*

Sexual Wilderness

In Victorian times, when the denial of sexual impulses, feelings, and drives was the mode and one would not talk about sex in polite company, an aura of sanctifying repulsiveness surrounded the whole topic. Males and females dealt with each other as though neither possessed sexual organs. William James, that redoubtable crusader who was far ahead of his time on every other topic, treated sex with the polite aversion characteristic of the turn of the century. In the whole two volumes of his epoch-making *Principles of Psychology*, only one page is devoted to sex, at the end of which he adds, "These details are a little unpleasant to discuss...."[1] But William Blake's warning a century before Victorianism, that "He who desires but acts not, breeds pestilence," was amply demonstrated by the later psychotherapists. Freud, a Victorian who did look at sex, was right in his description of the morass of neurotic symptoms which resulted from cutting off so vital a part of the human body and the self.

Then, in the 1920s, a radical change occurred almost overnight. The belief became a militant dogma in liberal circles that the opposite of repression—namely, sex education, freedom of talking, feeling, and expression—would have healthy effects, and obviously constituted the only stand for the enlightened person. In an amazingly short period following World War I, we shifted from acting as though sex did not exist at all to being obsessed with it. We now placed more emphasis on sex than any society since that of ancient Rome, and some scholars believe we are more preoccupied with sex than any other people in all of history. Today, far from not talking about sex, we might well seem, to a visitor from Mars dropping into Times Square, to have no other topic of communication.

And this is not solely an American obsession. Across the ocean in England, for example, "from bishops to biologists, everyone is in on the act." A perceptive front-page article in *The Times Literary Supplement*, London, goes on to point to the "whole turgid flood of post-Kinsey utilitarianism and post-Chatterley moral uplift. Open any newspaper, any day (Sunday in particular), and the odds are you will find some pundit treating the public to his views on contraception, abortion, adultery, obscene publications, homosexuality between consenting adults or (if all else fails) contemporary moral patterns among our adolescents."[2]

Partly as a result of this radical shift, many therapists today rarely see patients who exhibit repression of sex in the manner of Freud's pre-World War I hysterical patients. In fact, we find in the people who come for help just the opposite: a great deal of talk about sex, a great deal of sexual activity, practically no one complaining of cultural prohibitions over going to bed as often or with as many partners as one wishes. But what our patients do complain of is lack of feeling and passion. "The curious thing about this ferment of discussion is how little anyone seems to be *enjoying* emancipation."[3] So much sex and so little meaning or even fun in it!

Where the Victorian didn't want anyone to know that he or she had sexual feelings, we are ashamed if we do not.

Before 1910, if you called a lady "sexy" she would be insulted; nowadays, she prizes the compliment and rewards you by turning her charms in your direction. Our patients often have the problems of frigidity and impotence, but the strange and poignant thing we observe is how desperately they struggle not to let anyone find out they don't feel sexually. The Victorian nice man or woman was guilty if he or she did experience sex; now we are guilty if we *don't*.

One paradox, therefore, is that enlightenment has not solved the sexual problems in our culture. To be sure, there are important positive results of the new enlightenment, chiefly in increased freedom for the individual. Most external problems are eased: sexual knowledge can be bought in any bookstore, contraception is available everywhere except in Boston where it is still believed, as the English countess averred on her wedding night, that sex is "too good for the common people." Couples can, without guilt and generally without squeamishness, discuss their sexual relationship and undertake to make it more mutually gratifying and meaningful. Let these gains not be underestimated. External social anxiety and guilt have lessened; dull would be the man who did not rejoice in this.

But *internal* anxiety and guilt have increased. And in some ways these are more morbid, harder to handle, and impose a heavier burden upon the individual than external anxiety and guilt.

The challenge a woman used to face from men was simple and direct—would she or would she not go to bed?—a direct issue of how she stood vis-à-vis cultural mores. But the question men ask now is no longer, "Will she or won't she?" but "Can she or can't she?" The challenge is shifted to the woman's personal adequacy, namely, her own capacity to have the vaunted orgasm—which should resemble a *grand mal* seizure. Though we might agree that the second question places the problem of sexual decision more where it should be, we cannot overlook the fact that the first question is much easier for the person to handle. In my practice, one woman was afraid to go to bed for fear that the man "won't find me very good at making love." Another was afraid because "I don't even know how to do it," assuming that her lover would hold this against her. Another was scared to death of the second marriage for fear that she wouldn't be able to have the orgasm as she had not in her first. Often the woman's hesitation is formulated as, "He won't like me well enough to come back again."

In past decades you could blame society's strict mores and preserve your own self-esteem by telling yourself what you did or didn't do was society's fault and not yours. And this would give you some time in which to decide what you do want to do, or to let yourself grow into a decision. But when the question is simply how you can perform, your own sense of adequacy and self-esteem is called immediately into question, and the whole weight of the encounter is shifted inward to how you can meet the test.

College students, in their fights with college authorities about hours girls are to be permitted in the men's rooms, are curiously blind to the fact that rules are often a boon. Rules give the student time to find himself. He has the leeway to consider a way of behaving without being committed before he is ready, to try on for size, to venture into relationships tentatively—which is part of any growing up. Better to have the lack of commitment direct and open rather than to go into sexual relations under pressure —doing violence to his feelings by having physical commitment without psychological. He may flaunt the rules; but at least they give some structure to be flaunted. My point is true whether he obeys the rule or not. Many contemporary students, understandably anxious because of their new sexual freedom, repress this anxiety ("one should *like* freedom") and then compensate for the additional anxiety the repression gives them by attacking the parietal authorities for not giving them more freedom!

What we did not see in our short-sighted liberalism in sex was that throwing the individual into an unbounded and empty sea of free choice does not in itself give freedom, but is more apt to increase inner conflict. The sexual freedom to which we were devoted fell short of being fully human.

In the arts, we have also been discovering what an illusion it was to believe that mere freedom would solve our problem. Consider, for example, the drama. In an article entitled "Is Sex Kaput?," Howard Taubman, former drama critic of *The New York Times*, summarized what we have all observed in drama after drama: "Engaging in sex was like setting out to shop on a dull afternoon; desire had nothing to do with it and even curiosity was faint."[4] Consider also the novel. In the "revolt against the Victorians," writes Leon Edel, "the extremists have had their day. Thus far they have impoverished the novel rather than enriched it."[5] Edel perceptively brings out the crucial point that in sheer realistic "enlightenment" there has occurred a *dehumanization* of sex in fiction. There are "sexual encounters in Zola," he insists, "which have more truth in them than any D. H. Lawrence described—and also more humanity."[6]

The battle against censorship and for freedom of expression surely was a great battle to win, but has it not become a new strait jacket? The writers, both novelists and dramatists, "would rather hock their typewriters than turn in a manuscript without the obligatory scenes of unsparing anatomical documentation of their characters' sexual behavior. . . ."[7] Our "dogmatic enlightenment" is self-defeating: it ends up destroying the very sexual passion it set out to protect. In the great tide of realistic chronicling, we forgot, on the stage and in the novel and even in psychotherapy, that imagination is the life-blood of eros, and that realism is neither sexual nor erotic. Indeed, there is nothing *less* sexy than sheer nakedness, as a random hour at any nudist camp will prove. It requires the infusion of the imagination (which I shall later call intentionality) to transmute physiology and anatomy into *interpersonal* experience—into art, into passion, into eros in a million forms which has the power to shake or charm us.

Could it not be that an "enlightenment" which reduces itself to sheer realistic detail is itself an escape from the anxiety involved in the relation of human imagination to erotic passion?

Salvation Through Technique

A second paradox is that *the new emphasis on technique in sex and love-making backfires*. It often occurs to me that there is an inverse relationship between the number of how-to-do-it books perused by a person or rolling off the presses in a society and the amount of sexual passion or even pleasure experienced by the persons involved.

Certainly nothing is wrong with technique as such, in playing golf or acting or making love. But the emphasis beyond a certain point on technique in sex makes for a mechanistic attitude toward love-making, and goes along with alienation, feelings of loneliness, and depersonalization.

One aspect of the alienation is that the lover, with his age-old art, tends to be superseded by the computer operator with his modern efficiency. Couples place great emphasis on bookkeeping and timetables in their love-making—a practice confirmed and standardized by Kinsey. If they fall behind schedule they become anxious and feel impelled to go to bed whether they want to or not. My colleague, Dr. John Schimel, observes, "My patients have endured stoically, or without noticing, remarkably destructive treatment at the hands of their spouses, but they have experienced falling behind in the sexual timetable as a loss of love."[8] The man feels he is somehow losing his masculine status if he does not perform up to schedule, and the woman that she has lost her feminine attractiveness if too long a period goes by without the man at least making a pass at her. The phrase "between men," which women use about their affairs, similarly suggests a gap in time like the *entr'acte*. Elaborate accounting- and ledger-book lists—how often this week have we made love? did he (or she) pay the right amount of attention to me during the evening? was the foreplay long enough?—make one wonder how the spontaneity of this most spontaneous act can possibly survive. The computer hovers in the stage wings of the drama of love-making the way Freud said one's parents used to.

It is not surprising then, in this preoccupation with techniques, that the questions typically asked about an act of love-making are not, Was there passion of meaning or pleasure in the act? but, How well did I perform?[9] Take, for example, what Cyril Connolly calls "the tyranny of the orgasm," and the preoccupation with achieving a simultaneous orgasm, which is another aspect of the alienation. I confess that when people talk about the "apocalyptic orgasm," I find myself wondering, Why do they have to try so hard? What abyss of self-doubt, what inner void of loneliness, are they trying to cover up by this great concern with grandiose effects?

Even the sexologists, whose attitude is generally the more sex the merrier, are raising their eyebrows these days about the anxious overemphasis on achieving the orgasm and the great importance attached to "satisfying" the partner. A man makes a point of asking the woman if she "made it," or if she is "all right," or uses some other euphemism for an experience for which obviously no euphemism is possible. We men are reminded by Simone de Beauvoir and other women who try to interpret the love act that this is the last thing in the world a woman wants to be asked at that moment. Furthermore, the technical preoccupation robs the woman of exactly what she wants most of all, physically and emotionally, namely the man's spontaneous abandon at the moment of climax. This abandon gives her whatever thrill or ecstasy she and the experience are capable of. When we cut through all the rigmarole about roles and performance, what still remains is how amazingly important the sheer fact of intimacy of relationship is—the meeting, the growing closeness with the excitement of not knowing where it will lead, the assertion of the self, and the giving of the self—in making a sexual encounter memorable. Is it not this intimacy that makes us return to the event in memory again and again when we need to be warmed by whatever hearths life makes available?

It is a strange thing in our society that what goes into building a relationship—the sharing of tastes, fantasies, dreams, hopes for the future, and fears from the past—seems to make people more shy and vulnerable than going to bed with each other. They are more wary of the tenderness that goes with psychological and spiritual nakedness than they are of the physical nakedness in sexual intimacy.

The New Puritanism

The third paradox is that our highly-vaunted sexual freedom has turned out to be a new form of puritanism. I spell it with a small "p" because I do not wish to confuse this with the original Puritanism. That, as in the passion of Hester and Dimmesdale in Hawthorne's *The Scarlet Letter*, was a very different thing.[10] I refer to puritanism as it came down via our Victorian grandparents and became allied with industrialism and emotional and moral compartmentalization.

I define this puritanism as consisting of three elements. First, *a state of alienation from the body*. Second, *the separation of emotion from reason*. And third, *the use of the body as a machine*.

In our new puritanism, bad health is equated with sin.[11] Sin used to mean giving in to one's sexual desires; it now means not having full sexual expression. Our contemporary puritan holds that it is immoral *not* to express your libido. Apparently this is true on both sides of the ocean: "There are few more depressing sights," the London *Times Literary Supplement* writes, "than a progressive intellectual determined to end up in bed with someone from a sense of moral duty. . . . There is no more high-minded puritan in the world than your modern advocate of salvation through properly directed passion. . . ."[12] A woman used to be guilty if she went to bed with a man; now she feels vaguely guilty if after a certain number of dates she still refrains; her sin is "morbid repression," refusing to "give." And the partner, who is always completely enlightened (or at least pretends to be) refuses to allay her guilt by getting overtly angry at her (if she could fight him on the issue, the conflict would be a lot easier for her). But he stands broadmindedly by, ready at the end of every date to undertake a crusade to assist her out of her fallen state. And this, of course, makes her "no" all the more guilt-producing for her.

This all means, of course, that people not only have to learn to perform sexually but have to make sure, at the same time, that they can do so without letting themselves go in passion or unseemly commitment—the latter of which may be interpreted as exerting an unhealthy demand upon the partner. *The Victorian person sought to have love without falling into sex; the modern person seeks to have sex without falling into love.*

I once diverted myself by drawing an impressionistic sketch of the attitude of the contemporary enlightened person toward sex and love. I would like to share this picture of what I call the new sophisticate:

> The new sophisticate is not castrated by society, but like Origen is self-castrated. Sex and the body

are for him not something to be and live out, but tools to be cultivated like a T.V. announcer's voice. The new sophisticate expresses his passion by devoting himself passionately to the moral principle of dispersing all passion, loving everybody until love has no power left to scare anyone. He is deathly afraid of his passions unless they are kept under leash, and the theory of total expression is precisely his leash. His dogma of liberty is his repression; and his principle of full libidinal health, full sexual satisfaction, is his denial of eros: The old Puritans repressed sex and were passionate; our new puritan represses passion and is sexual. His purpose is to hold back the body, to try to make nature a slave. The new sophisticate's rigid principle of full freedom is not freedom but a new straitjacket. He does all this because he is afraid of his body and his compassionate roots in nature, afraid of the soil and his procreative power. He is our latter-day Baconian devoted to gaining power *over* nature, gaining knowledge in order to get more power. And you gain power over sexuality (like working the slave until all zest for revolt is squeezed out of him) precisely by the role of full expression. Sex becomes our tool like the caveman's bow and arrows, crowbar, or adz. Sex, the new machine, the *Machina Ultima*.

This new puritanism has crept into contemporary psychiatry and psychology. It is argued in some books on the counseling of married couples that the therapist ought to use only the term "fuck" when discussing sexual intercourse, and to insist the patients use it; for any other word plays into the patients' dissimulation. What is significant here is not the use of the term itself: surely the sheer lust, animal but self-conscious, and bodily abandon which is rightly called fucking is not to be left out of the spectrum of human experience. But the interesting thing is that the use of the once-forbidden word is now made into an *ought*—a duty for the moral reason of honesty. To be sure, it *is* dissimulation to deny the biological side of copulation. But it is also dissimulation to use the term fuck for the sexual experience when what we seek is a relationship of personal intimacy which is more than a release of sexual tension, a personal intimacy which will be remembered tomorrow and many weeks after tomorrow. The former is dissimulation in the service of inhibition; the latter is dissimulation in the service of alienation of the self, a defense of the self against the anxiety of intimate relationship. As the former was the particular problem of Freud's day, the latter is the particular problem of ours.

The new puritanism brings with it a depersonalization of our whole language. Instead of making love, we "have sex"; in contrast to intercourse, we "screw"; instead of going to bed, we "lay" someone or (heaven help the English language as well as ourselves!) we "are laid." This alienation has become so much the order of the day that in some psychotherapeutic training schools, young psychiatrists and psychologists are taught that it is "therapeutic" to use solely the four-letter words in sessions; the patient is probably masking some repression if he talks about making love; so it becomes our righteous duty—the new puritanism incarnate!—to let him know he only fucks. Everyone seems so intent on sweeping away the last vestiges of Victorian prudishness that we entirely forget that these different words refer to different kinds of human experience. Probably most people have experienced the different forms of sexual relationship described by the different terms and don't have much difficulty distinguishing among them. I am not making a value judgment among these different experiences; they are all appropriate to their own kinds of relationship. Every woman wants at some time to be "laid"—transported, carried away, "made" to have passion when at first she has none, as in the famous scene between Rhett Butler and Scarlett O'Hara in *Gone with the Wind*. But if being "laid" is all that ever happens in her sexual life, then her experience of personal alienation and rejection of sex are just around the corner. If the therapist does not appreciate these diverse kinds of experience, he will be presiding at the shrinking and truncating of the patient's consciousness, and will be confirming the narrowing of the patient's bodily awareness as well as his or her capacity for relationship. This is the chief criticism of the new puritanism: it grossly limits feelings, it blocks the infinite variety and richness of the act, and it makes for emotional impoverishment.

It is not surprising that the new puritanism develops smoldering hostility among the members of our society. And that hostility, in turn, comes out frequently in references to the sexual act itself. We say "go fuck yourself" or "fuck you" as a term of contempt to show that the other is of no value whatever beyond being used and tossed aside. The biological lust is here in its *reductio ad absurdum*. Indeed, the word fuck is the most common expletive in our contemporary language to express violent hostility. I do not think this is by accident.

Freud and Puritanism

How Freudian psychoanalysis was intertwined with both the new sexual libertarianism and puritanism is a fascinating story. Social critics at cocktail parties tend to credit Freud with being the prime mover of, or at least the prime spokesman for, the new sexual freedom. But what they do not see is that Freud and psychoanalysis reflected and expressed the new puritanism in both its positive and negative forms.

The psychoanalytic puritanism is positive in its emphasis on rigorous honesty and cerebral rectitude, as exemplified in Freud himself. It is negative in its providing a new system by which the body and self can be viewed, rightly or wrongly, as a mechanism for gratification by way of "sexual objects." The tendency in psychoanalysis to speak of sex as a "need" in the sense of a tension to be reduced plays into this puritanism.

We thus have to explore this problem to see how the new sexual values in our society were given a curious twist as they were rationalized psychoanalytically. "Psychoanalysis is Calvinism in Bermuda shorts," pungently stated Dr. C. Macfie Campbell, president of the American Psychiatric Association in 1936–37, discussing the philosophical aspects of psychoanalysis. The aphorism is only half true, but that half is significant. Freud himself was an excellent example of a puritan in the positive sense in his strength of character, control of his passions, and compulsive work. Freud greatly admired Oliver Cromwell, the Puritan commander, and named a son after him. Philip Rieff, in his study *Freud: The Mind of the Moralist*, points out that this "affinity for militant puritanism was not uncommon among secular Jewish intellectuals, and indicates a certain preferred character type, starched with independence and cerebral rectitude rather than a particular belief or doctrine."[13] In his ascetic work habits, Freud shows one of the most significant aspects of puritanism, namely the use of *science as a monastery*. His compulsive industry was rigorously devoted to achieving his scientific goals, which transcended everything else in life (and, one might add, life itself) and for which he sublimated his passion in a quite real rather than figurative sense.

Freud himself had a very limited sexual life. His own sexual expression began late, around thirty, and subsided early, around forty, so his biographer Ernest Jones tells us. At 41, Freud wrote to his friend Wilhelm Fliess complaining of his depressed moods, and added, "Also sexual excitation is of no more use to a person like me." Another incident points to the fact that around this age his sexual life had more or less ended. Freud reports in *The Interpretation of Dreams* that at one time, in his forties, he felt physically attracted to a young woman and reached out half-voluntarily and touched her. He comments on how surprised he was that he was "still" able to find the possibility for such attraction in him.[14]

Freud believed in the control and channeling of sexuality, and was convinced that this had specific value both for cultural development and for one's own character. In 1883, during his prolonged engagement to Martha Bernays, the young Freud wrote to his future wife:

> ... it is neither pleasant nor edifying to watch the masses amusing themselves; we at least don't have much taste for it. ... I remember something that occurred to me while watching a performance of *Carmen*: the mob gives vent to its appetites, and we deprive ourselves. We deprive ourselves in order to maintain our integrity, we economize in our health, our capacity for enjoyment, our emotions; we save ourselves for something, not knowing for what. And this constant suppression of natural instincts gives us the quality of refinement. ... And the extreme case of people like ourselves who chain themselves together for life and death, who deprive themselves and pine for years so as to remain faithful, who probably

wouldn't survive a catastrophe that robbed them of their beloved. . . .[15]

The basis of Freud's doctrine of sublimation lies in this belief that libido exists in a certain quantity in the individual, that you can deprive yourself, "economize" emotionally in one way to increase your enjoyment in another, and that if you spend your libido in direct sexuality you will not have it for utilization, for example, in artistic creation. In a positive statement of appreciation of Freud's work, Paul Tillich nevertheless remarks that the "concept of sublimation is Freud's most puritanical belief."[16]

I am not making a simple derogatory value judgment about psychoanalysis when I point out the association between it and puritanism. The *original* Puritan movement, in its best representatives and before its general deterioration into the moralistic compartments of Victorianism at the end of the nineteenth century, was characterized by admirable qualities of dedication to integrity and truth. The progress of modern science owes a great deal to it and, indeed, would probably not have been possible without these virtues of the secular monks in their scientific laboratories. Furthermore, a cultural development like psychoanalysis is always effect as well as cause: it *reflects* and *expresses* the emerging trends in the culture, as well as molds and influences these trends. If we are conscious of what is going on, we can, in however slight a way, influence the direction of the trends. We can then hopefully develop new values which will be relevant to our new cultural predicament.

But if we try to take the content of our values from psychoanalysis, we are thrown into a confusing contradiction not only of the values themselves but of our own self-image. It is an error to expect psychoanalysis to carry the burden of providing our values. Psychoanalysis can, by its unfolding and revealing of previously denied motives and desires and by enlarging consciousness, prepare the way for the patient's working out values by means of which he can change. But it can never, in itself, carry the burden for the value decisions which do change a person's life. The great contribution of Freud was his carrying of the Socratic injunction "Know thyself" into new depths that comprise, in effect, a new continent, the continent of repressed, unconscious motives. He also developed techniques in the personal relationships in therapy, based on the concepts of transference and resistance, for bringing these levels into conscious awareness. Whatever the ebb and flow of the popularity of psychoanalysis, it will remain true that Freud's discoveries and those of the others in this field are an invaluable contribution not only to the area of psychological healing but also to morality in clearing away hypocritical debris and self-deceit.

What I wish to make clear is that many people in our society, yearning for the nirvana of automatic change in their characters and relief from responsibility that comes from handing over one's psyche to a technical process, have actually in their values of "free expression" and hedonism simply *bootlegged in from psychoanalysis new contents to their old puritanism.* The fact that the change in sexual attitudes and mores occurred so quickly—virtually in the one decade of the 1920s—also argues for the assumption that we changed our clothes and our roles more than our characters. What was omitted was the opening of our senses and imaginations to the enrichment of pleasure and passion and the meaning of love; we relegated these to technical processes. In this kind of "free" love, one does not learn to love; and freedom becomes not a liberation but a new straitjacket. The upshot was that our sexual values were thrown into confusion and contradiction, and sexual love presented the almost insoluble paradoxes we are now observing.

I do not wish to overstate the case, nor to lose sight at any point of the positive benefits of the modern fluidity in sexual mores. The confusions we are describing go hand in hand with the real possibilities of freedom for the individual. Couples are able to affirm sex as a source of pleasure and delight; no longer hounded by the misconception that sex as a natural act is evil, they can become more sensitive to the actual evils in their relationships such as manipulation of each other. Free to a degree Victorians never were, they can explore ways of making their relationship more enriching. Even the growing frequency of divorce, no matter how sobering the problems it raises, has the positive psychological effect of making it harder for couples to rationalize a bad marriage by the dogma that they are "stuck" with each other. The possibility of finding a new lover makes it more necessary for us to accept the responsibility of choosing the one we *do* have if we stay with him or her. There is the possibility of developing a courage that is midway between—and includes both—biological lust on one hand and on the other the desire for meaningful relationship, a deepening awareness of each other, and the other aspects of what we call human understanding. Courage can be shifted from simply fighting society's mores to the inward capacity to commit one's self to another human being.

But these positive benefits, it is now abundantly clear, do not occur automatically. They become possible only as the contradictions which we have been describing are understood and worked through.

Motives of the Problem

In my function as a supervisory analyst at two analytic institutes, I supervise one case of each of six psychiatrists or psychologists who are in training to become analysts. I cite the six patients of these young analysts both because I know a good deal about them by now and also because, since they are not my patients, I can see them with a more objective perspective. Each one of these patients goes to bed without ostensible shame or guilt—and generally with different partners. The women—four of the six patients—all state that they don't feel much in the sex act. The motives of two of the women for going to bed seem to be to hang on to the man and to live up to the standard that sexual intercourse is "what you do" at a certain stage. The third woman has the particular motive of generosity: she sees going to bed as something nice you give a man—and she makes tremendous demands upon him to take care of her in return. The fourth woman seems the only one who does experience some real sexual lust, beyond which her motives are a combination of generosity to and anger at the man ("I'll *force* him to give me pleasure!"). The two male patients were originally impotent, and now, though able to have intercourse, have intermittent trouble with potency. But the outstanding fact is they never report getting much of a "bang" out of their sexual intercourse. Their chief motive for engaging in sex seems to be to demonstrate their masculinity. The specific purpose of one of the men, indeed, seems more to tell his analyst about his previous night's adventure, fair or poor as it may have been, in a kind of backstage interchange of confidence between men, than to enjoy the love-making itself.

Let us now pursue our inquiry on a deeper level by asking, What are the underlying motives in these patterns? What drives people toward the contemporary compulsive preoccupation with sex in place of their previous compulsive denial of it?

The struggle to prove one's identity is obviously a central motive—an aim present in women as well as men, as Betty Friedan in *The Feminine Mystique* made clear. This has helped spawn the idea of *egalitarianism* of the sexes and the *interchangeability* of the sexual roles. Egalitarianism is clung to at the price of denying not only biological differences—which are basic, to say the least—between men and women, but emotional differences from which come much of the delight of the sexual act. The self-contradiction here is that the compulsive need to prove you are identical with your partner means that you repress your own unique sensibilities—and this is exactly what undermines your own sense of identity. This contradiction contributes to the tendency in our society for us to become machines even in bed.

Another motive is the individual's hope to overcome his own solitariness. Allied with this is the desperate endeavor to escape feelings of emptiness and the threat of apathy: partners pant and quiver hoping to find an answering quiver in someone else's body just to prove that their own is not dead; they seek a responding, a longing in the other to prove their own feelings are alive. Out of an ancient conceit, this is called love.

One often gets the impression, amid the male's flexing of sexual prowess, that men are in training to become sexual athletes. But what is the great prize of the game? Not only men, but women struggle to prove their sexual power —they too must keep up to the timetable, must show passion, and have the vaunted orgasm. Now it is well accepted in psychotherapeutic circles that, dynamically, the overconcern with potency is generally a compensation for feelings of impotence.

The use of sex to prove potency in all these different

realms has led to the increasing emphasis on technical performance. And here we observe another curiously self-defeating pattern. It is that the excessive concern with technical performance in sex is actually correlated with the reduction of sexual feeling. The techniques of achieving this approach the ludicrous: one is that an anesthetic ointment is applied to the penis before intercourse. Thus feeling less, the man is able to postpone his orgasm longer. I have learned from colleagues that the prescribing of this anesthetic "remedy" for premature ejaculation is not unusual. "One male patient," records Dr. Schimel, "was desperate about his 'premature ejaculations,' even though these ejaculations took place after periods of penetration of 10 minutes or more. A neighbor who was a urologist recommended an anesthetic ointment to be used prior to intercourse. This patient expressed complete satisfaction with the solution and was very grateful to the urologist."[17] Entirely willing to give up any pleasure of his own, he sought only to prove himself a competent male.

A patient of mine reported that he had gone to a physician with the problem of premature ejaculation, and that such an anesthetic ointment had been prescribed. My surprise, like Dr. Schimel's, was particularly over the fact that the patient had accepted this solution with no questions and no conflicts. Didn't the remedy fit the necessary bill, didn't it help him turn in a better performance? But by the time that young man got to me, he was impotent in every way imaginable, even to the point of being unable to handle such scarcely ladylike behavior on the part of his wife as her taking off her shoe while they were driving and beating him over the head with it. By all means the man was impotent in this hideous caricature of a marriage. And his penis, before it was drugged senseless, seemed to be the only character with enough "sense" to have the appropriate intention, namely to get out as quickly as possible.

Making one's self *feel less* in order to *perform better!* This is a symbol, as macabre as it is vivid, of the vicious circle in which so much of our culture is caught. The more one must demonstrate his potency, the more he treats sexual intercourse—this most intimate and personal of all acts—as a performance to be judged by exterior requirements, the more he then views himself as a machine to be turned on, adjusted, and steered, and the less feeling he has for either himself or his partner; and the less feeling, the more he loses genuine sexual appetite and ability. The upshot of this self-defeating pattern is that, in the long run, *the lover who is most efficient will also be the one who is impotent.*

A poignant note comes into our discussion when we remind ourselves that this excessive concern for "satisfying" the partner is an expression, however perverted, of a sound and basic element in the sexual act: the pleasure and experience of self-affirmation in being able to *give* to the partner. The man is often deeply grateful toward the woman who lets herself be gratified by him—lets him give her an orgasm, to use the phrase that is often the symbol for this experience. This is a point midway between lust and tenderness, between sex and agapé—and it partakes of both. Many a male cannot feel his own identity either as a man or a person in our culture until he is able to gratify a woman. The very structure of human interpersonal relations is such that the sexual act does not achieve its full pleasure or meaning if the man and woman cannot feel they are able to gratify the other. And it is the inability to experience this pleasure at the gratification of the other which often underlies the exploitative sexuality of the rape type and the compulsive sexuality of the Don Juan seduction type. Don Juan has to perform the act over and over again because he remains forever unsatisfied, quite despite the fact that he is entirely potent and has a technically good orgasm.

Now the problem is not the desire and need to satisfy the partner as such, but the fact that this need is interpreted by the persons in the sexual act in only a technical sense—giving physical sensation. What is omitted even from our very vocabulary (and thus the words may sound "square" as I say them here) is the experience of giving feelings, sharing fantasies, offering the inner psychic richness that normally takes a little time and enables sensation to transcend itself in emotion and emotion to transcend itself in tenderness and sometimes love.

It is not surprising that contemporary trends toward the mechanization of sex have much to do with the problem of impotence. The distinguishing characteristic of the machine is that it can go through all the *motions* but it never *feels.* A knowledgeable medical student, one of whose reasons for coming into analysis was his sexual impotence, had a revealing dream. He was asking me in the dream to put a pipe in his head that would go down through his body and come out at the other end as his penis. He was confident in the dream that the pipe would constitute an admirably strong erection. What was entirely missing in this intelligent scion of our sophisticated times was any understanding at all that *what he conceived of as his solution was exactly the cause of his problem,* namely the image of himself as a "screwing machine." His symbol is remarkably graphic: the brain, the intellect, is included, but true symbol of our alienated age, his shrewd system bypasses entirely the seats of emotions, the thalamus, the heart and lungs, even the stomach. Direct route from head to penis—but what is lost is the heart![18]

I do not have statistics on hand concerning the present incidence of impotence in comparison with past periods, nor does anyone else so far as I have been able to discover. But my impression is that impotence is increasing these days despite (or is it because of) the unrestrained freedom on all sides. All therapists seem to agree that more men are coming to them with that problem—though whether this represents a real increase in the prevalence of sexual impotence or merely a greater awareness and ability to talk about it cannot be definitely answered. Obviously, it is one of those topics on which meaningful statistics are almost impossible to get. The fact that the book dealing with impotence and frigidity, *Human Sexual Response,* clung near the top of the best-seller lists for so many months, expensive and turgidly-written as it was, would seem to be plenty of evidence of the urge of men to get help on impotence. Whatever the reason, it is becoming harder for the young man as well as the old to take "yes" for an answer.

To see the curious ways the new puritanism shows itself, you have only to open an issue of *Playboy,* that redoubtable journal reputedly sold mainly to college students and clergymen. You discover the naked girls with silicated breasts side by side with the articles by reputable authors, and you conclude on first blush that the magazine is certainly on the side of the new enlightenment. But as you look more closely you see a strange expression in these photographed girls: detached, mechanical, uninviting, vacuous —the typical schizoid personality in the negative sense of that term. You discover that they are not "sexy" at all but that *Playboy* has only shifted the fig leaf from the genitals to the face. You read the letters to the editor and find the first, entitled "Playboy Priest," telling of a priest who "lectures on Hefner's philosophy to audiences of young people and numerous members of the clergy," that "true Christian ethics and morality are not incompatible with Hefner's philosophy," and—written with enthusiastic approbation—that "most clergymen in their fashionable parsonages live more like playboys than ascetics."[19] You find another letter entitled "Jesus was a playboy," since he loved Mary Magdalene, good food, and good grooming, and castigated the Pharisees. And you wonder why all this religious justification and why people, if they are going to be "liberated," can't just enjoy their liberation?

Whether one takes the cynical view that letters to the editor are "planted," or the more generous one that these examples are selected from hundreds of letters, it amounts to the same thing. An image of a type of American male is being presented—a suave, detached, self-assured bachelor, who regards the girl as a "Playboy accessory" like items in his fashionable dress. You note also that *Playboy* carries no advertising for trusses, bald heads, or anything that would detract from this image. You discover that the good articles (which, frankly, can be bought by an editor who wants to hire an assistant with taste and pay the requisite amount of money) give authority to this male image.[20] Harvey Cox concludes that *Playboy* is basically antisexual, and that it is the "latest and slickest episode in man's continuing refusal to be human." He believes "the whole phenomenon of which *Playboy* is only a part vividly illustrates the awful fact of the new kind of tyranny."[21] The poet-sociologist Calvin Herton, discussing *Playboy* in connection with the fashion and entertainment world, calls it the new sexual fascism.[22]

Playboy has indeed caught on to something significant in American society: Cox believes it to be "the repressed fear of involvement with women."[23] I go farther and hold that it, as an example of the new puritanism, gets its dynamic from a repressed anxiety in American men that underlies even the fear of involvement. This is the repressed anxiety about impotence. Everything in the magazine is beautifully concocted to bolster the *illusion of potency* without ever putting it to the test or challenge at all. Noninvolvement (like playing it cool) is elevated into the ideal model for the Playboy. This is possible because the illusion is air-tight, ministering as it does to men fearful for their potency, and capitalizing on this anxiety. The character of the illusion is shown further in the fact that the readership of *Playboy* drops off significantly after the age of 30 when men cannot escape dealing with real women. This illusion is illustrated by the fact that Hefner himself, a former Sunday-school teacher and son of devout Methodists, practically never goes outside his large establishment in North Chicago. Ensconced there, he carries on his work surrounded by his bunnies and amidst his nonalcoholic bacchanals on Pepsi-Cola.

The Revolt Against Sex

With the confusion of motives in sex that we have noted above—almost every motive being present in the act except the desire to make love—it is no wonder that there is a diminution of feeling and that passion has lessened almost to the vanishing point. This diminution of feeling often takes the form of a kind of anesthesia (now with no need of ointment) in people who can perform the mechanical aspects of the sexual act very well. We are becoming used to the plaint from the couch or patient's chair that "We made love, but I didn't feel anything." Again, the poets tell us the same things as our patients. T. S. Eliot writes in *The Waste Land* that after "lovely woman stoops to folly," and the carbuncular clerk who seduced her at tea leaves,

> She turns and looks a moment in the glass,
> Hardly aware of her departed lover;
> Her brain allows one half-formed thought to pass;
> "Well now that's done: and I'm glad it's over."
> When lovely woman stoops to folly and
> Paces about her room again, alone,
> She smooths her hair with automatic hand,
> And puts a record on the gramophone.
> (III:249–256)

Sex is the "last frontier," David Riesman meaningfully phrases it in *The Lonely Crowd*. Gerald Sykes, in the same vein, remarks, "In a world gone gray with market reports, time studies, tax regulations and path lab analyses, the rebel finds sex to be the one green thing."[24] It is surely true that the zest, adventure, and trying out of one's strength, the discovering of vast and exciting new areas of feeling and experience in one's self and in one's relations to others, and the validation of the self that goes with these are indeed "frontier experiences." They are rightly and normally present in sexuality as part of the psychosocial development of every person. Sex in our society did, in fact, have this power for several decades after the 1920s, when almost every other activity was becoming "other-directed," jaded, emptied of zest and adventure. But for various reasons—one of them being that sex by itself had to carry the weight for the validation of the personality in practically all other realms as well— the frontier freshness, newness, and challenge become more and more lost.

For we are now living in the post-Riesman age, and are experiencing the long-run implications of Riesman's "other-directed" behavior, the radar-reflected way of life. The last frontier has become a teeming Las Vegas and no frontier at all. Young people can no longer get a bootlegged feeling of personal identity out of revolting in sexuality since there is nothing there to revolt against. Studies of drug addiction among young people report them as saying that the revolt against parents, the social "kick of feeling their own oats" which they used to get from sex, they now have to get from drugs. One such study indicates that students express a "certain boredom with sex, while drugs are synonymous with excitement, curiosity, forbidden adventure, and society's abounding permissiveness."[25]

It no longer sounds new when we discover that for many young people what used to be called love-making is now experienced as a futile "panting palm to palm," in Aldous Huxley's predictive phrase; that they tell us that it is hard for them to understand what the poets were talking about, and that we should so often hear the disappointed refrain, "We went to bed but it wasn't any good."

Nothing to revolt against, did I say? Well, there is obviously one thing left to revolt against, and that is sex itself. The frontier, the establishing of identity, the validation of the self can be, and not infrequently does become for some people, a revolt against sexuality entirely. I am certainly not advocating this. What I wish to indicate is that the very revolt against sex—this modern Lysistrata in robot's dress—is rumbling at the gates of our cities or, if not rumbling, at least hovering. The sexual revolution comes finally back on itself not with a bang but a whimper.

Notes to Chapter Two

[1] William James, *Principles of Psychology* (New York, Dover Publications, 1950; originally published by Henry Holt, 1890), II, p. 439.

[2] *Atlas*, November, 1965, p. 302. Reprinted from *The Times Literary Supplement*, London.

[3] *Ibid*.

[4] Howard Taubman, "Is Sex Kaput?," *The New York Times*, sect. 2, January 17, 1965.

[5] Leon Edel, "Sex and the Novel," *The New York Times*, sect. 7, pt. I, November 1, 1964.

[6] *Ibid*.

[7] See Taubman.

[8] John L. Schimel, "Ideology and Sexual Practices," *Sexual Behavior and the Law*, ed. Ralph Slovenko (Springfield, Ill., Charles C Thomas, 1965), pp. 195, 197.

[9] Sometimes a woman patient will report to me, in the course of describing how a man tried to seduce her, that she cites as part of his seduction line how efficient a lover he is, and he promises to perform the act eminently satisfactorily for her. (Imagine Mozart's Don Giovanni offering such an argument!) In fairness to elemental human nature, I must add that as far as I can remember, the women reported that this "advance billing" did not add to the seducers' chances of success.

[10] That the actual Puritans in the sixteenth and seventeenth centuries were a different breed from those who represented the deteriorated forms in our century can be seen in a number of sources. Roland H. Bainton in the chapter "Puritanism and the Modern Period," of his book *What Christianity Says About Sex, Love and Marriage* (New York, Reflection Books, Association Press, 1957), writes "The Puritan ideal for the relations of man and wife was summed up in the words, 'a tender respectiveness.'" He quotes Thomas Hooker: "The man whose heart is endeared to the woman he loves, he dreams of her in the night, hath her in his eye and apprehension when he

awakes, museth on her as he sits at table, walks with her when he travels and parlies with her in each place he comes." Ronald Mushat Frye, in a thoughtful paper, "The Teachings of Classical Puritanism on Conjugal Love," *Studies from the Renaissance*, II (1955), submits conclusive evidence that classical Puritanism inculcated a view of sexual life in marriage as the "Crown of all our bliss," "Founded in Reason, Loyal, Just, and Pure" (p. 149). He believes that "the fact remains that the education of England in a more liberal view of married love in the sixteenth and early seventeenth centuries was in large part the work of that party within English Protestantism which is called Puritan" (p. 149). The Puritans were against lust and acting on physical attraction outside of marriage, but they as strongly believed in the sexual side of marriage and believed it the duty of all people to keep this alive all their lives. It was a later confusion which associated them with the asceticism of continence in marriage. Frye states, "In the course of a wide reading of Puritan and other Protestant writers in the sixteenth and early seventeenth centuries, I have found nothing but opposition to this type of ascetic 'perfection'" (p. 152).

One has only to look carefully at the New England churches built by the Puritans and in the Puritan heritage to see the great refinement and dignity of form which surely implies a passionate attitude toward life. They had the dignity of controlled passion, which may have made possible an actual living with passion in contrast to our present pattern of expressing and dispersing all passion. The deterioration of Puritanism into our modern secular attitudes was caused by the confluence of three trends: industrialism, Victorian emotional compartmentalization, and the secularization of all religious attitudes. The first introduced the specific mechanical model; the second introduced the emotional dishonesty which Freud analyzed so well; and the third took away the depth-dimensions of religion and made the concerns how one "behaved" in such matters as smoking, drinking, and sex in the superficial forms which we are attacking above. (For a view of the delightful love letters between husband and wife in this period, see the two-volume biography of John Adams by Page Smith. See also the writings on the Puritans by Perry Miller.)

[11] This formulation was originally suggested to me by Dr. Ludwig Lefebre.

[12] *Atlas*, November, 1965, p. 302.

[13] Philip Rieff, *Freud: The Mind of the Moralist* (New York, Viking Press, 1959), quoted in James A. Knight's "Calvinism and Psychoanalysis: A Comparative Study," *Pastoral Psychology*, December, 1963, p. 10.

[14] Knight, p. 11.

[15] Cf. Marcus, *The Other Victorians*, pp. 146–147. Freud's letter goes on: "Our whole conduct of life presupposes that we are protected from the direst poverty and that the possibility

exists of being able to free ourselves increasingly from social ills. The poor people, the masses, could not survive without their thick skins and their easy-going ways. Why should they scorn the pleasures of the moment when no other awaits them? The poor are too helpless, too exposed, to behave like us. When I see the people indulging themselves, disregarding all sense of moderation, I invariably think that this is their compensation for being a helpless target for all the taxes, epidemics, sickness, and evils of social institutions."

[16] Paul Tillich, in a speech, "Psychoanalysis and Existentialism," given at the Conference of the American Association of Existential Psychology and Psychiatry, February, 1962.

[17] Schimel, p. 198.

[18] Leopold Caligor and Rollo May, in *Dreams and Symbols* (New York, Basic Books, 1968), p. 108n, similarly maintain that today's patients, as a whole, seem to be preoccupied with the head and genitals in their dreams and leave out the heart.

[19] *Playboy*, April, 1957.

[20] These articles by notable people can be biased, as was Timothy Leary's famous interview which *Playboy* used broadly in its advertising, holding that LSD makes possible a "hundred orgasms" for the woman, and that "an LSD session that doesn't involve an ultimate merger isn't really complete." Actually, LSD seemingly temporarily "turns off" the sexual functions. This interview inspired a rejoinder from a writer who is an authority on both LSD and sex, Dr. R. E. L. Masters, who wrote, "Such claims about LSD effects are not only false, they are dangerous. . . . That occasional rare cases might support some of his claims, I don't doubt; but he suggests that he is describing the rule, not the exception, and that is altogther false" (mimeographed letter privately circulated).

[21] "*Playboy's* Doctrine of the Male," in *Christianity and Crisis*, XXI/6, April 17, 1961, unpaged.

[22] Discussion in symposium on sex, Michigan State University, February, 1969.

[23] *Ibid*.

[24] Gerald Sykes, *The Cool Millennium* (New York, 1967).

[25] A survey of students on three college campuses in the New York/New Jersey area conducted by Dr. Sylvia Hertz, Chairman of the Essex County Council on Drug Addiction, reported in *The New York Times* on November 26, 1967, that "The use of drugs has become so prominent, that it has relegated sex to second place."

As sex began to lose its power as the arena of proving one's individuality by rebellion and merged with the use of drugs as the new frontier, both then became related to the preoccupation with acts of violence. Efforts crop up anachronistically here and there to use sex as the vehicle for revolt against society. When I was speaking at a college in California, my student chauffeur to the campus told me that there was a society at the college dedicated, as its name indicates, to "Sex Unlimited." I remarked that I hadn't noticed anybody in California trying to limit sex, so what did this society do? He answered that the previous week, the total membership (which turned out to be six or seven students) got undressed at noon and, naked, jumped into the goldfish pool in the center of the campus. The city police then came and hiked them off to jail. My response was that if one wanted to get arrested, that was a good way to do it, but I couldn't see that the experience had a thing in the world to do with sex.

The Psychiatrists vs. Masters and Johnson

by Vivian Cadden

EDITORS' NOTE: *Mrs. Cadden is a former editor of McCall's and Redbook magazines. She was formerly on the board of the Sex Information and Educational Council (SIECUS). She has written widely on psychiatric subjects and here presents a roundup of authoritative opinion on the Masters and Johnson project.*

Once upon a time—and it seems like a long time ago—there was no doubt in anyone's mind that sex problems were the result of a childhood gone astray. Mother and Father were the villains, of course, and it was certain that the impotent man and what used to be called the "frigid" woman, got that way around the age of three or four, reinforced by some further horrendous experiences during adolescence.

It followed, therefore, like the night upon the day, that the only way to unravel a current sexual dilemma was indeed to unravel it—to take the long, long trail from the unsatisfactory marriage bed back to childhood and Mother and there find the source of the trouble. This meant some kind of therapy, whether psychoanalysis or less ambitious forms, which dealt not only, or even specifically with the sex problem at issue, but which ranged over a whole gamut of recollections, experiences and problems.

Today, while many experts would give at least a nodding agreement to the first proposition—that sexual inadequacy probably has some origins in the whole web of an adult's childhood experiences, there are nevertheless an increasing number who find the second proposition a nonsequitur. Even if Mother is the culprit, they don't believe that it is necessary or even wise to dredge up the details of her villainy. They believe that most sex problems can be treated in the here and now.

Dr. William Masters and Mrs. Virginia Johnson are the apotheosis of the here-and-now treatment of sex problems. Their two-week clinic sessions in St. Louis with couples seeking help spend a minimum of time excavating the past. True, Masters and Johnson take a very detailed sexual history and their account of the treatment process contained in their new book, *Human Sexual Inadequacy*, has passing references to such familiar and baleful factors and figures as The Dominant Mother, The Dominant Father, Religious Orthodoxy and GUILT. Nevertheless Masters and Johnson are committed to the treatment of sexual dysfunction regardless of its origin. And it is this short shrift that they give to the sources of the problem and their belief that in a sense sexual problems can be isolated from other problems that first earned them the enmity of those specialists in origins and interrelatedness, the psychoanalysts and psychoanalytically oriented therapists.

The rift between Masters and Johnson and certain wings of psychiatry got off to an early start even before the publication of their first book, *Human Sexual Response*. In a brilliant and often uproariously funny article, entitled, "I'm Sorry, Dear," Dr. Leslie H. Farber, a Washington, D. C. psychoanalyst, mercilessly spoofed the cult of simultaneous, self-conscious, split-second satisfaction, used Masters and Johnson as the prime examples of his thesis that "sex for the most part has lost its viability as a human experience" and delivered a withering blast against what he considered the tasteless and atypical aspects of sex as studied in the laboratory.

Farber was followed, upon publication of the book, by a goodly number of others. "Mechanical," "mechanistic," "dehumanizing," "depersonalizing" were among the favorite words of the critics.

Now, with the publication of *Human Sexual Inadequacy* the battle lines have been drawn again but with one very important difference. In the four years between the appearance of these two books there has been a significant shift within psychiatry from the long-term delving into the origins of problems and the global aim of changing "the whole person" to the here and now treatment of current difficulties. This applies not only to sex problems but to many, varied, specific complaints and distresses that patients may bring to a therapist.

"Mechanical," "mechanistic," "dehumanizing," and "depersonalizing" are still the favorite adjectives of the critics of the new Masters and Johnson study. But there are fewer voices and even those that are heard are, for the most part, somewhat muted.

One pillar of psychoanalytic orthodoxy still remains to state the pure, classical position. Dr. Natalie Shainess, a New York psychoanalyst, was one of the most vocal critics of the earlier study. Not surprisingly, reporters sought her out upon publication of the new book and Dr. Shainess was quoted as calling the study "oversimplistic and naive." It was, she said, merely a way of "papering over" symptoms, which, because they arose from deep seated and fundamental problems, would be certain to reappear.

Dr. Shainess feels something of a sense of mission in her attack on the whole range of Masters' and Johnson's work. She is particularly blistering about their therapy for the problem of premature ejaculation, since it involves a specific technique that can be easily taught, is reportedly almost 100 percent foolproof and has all the hallmarks of a sexual "gimmick."

"Is that sex?" Dr. Shainess asks with withering scorn. "That's manipulation! What happens to a person's ego in that kind of sex? A man must feel like a puppet. What kind of ongoing process can it be when a woman must do this or do that? That's just a parody of sexual intercourse! Press here. Touch there. That's joyless sex!"

Behind sexual inadequacy, Dr. Shainess believes, there is always anxiety, fear, hatred or rage—or a combination of these. The genesis of sexual disturbances lies somewhere deep in the past and there are no shortcuts to their alleviation. While Dr. Shainess does not claim that psychiatry is always successful in freeing people so that they may know joyful sex, she dismisses the Masters and Johnson approach as a kind of "Coaching that reduces one partner to a push-button operator."

But, as Dr. Shainess is the first to admit, hers is fast becoming an extreme minority position within her profession. "I'm on lonely ground," she says. "I don't know why the psychiatrists are jumping on the Masters and Johnson bandwagon. I wish I knew. They seem glad to have a sexual bible."

If not all psychiatrists have "jumped on the bandwagon" it is true that most of them are viewing the Masters and Johnson work with greater respect than they did four years ago. The change has paralleled their greater respect for the treatment of symptoms, behavioral problems and inadequate functioning of all kinds, apart from and regardless of their source. It is not that they have altogether given up their search for reasons and origins and sources but rather their growing conviction that help need not wait upon complete understanding.

John H. Gagnon, associate professor of sociology at State University of New York, and formerly a senior research fellow at the Kinsey Institute points out that what Masters and Johnson are doing is akin to "behavior therapy".

"Behavior therapy," Gagnon says, "treats the presenting problem. If you have a phobia about rats, it tries to desensitize you to rats. If you have a fear of high places, it tries to tackle that fear of high places. No need to drag Mother into it."

Gagnon believes that the trouble with traditional psychoanalysis is that it assumed too much continuity between childhood and adulthood. The man who is afraid of flying may never have fallen out of the apple tree as a child and even if he did, and now understands that he did and remembers how unpleasant that was, it may have very little bearing on his ability to muster the strength to board a plane. A kind of psychiatric Dramamine (plus Dramamine) might be of greater help.

Until relatively recently, Gagnon says, psychiatry has proceeded on the premise that if you understand something, you can do something about it. If you know how someone made a lock you can then make keys to open it. If you understand the etiology of a symptom or a disease— if you know how it came about—you can cure it. "But," Gagnon says, "it's not necessarily so—as psychiatrists are more and more admitting."

"What Masters and Johnson (and behavior therapy) recognize is that the symptom takes on a life of its own, a functional autonomy, that in turn creates other problems. Regardless of where it came from—and obviously sexual inadequacy can come from a myriad of sources—it's there, operating as a here-and-now factor in a marriage. And if the symptom can be treated who are we to say that this is not a *profound* change in the life of a human being."

Gagnon believes that some psychiatrists, "particularly run-of-the-mill ones," have had a tendency to be "uptight" about Masters and Johnson because prior to their advent it was the psychiatrist and the psychiatrist alone who was "Dr. Sex."

"It was threatening enough to the profession when Masters and Johnson set about with their original research into the nature of sexual response. But now that they have gone into therapy many traditional therapists will be as jittery as the plumbers union is when faced with a possible incursion of blacks into their ranks."

Gerald Caplan, Professor of Clinical Psychiatry at the Harvard Medical School and Director of the Laboratory of Community Psychiatry, feels that the point of view exemplified by Dr. Shainess is probably related to the very skewed sample of the population that analysts are likely to see.

"These are often extremely disturbed people whose sex problems are only one part of some very deep pathology," Dr. Caplan says. "I can understand how in such cases dealing with the sex problem can be thought of as merely 'papering over' symptoms—although in some cases that in itself can be helpful. In other cases, if the sex problem is the only outlet for the pathology, removing it might make matters even worse.

"There are fat people whose obesity is one expression of deep disturbances. Solving the obesity problem would 'paper over' other problems yet it might be a positive step forward. There are other fat people whose fatness is the *sole* expression of deep disturbances. If you take away their obesity, they might become depressed and psychotic."

But such considerations, Dr. Caplan believes, whether about sex or obesity, apply only to a very tiny minority—perhaps 5 percent—of the people who need help.

"For most people," Dr. Caplan says, "sex problems may

very well have emerged from relatively mild conflicts. The symptoms have then perpetuated themselves and thus brought on secondary symptoms. Removing such symptoms is not only possible, it produces an ego strength that is good. It makes people feel better."

Dr. Caplan estimates that at least 60 percent of sexual problems arise out of problems that are not longer active—ignorance at some past time, failing on a wedding night and having failed once, failing twice and feeling then psychologically inept.

"Masters' and Johnson's approach is a re-education approach," Dr. Caplan says, "a kind of re-training approach. To call it 'mechanistic' plainly misses the pole. It is certainly true that sexual intercourse has its basis in instinctual life. It is a form of human interaction. But people often have to learn modes of interaction; they don't necessarily spring forth in full bloom. One might say that dancing and singing together are forms of human interaction—very ancient and important forms indeed—yet they can be learned.

"And sexual intercourse, like almost everything else is a learned experience. Nor is there any inherent conflict between training and spontaneity. At the moment of being trained one must be highly conscious. But that training having been accomplished, one can be entirely spontaneous. One might even say that the training of a ballet dancer or a pianist or an actor is precisely what frees him to be spontaneous. Having mastery, he can throw away the book."

Dr. Caplan thinks that Masters and Johnson are up to something besides behavior therapy or symptom relief. In many cases of sexual inadequacy, the failing is not necessarily a "symptom." It's what Dr. Caplan calls "ineffective behavior." Masters and Johnson, he believes, are modifying ineffective behavior.

Traditional psychiatry and Masters and Johnson are at odds not only on the importance of the origins of sexual inadequacy and the efficacy of treating it *ad hoc* but also on the question of whether to treat one or both partners.

It is a cornerstone of the Masters and Johnson method that both partners in a marriage or a sexual relationship be treated together even though it may seem that only one has the problem. Not only do Masters and Johnson consider this approach crucial to their work; they suggest that the failure of traditional therapy in problems of sexual inadequacy can be laid at the door of the single-partner-treatment concept.

If only one partner is in treatment, Masters and Johnson say, the other partner may "destroy or negate" the treatment simply because he or she is not privy to what is going on and has no clues on how to act.

"For example," Masters and Johnson say, "if little or no information of sexual import, or for that matter of total treatment progress, reaches the wife of an impotent husband, she is in a quandary as to the most effective means of dealing with the ongoing marital relationship while her husband is in therapy. She does not know when, or if, or how, or under what circumstances to make sexual advances, or whether she should make advances at all. Would it be better to be simply a 'good wife' available to her husband's expression of sexual intent, or on occasion should she take the sexual initiative? During actual sexual functioning should she maintain a completely passive, a somewhat active, or a mutually participating role? None of these questions, all of which inevitably arise in the mind of any intelligent woman contending with the multiple anxieties and performance fears of an impotent husband, finds answers in the inevitable communications void that develops between husband and wife when one is isolated as a participant in therapy."

Dr. Caplan agrees completely with Masters and Johnson on the importance of treating both partners. But he feels that so many of his colleagues share this point of view that Masters and Johnson are "beating a dead horse" on this point. "I wouldn't conceive of treating a married couple or a pair of lovers with sexual problems without seeing each individually and/or both together," he says.

Harold Lief, Professor of Psychiatry and Director of the Division of Family Study at the University of Pennsylvania School of Medicine, and one of the earliest and most enthusiastic supporters of the Masters and Johnson research, also concurs heartily that sexual problems can best be treated within the context of the marriage relationship. Dr. Lief, who is also President of the Sex Information and Education Council of the United States (SIECUS), feels that the chances for success are much greater when both partners are involved.

"There are occasional exceptions as when one partner has deep-seated fears and phobias and inhibitions," Dr. Lief says. "Here psychiatry for that person seems to be indicated. But there's no guarantee that psychiatry will be able to do any better with such cases. For the vast bulk of cases of sexual inadequacy it makes eminently good sense to treat the couple."

Dr. Lief tells of a woman patient whom he had had in therapy for a long while, with no success. He referred her and her husband to Masters and Johnson and they went out to St. Louis for two weeks.

"She was paranoid, in a constant state of rage against her husband and what she described as his cruelty to her," Dr. Lief says. "He was an obsessive-compulsive and if not cruel, at least wholly insensitive to her needs."

After the couple had been in St. Louis for 11 days, Mrs. Johnson called Dr. Lief to report that the couple was having successful sexual relations for the first time in many years.

But five months later the wife was in a lawyer's office, raging again, and instituting divorce proceedings against her husband. Mrs. Johnson had taught them some tricks, she said. But that was the extent of it.

"Well," Dr. Lief remarks, "here was a case where we all failed."

No one knows better than Masters and Johnson that there will be failures. And indeed, it is probably the disarming modesty of their claims that will eventually serve to erase any conflict of interest between them and the psychiatrists.

The New York Times, headlined its front-page story on the publication of *Human Sexual Inadequacy,* "80% Success Claimed for Sex Therapy." But that was the *Times* interpretation of Masters' and Johnson's report of a 20 percent failure rate in their work. Masters and Johnson know that "success" is not the opposite of failure. By talking about failure, Masters and Johnson carefully put a limit on their goals. With calculated understatement, Masters and Johnson in effect define their objective as seeing to it that a sexually dysfunctional couple with a presenting complaint of say, secondary impotence, does not have that complaint upon leaving St. Louis after two weeks of therapy and continues not to have that complaint five years later.

The Masters and Johnson "successes" as some people call them, or non-failures, as Masters and Johnson would call them, may indeed find that "success" is not all that it is advertised to be. The non-orgasmic woman, orgasmic after therapy, may find that this experience is not the be-all and end-all of marriage. She may find that it's not sufficient to have a fundamentally poor relationship. The happy-go-lucky premature ejaculator may turn into a responsible, anxious, joyless provider of satisfaction to a wife who doesn't know which version of him is preferable. Possible. But Masters and Johnson have never pretended to solve all the ills of mankind, or even to save marriages.

Bibliography of the Reproductive Biology Research Foundation

1. Masters, W. H., Grody, M. H., and Robinson, D. W., Management and treatment of infertility. J.M.S.M.A., 49:327–337, 1952.

2. Grody, M. H., Robinson, D. W., and Masters, W. H., The cervical cap: an adjunct in the treatment of male infertility. J.A.M.A., 149:427–431, 1952.

3. Masters, W. H., Magallon, D. T., and Grody, M. H., Gonadotrophin titer in the adult human male: the effect of ejaculation. J. Urol., 67:1028–1036, 1952.

4. Goldhar, A., Grody, M. H., and Masters, W. H., The vaginal smear as an ovulatory index. Fertil. & Steril., 3:376–392, 1952.

5. Ballew, J. W., and Masters, W. H., Mumps: a cause of infertility, I. present considerations. Fertil. & Steril., 5:536–543, 1954.

6. Lampe, E. H., and Masters, W. H., Problems of male fertility, II. effect of frequent ejaculation. Fertil. & Steril., 7:123–127, 1956.

7. Riley, F. J., and Masters, W. H., Problems of male fertility, III. bacteriology of human semen. Fertil. & Steril., 7:128–132, 1956.

8. Masters, W. H., The infertile couple: a basic evaluation technique. J. Okla. S.M.A., 49:517–521, 1956.

9. Masters, W. H., Maze, L. E., and Gilpatrick, T. S., Etiological approach to habitual abortion. Am. J. Obst. & Gynec., 73:1022–1032, 1957.

10. Masters, W. H., Infertility—a family unit problem. Minn. Med., 40:842–846, 1957.

11. Masters. W. H., Infertility—a family unit problem. Medical Times, 86:825–832, 1958.

12. Masters, W. H., The infertile male—an obstetrical problem. S. Dakota J. Med. & Pharm., 12:131–134, 1959.
13. Masters, W. H., The sexual response cycle of the human female: vaginal lubrication. Ann. N. Y. Acad. Sci., 83:301–317, 1959.
14. Masters, W. H., and Johnson, V. E., The human female: anatomy of sexual response. Minn. Med., 43:31–36, 1960.
15. Masters, W. H., The sexual response cycle of the human female; I. gross anatomic considerations. West J. Surg., Obst. & Gynec., 68:57–72, 1960
16. Masters, W. H., "Influence of Male Ejaculate on Vaginal Acidity," *Endocrine Dysfunction and Infertility*, Report of the Thirty-fifth Ross Conference on Pediatric Research, 76–78, 1960.
17. Masters, W. H., and Johnson, V. E., "Orgasm, Anatomy of the Female," *The Encyclopedia of Sexual Behavior*, Vol. II (Ellis, A., and Abarbanel, A., eds.), 788–793, Hawthorn Books, Inc., New York, 1961.
18. Masters, W. H., and Johnson, V. E., The physiology of the vaginal reproductive function. West. J. Surg., Obst. & Gynec., 69:105–120, 1961.
19. Masters, W. H., and Johnson, V. E., The artificial vagina: anatomic, physiologic, psychosexual function. West J. Surg., Obst. & Gynec., 69:192–212, 1961.
20. Johnson, V. E., and Masters, W. H., Treatment of the sexually incompatible family unit. Minn. Med., 44:466–471, 1961.
21. Masters, W. H., and Johnson, V. E., Intravaginal environment, I. a lethal factor. Fertil. & Steril., 12:560–580, 1961.
22. Johnson, V. E., and Masters, W. H., Intravaginal contraceptive study, phase I. anatomy. West. J. Surg., Obst. & Gynec., 70:202–207, 1962.
23. Masters, W. H., and Johnson, V. E., The sexual response cycle of the human female, III. the clitoris: anatomic and clinical considerations. West. J. Surg., Obst. & Gynec., 70:248–257, 1962.
24. Masters, W. H., and Johnson, V. E., The sexual response cycle of the human male, I. gross anatomic considerations. West. J. Surg., Obst. & Gynec., 71:85–95, 1963.
25. Johnson, V. E., and Masters, W. H., Intravaginal contraceptive study, phase II. physiology (a direct test for protective potential). West. J. Surg., Obst. & Gynec., 71:144–153, 1963.

26. Masters, W. H., and Johnson, V. E., "The Clitoris: an Anatomic Baseline for Behavioral Investigation," *Determinants of Human Sexual Behavior* (Winokur, G. W., ed.), 3:44–51, Charles C Thomas, Springfield, Illinois, 1963.

27. Johnson, V. E., Masters, W. H., and Lewis, K. C., "The Physiology of Intravaginal Contraceptive Failure," *Manual of Contraceptive Practice* (Calderone, M. E., ed.), 6:138–150, The Williams and Wilkins Co., Baltimore, 1964.

28. Masters, W. H., and Johnson, V. E., "Sexual response: Part II. Anatomy and Physiology," *Human Reproduction and Sexual Behavior* (Lloyd, C. W., ed.), 25:460–472, Lea & Febiger, Philadelphia, 1964.

29. Johnson, V. E., and Masters, W. H., "Sexual Incompatibility: Diagnosis and Treatment," *Human Reproduction and Sexual Behavior* (Lloyd, C. W., ed.), 26:474–489, Lea & Febiger, Philadelphia, 1964.

30. Johnson, V. E., and Masters, W. H., A team approach to the rapid diagnosis and treatment of sexual incompatibility. Pac. Med. & Surg., 72:371–375, 1964.

31. Masters, W. H., and Johnson, V. E., "Counseling with Sexually Incompatible Marriage Partners," *Counseling in Marital and Sexual Problems (A Physician's Handbook)* (Klemer, R. H., ed.), 13:126–137, Williams & Wilkins, Baltimore, 1965.

32. Masters, W. H., and Johnson, V. E., "The Sexual Response Cycle of the Human Female: I. Gross Anatomic Considerations," *Sex Research-New Developments* (Money, J., ed.), 3:53–89, Holt, Rinehart & Winston, Inc., New York, 1965.

33. Masters, W. H., and Johnson, V. E., "The Sexual Response Cycle of the Human Female: II. The Clitoris: Anatomic and Clinical Considerations," *Sex Research-New Developments* (Money, J., ed.), 4:90–112, Holt, Rinehart & Winston, Inc., New York, 1965.

34. Johnson, V. E., and Masters, W. H., A product of dual import: intravaginal infection control and conception control. Pac. Med. & Surg., 73:267–271, 1965.

35. Masters, W. H., and Johnson, V. E., "The Sexual Response Cycles of the Human Male and Female: Comparative Anatomy and Physiology," *Sex & Behavior* (Beach, F. A. ed.), 21:512–534, John Wiley & Sons, Inc., New York, 1965.

36. Masters, W. H., and Johnson, V. E., *Human Sexual Response*, Little, Brown and Co., Boston, 1966.

37. Masters, W. H., Clinical significance of the study of human sexual response. Med. Aspects of Human Sexuality, 1:14–20, 1967.

38. Masters, W. H., and Johnson, V. E., "Clinical Parameters of Human Reproduction and Sexual Behavior," *Perspectives in Reproduction and Sexual Behavior* (Diamond, M., ed.), Indiana University Press. In print.

39. Masters, W. H., and Johnson, V. E., The scientist and his interpreters. Bull. Am. Med. Writers Assoc. (Dailey, E. G., ed.), Vol. XVII, No. 5, pp. 4–9, 1967.

40. Bauer, J. D., Ackerman, P. G., and Toro, G., *Bray's Clinical Laboratory Methods*, (7th ed.), C. V. Mosby, St. Louis, 1968.

41. Masters, W. H., Toro, G., Ackerman, P. G., and Johnson, V. E., Biochemistry of human vaginal lubrication, 1. enzymology. J. Fertil. & Steril., in print. 1968.

42. Masters, W. H., and Johnson, V. E., "Human Sexual Response: the Aging Female and the Aging Male," *Middle Age and Aging* (Neugarten, B. L., ed.) Chicago and London: University of Chicago Press, 30:269–279, 1968.

Directors' Professional Bibliography

1. Masters, W. H., and Allen, W. M., Female sex hormone replacement in the aged woman. J. Gerontol., 3:183–190, 1948.

2. Masters, W. H., Caudal analgesia. J.M.S.M.A., 45:592–597, 1948.

3. Masters, W. H., Continuous caudal analgesia (a report of 1,500 cases). Am. J. Obst. & Gynec., 56:756–761, 1948.

4. Masters, W. H., "The Advantages of Conduction Anesthesia in Premature Labor and Delivery," *Control of Pain in Childbirth* (Lull and Hingson, eds.), 473–476, 3rd ed., J. B. Lippincott Co., Philadelphia, 1948.

5. Masters, W. H., Ectopic pregnancy. J.M.S.M.A., 46:405–410, 1949.

6. Masters, W. H., and Allen, W. M., "Investigation of Sexual Regeneration in Elderly Women," Conference on Problems of Aging, Transactions of the Tenth and Eleventh Conferences, February 1948, and April 1949, 21–29, Josiah Macy Jr. Foundation, New York.

7. Masters, W. H., and Ross, R. W., Conduction anesthesia (protection afforded the premature infant). J.A.M.A., 141:909–912, 1949.

8. Masters, W. H., and Magallon, D. T., Androgen administration in the postmenopausal woman. J. Clin. Endocrinol., 10:348–358, 1950.

9. Masters, W. H., and Magallon, D. T., "Hormone Replacement" Therapy in the Aged Female—Estrogen Bioassay," Proceedings of the Soc. for Exp. Biol. and Med., 73:672–676, 1950.

10. Masters, W. H., and Magallon, D. T., The experimental production of irregular shedding of the endometrium. Am. J. Obst. & Gynec., 59:970–978, 1950.

11. Magallon, D. T., and Masters, W. H., Basal temperature studies in the aged female: influence of estrogen, pro-

gesterone and androgen. J. Clin. Endocrinol., 10:511–518, 1950.

12. Masters, W. H., The rationale and technique of sex hormone replacement in the aged female and a preliminary result report. S. Dakota J., 4:296–300, 1951.

13. Masters, W. H., "The Female Reproductive System," *Cowdry's Problems of Aging*, 25:651–685, 3rd ed., The Williams and Wilkins Co., Baltimore, 1952.

14. Masters, W. H., Grody, M. H., and Robinson, D. W., Management and treatment of infertility. J.M.S.M.A., 49:327–337, 1952.

15. Grody, M. H., Robinson, D. W., and Masters, W. H., The cervical cap: an adjunct in the treatment of male infertility. J.A.M.A., 149:427–431, 1952.

16. Masters, W. H., Magallon, D. T., and Grody, M. H., Gonadotrophin titer in the adult human male: the effect of ejaculation. J. Urol., 67:1028–1036, 1952.

17. Goldhar, A., Grody, M. H., and Masters, W. H., The vaginal smear as an ovulatory index. Fertil. & Steril., 3:376–392, 1952.

18. Masters, W. H., Grody, M. H., and Magallon, D. T., Progesterone in aqueous crystalline suspension vs. progesterone in oil: comparable withdrawal bleeding experiments in the human female. J. Clin. Endocrinol. & Metabol., 12:1445–1453, 1952.

19. Masters, W. H., Long-rang sex steroid replacement—target organ regeneration. J. Gerontol., 8:33–39, 1953.

20. Lamb, W. M., Ulett, G. A., Masters, W. H., and Robinson, D. W., Premenstrual tension: EEG, hormonal, and psychiatric evaluation. Am. J. Psychiat., 109:840–848, 1953.

21. Grody, M. H., Lampe, E. H., and Masters, W. H., Estrogen-androgen substitution therapy in the aged female, I. uterine bioassay report. Obst. & Gynec., 2:36–45, 1953.

22. Masters, W. H., and Grody, M. H., Estrogen-androgen substitution therapy in the aged female, II. clinical response. Obst. & Gynec., 2:139–147, 1953.

23. Goldhar, A., and Masters, W. H., Continuous caudal analgesia—housestaff management of 5,000 consecutive cases. Miss. V. Med. J., 75: 1953.

24. Masters, W. H., The abdominal approach to cystourethrocele repair. Am. J. Obst. & Gynec. 67:85–91, 1954.

25. Ballew, J. W., and Masters, W. H., Mumps: a cause of infertility, I. present considerations. Fertil. & Steril., 5:536–543, 1954.

26. Masters, W. H., and Ballew, J. W., The third sex. Geriatrics, 10:1–4, 1955.
27. Masters, W. H., and Ballew, J. W., "The Third Sex," *Proceedings of the 3rd International Congress of Gerontology: Old Age in the Modern World*. E. & S. Livingstone Ltd., London, 1955.
28. Masters, W. H., "Sex Life of the Aging Female," *Sex in Our Culture*. Emerson Books, Inc., New York, 1955.
29. Masters, W. H., Rationale of sex steroid replacement in the "neutral gender." J. Geriatrics, 3:389–395, 1955.
30. Allen, W. M., and Masters, W. H., Traumatic laceration of uterine support: the clinical syndrome and the operative treatment. Am. J. Obst. & Gynec., 70:500–513, 1955.
31. Masters, W. H., "Sex Steroid Replacement in the Aging Individual," *Hormones and the Aging Process*, 241–251, Academic Press Inc., New York, 1956.
32. Lampe, E. H., and Masters, W. H., Problems of male fertility, II. effect of frequent ejaculation. Fertil. & Steril. 7:123–127, 1956.
33. Riley, F. J., and Masters, W. H., Problems of male fertility, III. bacteriology of human semen. Fertil. & Steril., 7:128–132, 1956.
34. Masters, W. H., Endocrine therapy in the aging individual. Obst. & Gynec., 8:61–67, 1956.
35. Masters, W. H., The present status of the estrogen-androgen replacement experiments. J. Miss. V. Med., 78:177–178, 1956.
36. Masters, W. H., The infertile couple: a basic evaluation technique. J. Okla. S.M.A., 49:517–521, 1956.
37. Masters, W. H., The surgeon's role in geriatric female endocrinology. J. Int. Col. Surg., 27:189–192, 1957.
38. Masters, W. H., Maze, L. E., and Gilpatrick, T. S., Etiological approach to habitual abortion. Am. J. Obst. & Gynec., 73:1022–1032, 1951.
39. Masters, W. H., Sex steroid influence on the aging process, Am. J. Obst. & Gynec., 74:733–746, 1957.
40. Masters, W. H., Infertility—a Family unit problem. Minn. Med., 40:842–846, 1957.
41. Masters, W. H., "Amenorrhea," *Current Therapy* (Conn, H. F., ed.), 679–682, W. B. Saunders Co., 1958.
42. Masters, W. H., Menopause and thereafter. Minn. Med., 41:1–4, 1958.
43. Masters, W. H., Infertility—a family unit problem. Medical Times, 86:825–832, 1958.

44. Masters, W. H., The infertile male—an obstetrical problem. S. Dakota J. Med. & Pharm., 12:131–134, 1959.

45. Masters, W. H., The sexual response cycle of the human female: vaginal lubrication. Ann. N. Y. Acad. Sci., 83: 301–317, 1959.

46. Dunnihoo, D. R., and Masters, W. H., Ectopic pregnancy: a report of 219 cases. Minn. Med., 42:1768–1772, 1959.

47. Masters, W. H., and Johnson, V. E., The human female: anatomy of sexual response. Minn. Med., 43:31–36, 1960.

48. Masters, W. H., The sexual response cycle of the human female: I. gross anatomic considerations. West. J. Surg., Obst. & Gynec., 68:57–72, 1960.

49. Masters, W. H., "Influence of Male Ejaculate on Vaginal Acidity," *Endocrine Dysfunction and Infertility*, Report of the Thirty-fifth Ross Conference on Pediatric Research, 76–78, 1960.

50. Masters, W. H., and Johnson, V. E., "Orgasm, Anatomy of the Female," *The Encyclopedia of Sexual Behavior*, Vol. II (Ellis, A., and Abarbanel, A., eds.), 788–793, Hawthorn Books, Inc., New York, 1961.

51. Masters, W. H., and Johnson, V. E., The physiology of the vaginal reproductive function. West J. Surg., Obst. & Gynec., 69:105–120, 1961.

52. Holmes, D. R., and Masters, W. H., Ectopic pregnancy. Clin. Med., 8:899–903, 1961.

53. Masters, W. H., and Johnson, V. E., The artificial vagina: anatomic, physiologic, psychosexual function. West. J. Surg., Obst. & Gynec., 69:192–212, 1961.

54. Johnson, V. E., and Masters, W. H., Treatment of the sexually incompatible family unit. Minn. Med., 44:466–471, 1961.

55. Masters, W. H., and Johnson, V. E., Intravaginal environment, I. a lethal factor. Fertil. & Steril., 12:560–580, 1961.

56. Johnson, V. E., and Masters, W. H., Intravaginal contraceptive study, phase I. anatomy. West. J. Surg., Obst. & Gynec., 70:202–207, 1962.

57. Masters, W. H., and Johnson, V. E., The sexual response cycle of the human female, III. the clitoris: anatomic and clinical considerations. West. J. Surg., Obst. & Gynec., 70:248–257, 1962.

58. Masters, W. H., and Johnson, V. E., The sexual response cycle of the human male, I. gross anatomic considerations. West. J. Surg., Obst. & Gynec., 71:85–95, 1963.

59. Johnson, V. E., and Masters, W. H., Intravaginal contraceptive study, phase II. physiology (a direct test for protective potential). West. J. Surg., Obst. & Gynec., 71:144–153, 1963.

60. Masters, W. H., and Johnson, V. E., "The Clitoris: an Anatomic Baseline for Behavioral Investigation," *Determinants of Human Sexual Behavior* (Winokur, G. W., ed.), 3:44–51, Charles C Thomas, Springfield, Illinois, 1963.

61. Johnson, V. E., Masters, W. H., and Lewis, K. C., "The Physiology of Intravaginal Contraceptive Failure," *Manual of Contraceptive Practice* (Calderone, M. E., ed.), 6:138–150, The Williams & Wilkins Co., Baltimore, 1964.

62. Masters, W. H., and Johnson, V. E., "Sexual Response: Part II. Anatomy and Physiology," *Human Reproduction and Sexual Behavior* (Lloyd, C. W., ed.), 25:460–472, Lea & Febiger, Philadelphia, 1964.

63. Johnson, V. E., and Masters, W. H., "Sexual Incompatibility: Diagnosis and Treatment," *Human Reproduction and Sexual Behavior* (Lloyd, C. W., ed.), 26:474–489, Lea & Febiger, Philadelphia, 1964.

64. Johnson, V. E., and Masters, W. H., A team approach to the rapid diagnosis and treatment of sexual incompatibility. Pac. Med. & Surg., 72:371–375, 1964.

65. Masters, W. H., and Johnson, V. E., "Counseling with Sexually Incompatible Marriage Partners," *Counseling in Marital and Sexual Problems (A Physician's Handbook)* (Klemer, R. H., ed.), 13:126–137, The Williams & Wilkins Co., Baltimore, 1965.

66. Masters, W. H., and Johnson, V. E., "The Sexual Response Cycle of the Human Female: I. Gross Anatomic Considerations", *Sex Research-New Developments* (Money, J., ed.), 3:53–89, Holt, Rinehart & Winston, Inc., New York, 1965.

67. Masters, W. H., and Johnson, V. E., "The Sexual Response Cycle of the Human Female: II. The Clitoris: Anatomic and Clinical Considerations," *Sex Research-New Developments* (Money, J. ed.), 4:90–112, Holt, Rinehart & Winston, Inc., New York, 1965.

68. Johnson, V. E., and Masters, W. H., A product of dual import: intravaginal infection control and conception control. Pac. Med. & Surg., 73:267–271, 1965.

69. Masters, W. H., and Ballew, J. W., "The Third Sex," *Problems of the Middle-Aged* (Vedder, C. G., ed.), 134–140, Charles C Thomas, Springfield, Illinois, 1965.

70. Masters, W. H., and Johnson, V. E., "The Sexual Response Cycles of the Human Male and Female: Comparative Anatomy and Physiology," *Sex & Behavior* (Beach, F. A., ed.), 21:512–534, John Wiley & Sons, Inc., New York, 1965.

71. Masters, W. H., and Johnson, V. E., *Human Sexual Response,* Little, Brown and Co., Boston, 1966.

72. Masters, W. H., Clinical significance of the study of human sexual response: Med. Aspects of Human Sexuality, 1:14–20, 1967.

73. Masters, W. H., and Johnson, V. E., "Clinical Parameters of Human Reproduction and Sexual Behavior," *Perspectives in Reproduction and Sexual Behavior* (Diamond, M., ed.), Indiana University Press. In print.

74. Masters, W. H., and Johnson, V. E., The scientist and his interpreters. Bull. Am. Med. Writers Assoc. (Dailey, E. G., ed.), Vol. XVII, No. 5, pp. 4–9, 1967.

75. Masters, W. H., Toro, G., Ackerman, P. G., and Johnson, V. E., Biochemistry of human vaginal lubrication, 1. enzymology. J. of Fertil. and Steril., in print, 1968.

76. Masters, W. H., and Johnson, V. E., "Human Sexual Response: the Aging Female and the Aging Male," *Middle Age and Aging* (Neugarten, B. L., ed.) Chicago and London: University of Chicago Press, 30:269–279, 1968.

Other SIGNET Marriage Manuals

- [ ] **SEXUAL FREEDOM IN MARRIAGE edited by Isadore Rubin.** A personal guide to a satisfactory sex life. (#Q3995—95¢)

- [ ] **LOVE AND ORGASM by Alexander Lowen, M.D.** A distinguished psychiatrist examines the physical and psychic conditions and effects of complete sexual satisfaction, presenting a revolutionary view of the role of love in sex. (#Q3227—95¢)

- [ ] **PREGNANCY AND BIRTH by Alan F. Guttmacher, M.D.** A handbook for expectant parents by the Director of Gynecology and Obstetrics, Mount Sinai Hospital, New York. (#Q4508—95¢)

- [ ] **LIFE BEFORE BIRTH by Ashley Montagu.** Vital information for the mother-to-be to increase her chances of bearing a normal, healthy baby. Introduction by Dr. Alan E. Guttmacher. (#T2690—75¢)

THE NEW AMERICAN LIBRARY, INC., P.O. Box 2310, Grand Central Station, New York, New York 10017

Please send me the SIGNET BOOKS I have checked above. I am enclosing $_____(check or money order—no currency or C.O.D.'s). Pleaes include the list price plus 10¢ a copy to cover mailing costs. (New York City residents add 6% Sales Tax. Other New York State residents add 3% plus any local sales or use taxes.)

Name_____

Address_____

City_____State_____Zip Code_____

Allow at least 3 weeks for delivery

☐ **SEX AND THE OVERWEIGHT WOMAN by Dr. Eugene Scheimann with Paul Neimark.** Fact is separated from fiction in this penetrating study of sex and the overweight woman. (#T4127—75¢)

☐ **LOVE WITHOUT FEAR by Dr. Eustace Chesser.** A noted physician and marriage counselor offers scientific information on how to achieve sexual happiness in marriage. (#Q4367—95¢)

☐ **HUSBAND AND LOVER: The Art of Sex for Men by Robert Chartham.** A frank, authoritative guide describing in clear, everyday language the sex techniques every man should know in order to achieve a happy and satisfying marriage. (#T3293—75¢)

☐ **THE ENJOYMENT OF LOVE IN MARRIAGE by LeMon Clark, M.D.** An honest guide to sexual harmony—illustrated with line drawings demonstrating positions in intercourse. (#T3886—75¢)

THE NEW AMERICAN LIBRARY, INC., P.O. Box 2310, Grand Central Station, New York, New York 10017

Please send me the SIGNET BOOKS I have checked above. I am enclosing $_____(check or money order—no currency or C.O.D.'s). Please include the list price plus 10¢ a copy to cover mailing costs. (New York City residents add 6% Sales Tax. Other New York State residents add 3% plus any local sales or use taxes.)

Name_____

Address_____

City_____State_____Zip Code_____

Allow at least 3 weeks for delivery

Other SIGNET Titles of Special Interest

☐ **LET'S COOK IT RIGHT by Adelle Davis.** For the first time in paperback, and completely revised and updated, the celebrated cookbook dedicated to good health, good sense and good eating. Contains 400 easy-to-follow basic recipes, a table of equivalents and an index.
(#W4383—$1.50)

☐ **THE ROOTS OF HEALTH by Leon Petulengro.** The passport to good health is in the natural food that grows all around in the fields, hedges and gardens. The author tells you how to keep healthy by using the right foods, truly "the roots of health." (#T4267—75¢)

☐ **JOGGING, AEROBICS AND DIET: One is Not Enough—You Need All Three by Roy Ald with a Foreword by M. Thomas Woodall, Ph.D.** A personalized prescription for health, vitality, and general well-being based on a revolutionary new theory of exercise. (#T3703—75¢)

☐ **THE NEW AMERICAN MEDICAL DICTIONARY AND HEALTH MANUAL by Robert Rothenberg, M.D.** Over 7500 definitions of medical terms, disorders, and diseases, with more than 300 illustrations, make this the most complete and easy-to-understand book of its kind. Also includes a comprehensive first-aid section and guides to better health. (#Y4016—$1.25)

THE NEW AMERICAN LIBRARY, INC., P.O. Box 2310, Grand Central Station, New York, New York 10017

Please send me the SIGNET BOOKS I have checked above. I am enclosing $_____ (check or money order—no currency or C.O.D.'s). Please include the list price plus 10¢ a copy to cover mailing costs. (New York City residents add 6% Sales Tax. Other New York State residents add 3% plus any local sales or use taxes.)

Name_____

Address_____

City_____ State_____ Zip Code_____
Allow at least 3 weeks for delivery